"This book is a beautiful, profound, and deeply to[...] spiritual writing that heals and reveals ourselves to us in our full humanity. Nothing moves me more than women telling the truth about their real lives—their families, relationships, choices, inspirations, losses, transformation, survival, their histories and their immersion in the now. And these writers are a stunning gathering of women, a quilt of rich, wise voices."

—ANNE LAMOTT
Author of *Traveling Mercies*

"When I put this wonderful and wise book down (having read it straight through), I felt an unusual feeling: stirred up, but contemplatively so. *Chapters of the Heart* is for anyone who wants to find the holy in the ordinary, for anyone who wants to read the sacred texts of her own life with more attentiveness, more generosity, and more curiosity."

—LAUREN F. WINNER
Author of *Girl Meets God*

"I have long encouraged women to share their journeys toward holiness; *Chapters of the Heart* brings together a remarkable circle of women who share their Jewish wisdom with insight and humor, taking their place in the tradition of sacred storytelling."

—RABBI ZALMAN M. SCHACHTER-SHALOMI
Founder, Jewish Renewal Movement

"This marvelous collection reminds me how much I have learned (and am still learning) from my Jewish sisters. Thank you for sharing your stories and wisdom with us."

—REV. DR. MARIE M. FORTUNE
Founder, FaithTrust Institute

"This book brings together extraordinary explorers of life who mix truth, courage, wisdom, grace, surprise, delight, and love in a magic alchemy . . . Read this book and you will be enlightened, enchanted, and enlivened, and you will feel blessed to be living in an era of such teachers."

—RABBI IRWIN KULA
President, National Jewish Center fo[...]

Chapters of the Heart

Chapters of the Heart

Jewish Women Sharing the Torah of Our Lives

Edited by
Sue Levi Elwell
and
Nancy Fuchs Kreimer

CASCADE *Books* · Eugene, Oregon

CHAPTERS OF THE HEART
Jewish Women Sharing the Torah of Our Lives

All scripture translations are either from the contributing authors themselves or, in some cases, from the TANAKH: The Holy Scriptures: The New JPS Translation According to the Traditional Hebrew Text (NJPS), © 1985 Jewish Publication Society, Philadelphia.

Cascade Books
An Imprint of Wipf and Stock Publishers
199 W. 8th Ave., Suite 3
Eugene, OR 97401

www.wipfandstock.com

ISBN 13: 978-1-62032-013-6

Cataloguing-in-Publication data:

Chapters of the heart : Jewish women sharing the Torah of our lives / edited by Sue Levi Elwell and Nancy Fuchs Kreimer.

xviii + 206 pp. ; 23 cm. Includes bibliographical references.

ISBN 13: 978-1-62032-013-6

1. Jewish women—Religious life. 2. Jewish women—Biography. 3. Judaism. 4. Spirituality. I. Elwell, Ellen Sue Levi. II. Fuchs, Nancy. III. Title.

BM43 C25 2013

Manufactured in the U.S.A.

Cover art used with permission of Yair Emanuel and Women of the Wall.

For our teachers and our students and the students of our students.

Contents

Gratitude

WITH FULL HEARTS, WE thank the many hands and minds that helped to "midwife" this book. Rabbi Maurice Harris read and formatted every word; we thank him for focusing his keen eye and discerning spirit on this work. Our thanks go to Christian Amondson, K. C. Hanson, James Stock and the entire team at Cascade Books who helped us bring this project to completion. One of our authors, Ellen Frankel, Editor-in-Chief Emerita at Jewish Publication Society, has been especially generous with her time and good counsel.

This book began over three years ago, sitting on the floor in an overcrowded Amtrak train heading for New York. Having known each other as friends for over thirty years, the two of us began to dream of putting together a book—a volume that each of us wished we had to give to students and other seekers.

We were blessed with an extraordinary group of colleagues who came together to create this book. Not only did they graciously accept our invitation to write, over half joined us in Philadelphia for a working retreat in which we, in the words of Nelle Morton, "heard each other into speech." Both of us grew through the course of planning, writing, and editing these chapters, learning from each of our contributors and from each other.

Like many of our authors, we are indebted to our own families, for the stories we share are their stories as well. We thank our beloveds for their patience with us as we devoted ourselves to this project. And we appreciate the generosity of Lili Perski, Mary Dratman, MD, and Linda and Jim Wimmer, as well as many other friends who believed in us and in the power of women's writing to turn hearts to one another.

Sue Levi Elwell
Nancy Fuchs Kreimer

Introduction

What would happen if a woman told the truth about her life?

—Kathe Kollowitz (1865–1945)

Everyone seeks a home, a refuge. And I am always in search of a few words.

—Etty Hillesum (1914–1943)

W E ASKED A GROUP of Jewish women to tell us the truth about their lives and to do so with a few Jewish words. We, two rabbis who love both Jewish words and talking with other women about the truth of their lives, rounded up some friends who are professionals in the Jewish "word business"—rabbis, scholars, writers, theologians. We asked each woman to open her heart, to delve into her considerable Jewish vocabulary, and to tell us what she found. They, and we, are not beginners; we are almost all over fifty, and many of us a decade or two more. Nevertheless, like everyone else, when it comes to our own lives, we are still trying to figure out how to live with grace. And each of us, in our own way, is still exploring what it all means. Our stories are not ours alone. Reading them, you may recognize yourself or someone you know.

We tried to share with you our hearts and minds, or as much as we are capable of accessing. We want to highlight where Jewish tradition has helped us make meaning and where, on occasion, it has come up empty. And we wanted to crack open the texts for you, show you how they have revealed their gifts to us, sometimes in a moment of surprise and delight, sometimes as a sober, grounding insight. For some, a particular phrase or a story becomes a touchstone for a life. For others, there is a long journey, the text and the reader keep changing as the relationship grows.

What are these texts? First and foremost, the Torah, a book whose style is so "fraught with background" that it has, throughout its history, engaged the listener or reader in an effort to fill in the blanks, to explain discrepancies, to repair, to reinvent. In this book, you will discover teachings created by generations of rabbis who added their voices to the ongoing conversation. You will also find contemporary *midrash*, including one that the author wrote herself to fill a gap in the tradition. Our authors read their lives through multiple sources: Hasidic stories, American Jewish literature, and contemporary psychology. One author's text is a well-known line from a contemporary Jewish theologian, her husband. Others find their texts in the Passover *Haggadah*, still others in Buddhist writings, writings that help them notice something they had not seen before in Jewish teaching or practice.

We begin the volume, as the Torah does, with our first and most intimate relationships, with our families, our homes, the ordinary, the quotidian. Like the other groupings in the book, this one is somewhat arbitrary. Our authors chose topics that compelled them. Only afterwards we, the editors, gathered them into sections, using phrases from psalms as suggestive hints, not neat, well-boundaried categories. We named our first section "All the Days of Our Lives," an echo from Psalm 27, in which we hear the poet speak of one and only wish, to "dwell in the house of God." The reader may assume that sounds like a wish for a good afterlife, but—no!—the poet's request is that this happen "all the days of my life," in other words, right now.

Our first essay, by Vanessa Ochs, an anthropologist who studies Jewish ritual, appears to be about dishes, but is about much more—how we need protection in our homes from demons of all kinds, not unlike the Talmudic rabbis who, despite their own theological misgivings, report on the potions, amulets, and superstitions that Jewish women practiced in their day. We turn then to specific relationships—Hara Person writing about her relationship with her son, Ellen Umansky with her sister, Nancy Kreimer with her husband. Learning to love one's own family members well presents an essential spiritual challenge. Whether it is a parent, a child, a sibling, or a partner, the challenge is not only about those intimate "others," but also about ourselves. Vivian Mayer, looking back on her life of immersion in Jewish stories and prayer, recalls how she first idealized and then reviled the all-too-human matriarchs in the Torah. In the end, Vivie learns something about God's love from their stories, but not before realizing that she "knew each one of these mothers from the inside out," and that being on guard against them meant being on guard against herself. We conclude this section with Julie Greenberg who reflects, like Vanessa, on the physical—a child's belt buckle, a heap of laundry—small things in a home, in a family life, portals to the sacred.

In the next section, "Out of the Narrow Places," four authors recall times when they were, to use Ellen Frankel's word, "ambushed" by life. The psalmist's narrow place, the same word that is the name for Egypt, comes to mean a place of difficulty, a place from which one cries out to God. In Ellen's case it was a hysterectomy at age twenty-six with life-long implications. Amy Eilberg and Ruth Sohn describe living through a loved one's illness, in Amy's case, a daughter, in Ruth's, her husband. Rachel Adler writes of a different time of trouble, watching her mother's deterioration and eventual death from Alzheimer's. In navigating these straits, each of these women in their own way discovers new meanings in texts and new meanings in life. We conclude with an essay by Judith Plaskow, the first Jewish feminist theologian, who shares a piece of her intellectual and spiritual autobiography. Judith returns to the book of Job to explore an issue that has compelled her since her childhood, "God and evil."

The title of the third part, "Opening the Gates," alludes to the psalmists "gates of justice," as our authors describe their going out into a world that is not yet just, a world that includes oppressions of various kinds from gender inequality to war. All four of the writers in this section see ways in which the world is different from how they would wish it to be. Sue Levi Elwell and Wendy Zierler grapple with issues as Jewish women and feminists. Blu Greenberg and Margaret Holub focus on a world beyond the Jewish community, a world they seek to change as social/interfaith activists. For Blu, a lifelong Orthodox Jew in her seventies, the Nazi Holocaust is a lens through which she sees the world. Forty years of interfaith encounters have opened her heart to non-Jews and their suffering, but the final word is always the Jewish people's survival. She feels most deeply how vulnerable Israel is, how the poison of anti-Semitism is spreading. Margaret, several decades younger than Blu, living in leftist political community, also reads current events through her Jewish eyes, but what compels her—with no less passion than Blu's—is a sense of her "pharaoh-ness" as a privileged American and as a Jew. Both take with utmost seriousness their responsibility as Jews to open the gates of justice.

The fourth section, "Be Still and Know," brings together four reflections by women continuing to grow through life's latter stages. These are times when wisdom increasingly comes from knowing not only when to take hold but also when to let go. As Barbara Breitman realized after the death of her husband, within one lifetime, we sometimes need to die to an old self and give birth to a new one. It could be weaning a child, undergoing a humiliating divorce, reimagining a career trajectory, coping with the realities of an aging body, or living into a radically new life. Images from the tradition abound: smashed tablets, shattered vessels, broken hearts. Whether we speak of a gap year or of mindfulness meditation, we need to metaphorically or literally sit still in order to resume movement. Dayle

Friedman pauses in midlife to assess; Laura Geller contemplates upcoming retirement by considering what she has learned from the weanings she has already completed. Sheila Weinberg reminds us that growing older is simply another opportunity to learn to be with what is without contention. Barbara's essay weaves these themes together with her understanding of *teshuvah*.

According to rabbinic tradition, a sermon, however difficult the topic, should end with a *nechemta*, a bit of solace. Our writers take us to some harsh places in their lives; we close by offering Tamara Eskenazi's love song to a cherished text as *nechemta*. A renowned scholar of the Hebrew Bible, Tamara published her first article in 1981, "The Song of Songs as an Answer to the Book of Job." In the essay she wrote for us, she shares her own personal story, how she has lived with and loved three husbands, and found her own meaning "With the Song of Songs in Our Hearts." Her title says what this project is all about—how an ancient text, despite suffering what Buber called the "leprosy of fluency" as well as the indignity of dissection in scholarly articles, can still live inside a heart. Or, to put it a different way, a person can live inside a text. Tamara's husband Bill, also a scholar of the Hebrew Bible, shared her love of the Song. About Bill's death from cancer, Tamara writes, "the text he inhabited stood by him and within him, to the end. I do not need to wish . . . that he 'may rest in the Garden of Eden.' I know that the Garden of Eden was his final stop, even when breath was still in him."

Many of our authors worked hard to stretch or contract to fit the vision of this book. On the contracting side, for some of our academic scholars, it was a true sacrifice to give up beloved forays into scholarship in the interest of readability. For others it was a challenge to be more reticent. As for the stretching, we asked each writer, both the reference lovers and those comfortable with confiding, to reflect on the intersection of life and text. We were ruthless in requiring the sacrifice of beloved footnotes. We tried to stamp out the pulpit voice where we heard its "stained glass" tones, what one of our authors refers to as "rabbinese."

Every spring, during the six weeks between Passover and Shavuot, Jewish tradition invites us to read—one chapter each week—a collection of sayings by the rabbis of the first and second centuries entitled *Pirkei Avot*, literally Chapters (*pirkei*) of the Fathers (*avot*). Some translators call it Ethics of the Fathers, in order to communicate what those chapters do in fact contain—adages concerning right behavior, including some of the most famous ethical teachings of Judaism, such as *If not now, when?* and *You are not required to complete the task.* We named our book, *Pirke Levavot*, echoing the name in Hebrew, translated into English as "Chapters of the Heart."

Pirke Avot begins: "Moses received the Torah from Sinai and handed it over to Joshua. Joshua gave it over to the Elders, the Elders to the Prophets, and the Prophets handed it over to the Men of the Great Assembly."

We feel blessed to be among the first generation of Jewish women who have been welcomed into the study of Torah with opportunities for formal Jewish learning (and titles!) our mothers and grandmothers barely imagined. We see ourselves as part of that great chain of tradition and connect ourselves to it, quoting Torah, the rabbis, and each other.

Some of us have been in conversation with one another for years, and many of us gathered for a day of sharing during which we developed our chapters for this book. You will notice some of us citing one another's teachings with appreciation. Taking special note of the role of a teacher or friend in transmitting a text or an insight has roots deep in Jewish tradition: *Ha'omer davar b'shem omro*, one who says something in the name of the one who originally said it brings redemption to the world (*Pirkei Avot* 6:6). We not only take delight in crediting our teachers and colleagues, we also see ourselves as part of an ongoing process of repair. Many of us spoke with the people in our lives who appear in the stories we tell. In one case, Amy Eilberg's chapter, you will hear from the family member herself.

To our Jewish women colleagues: Obviously, we could have filled several more volumes with writers as learned and insightful as the ones who happened to end up in this one. So much in life is random. We beg your forgiveness and ask you to judge us on the scale of merit. As for the increasingly large numbers of younger women who are engaging in serious Jewish studies and whose stories are just unfolding, we hope that our words will spark yours and that the chain of tradition will continue. We take comfort in knowing that it is not incumbent upon us to complete the task. We rest assured that you will continue it.

To all our readers: We offer these chapters hoping you will read them in the spirit in which they were written. These are the places where our authors have found a few good Jewish words. They welcome the opportunity to share them with you, albeit some of them needed to overcome their shyness to reach out in this way. As editors we had no thesis to prove, no argument to win. If we had an agenda, it was to persuade you that hearing and telling stories while in conversation with sacred texts can be a good thing. Perhaps reading this book you will gain some new insights into Judaism or into your own religious tradition. You will surely see things in these stories that neither we nor our authors could see. Perhaps you will see something in your own life in a new way. Do not hesitate to write and tell us about it all. In the meantime, in the words of the Song of Songs, as quoted by Tamara at the end of her essay, "Arise my friend, my beautiful one, and go forth. It is time to hear *your* voice and it is time for *you* to blossom."

Editors' Note to Readers

We wanted to make this volume as accessible as possible to readers from different backgrounds. Since our authors sometimes use words from a Jewish context that are not be familiar to everyone, we have provided a glossary in the back. In addition, we realize that our audience will include different kinds of readers. We imagine that some of our readers will enjoy simply reading an unencumbered text. Others, however, may want to follow up specific citations. Still others may become curious and want ideas for further reading. We have chosen to place all the bibliographic references in a section titled "Authors' Endnotes." We hope that this arrangement provides each of you with what you need. We invite you to visit us online at www.chaptersoftheheart.com to continue the conversation.

Abbreviations

BT   Babylonian Talmud

m.   Mishnah

NJPS   TANAKH: The Holy Scriptures: Jewish Publication Society, 1985

I

All the Days of Our Lives
(Psalm 27:4)

1

A Life with Things

Vanessa L. Ochs

Soon after my engagement, my future mother-in-law kept me lingering at her breakfast table in Lloyd Neck, New York. These people were technically Jews by birth and by a strong ethnic pride, yet it was a "WASPy" home, the first "WASPy" home I had ever been in. Their son, my fiancé, was in rabbinical school, a situation that so dismayed his father, a man who ran from the old-world Jewish chicken-bone nonsense he had grown up with into the arms of science. He was metaphorically sitting *shiva* for his son until the blessed day he left seminary to work on a doctorate in philosophy.

Mrs. Ochs (which is what I called her) dressed in a pale blue lingerie set with matching pale blue leather slippers. For breakfast, after cut-up grapefruit, she served homemade blueberry pancakes with softened butter in a ramekin and warmed syrup in a crystal pitcher. In a hand-painted Italian ceramic creamer she had found at a fancy estate sale, she served what she called, "hoff and hoff," as native Bostonians do. Every food needed a proper container once it was transported to the table. Even cereals were redistributed from their packages into Tupperware, and the milk for the cereal was properly jugged.

"I trust you have registered for China?" she asked rhetorically. She had paused, mid-sentence to hold her face, to address the pain of *tic douleroux*. But she never said anything about it; this too was part of the household decorum. To *kvetch*, even when justified, was not done.

What did it mean to register for a country, a communist country at that? I had never mentioned a particular interest in China, even though

3

Nixon, Kissinger, and Ford were making social trips there and were seeing what the officials wanted them to see. Maybe if she had asked me when the whole world was turning toward China during the Olympics, first with smog and human rights violations on our minds, and later, with Michael Phelps and the prepubescent Chinese gymnasts seizing our attention, I could have impressed her favorably and fudged an appropriate response. That mattered to me in the early years, before I gave up trying to fly under her critical radar. Still, I felt lucky she had brought up China, presuming we were going to have a discussion of substance about geography or politics, and avoid invitations or guest lists. I was just nineteen, and even though I had just become engaged, I could give a fig about things that would fill a home. I was in love. The only thing I wanted was to have this boy forever.

Mrs. Ochs went on to explain. "You need to give thought to selecting your china pattern, because it's forever."

"You don't say," I said, copying the expression she most fancied. It dawned on me that I might spend years ahead feigning interest in elegantly intrusive orations on home furnishings, upholstery, and the proper way to rear children (her way, 1950s style, with mother at home and children in playpens).

The next day, back home on the South Shore of Long Island, the Five Towns to be specific, Hewlett Harbor to be precise, I told my mother about what Mrs. Ochs had counseled me to do. My mother had heard of gift registries and she, an artist, who wore a mink coat with sneakers, shared my disdain. We agreed that it was rude, greedy, and presumptuous. Perhaps this business of registering for china was what WASPs did, another one of their quirks, like having trust funds but still driving beat-up station wagons.

"Failing to register, you'll end up with gifts you don't want," Mrs. Ochs went on to say the next time I visited, sensing she might appeal to my pragmatism.

"You don't say," I said again, moving the conversation along.

I didn't know we'd be getting wedding presents. I had been to only one wedding as the flower girl. My aunt had taught me about going down the aisle dropping petals from a basket (step, together, drop, repeat), but she had mentioned nothing about brides signing up at Tiffany, Bloomingdale's, or Fortunoff so that they could outfit their real-life "Barbie's Dream Houses" with the objects they desired, and in the patterns they preferred. Perhaps I just wasn't listening.

A college junior, I had no idea just how many objects were necessary for daily life outside of a dorm. Didn't we already have more than everything we needed? There was my parent's cast-off furniture in their basement; the pots and pans, bun-warmer and yogurt-maker my grandparents had gotten as premiums for starting new checking accounts in several banks; the

Chagall poster from my dorm room, and "Christina's World" from my fiancé's. In his seminary room, my fiancé had four dishes for meat and four for milk; among his classmates, with his hot plate, he was practically the Jewish Galloping Gourmet. Maybe we'd need a cookbook other than *The Vegetarian Epicure*, a glass measuring cup, and more cinderblock shelves, but we certainly didn't need to fill a grad school flat with symbols of respectability.

Mrs. Ochs would not be giving up; her lectures grew impassioned. China, she explained, meant dishes, dishes you didn't use for everyday, dishes that symbolized an enduring marriage. The steps you took to preserve your china in a hutch mirrored those you took to preserve your marriage. That your dishes came from many people reflected the community's investment in your relationship. "With the china," taking a less foreboding approach, she concluded, "you celebrate and make an impression." She used a phrase I couldn't parse: "Your wedding china is for 'best.'" She clarified, "China is for company."

My family did not, as a rule, have company, with the exception of the few times that my uncles Effie or Shep came for *Shabbes* so we could fix them up on Saturday night with my grade-school teachers who wore their hair teased way up in beehives. My mother bought Southern-fried chicken in a bag from the new Kosher take-out place, along with foil containers of egg-mushroom "barley," potato and spinach knishes wrapped in wax paper, containers of "health" salad, coleslaw and potato salad, and a thick slice of *kishke* that was rationed off in slivers, lest too much kill a person with indigestion. She served this all up on paper plates for *Shabbes* dinner, *Shabbes* lunch, and Saturday night dinner. At the end of each meal, she was sucking the marrow out of the heap of bones on her grease-stained plate, making flute sounds.

Uncle Effie had married a woman from Montclair, *une petite peu* WASPy herself, and he called to say they were stopping by to visit on Saturday night, even though my mother told him explicitly not to come as she was going to bed early. It happened that she was annoyed with him, as usual, for some miniscule brotherly infraction, a failure to show respect. They came anyways, and my mother, already in pajamas, dimmed the lights in the dining room when she saw his car light coming around the bend. She told me lie low and do not laugh. She said, "Effie is in the doghouse." Being a literalist, I said, "He's not in a doghouse. He and Auntie Bobbie are at the front door and they are wearing sleeping hats and bathrobes and I'm letting them in." Despite an awkward start, we all sat around the dining room table having a good time together, picking off pieces of a Wall's marble cake still in the box, and using paper towels ripped off the roll as our plates.

My uncle and aunt, who sort of spoke together as a Greek chorus, both on and off the phone, threatened my mother: "One day, your daughter's future in-laws will make their first visit to your house to meet you, and they'll be eating off your mix and match plates, or God forbid, paper plates. Look at this—paper towels! Like peasants! They'll be drinking some fancy French wine they brought you out of your *yartzeit* glasses. Do you know what they'll think? They'll think that the girl their son wants to marry was raised by wolves, that's what they'll think. They'll pull him out of your house by the scruff of his neck. You'll never marry her off!"

As for good dinnerware, we did not have any, unless you counted the paper plates that were extra-strength. (This predated knowing there were carbon footprints to minimize. It came before recycling, unless you count using an empty borscht jar to store chicken soup so that the fat would rise to the top when you placed it in the refrigerator all night.) For everyday use, only we in my family could tell our milk and meat sets apart. I'm not sure how, for none of the dishes matched, except for a few odd pieces, such as cups and saucers, items we never used as pairs. I suspect there may have originally been two full sets, but my mother was notoriously clumsy, breaking and chipping dishes regularly, particularly when she washed up. They had fallen in the act of kitchen duty. Her siblings called her *gelengtere*, which she said meant "the clumsy one." At one point, she said, she thought it was her name. Their appellation condemned her, but also was liberatory, permitting her to act without worrying what others thought. The ranks of our diminished dish sets were filled out with odd lots she had picked up at a store she said was called Six-Fifteen, calling her trips there for bargains her "fix," a tiny nod to the drug culture passing us all by.

As for beverage service, we drank our juice out of *yartzeit* glasses that my mother had washed out after the dead had been properly remembered, the wax had melted, and the wick and its metal tag had been fished out. This was as close to a complete, matching set of anything we possessed. The glasses were so sturdy that they bounced off the mock-brick linoleum each time my mother dropped them. And with each year, our glass cemetery increased: one glass burned for the day of death, three burned for the festivals, and another, if I recall, around the time of the High Holidays, which was when the ancestors had been visited at their cemeteries in Queens or Brooklyn. Drinking out of *yartzeit* glasses was simply too creepy for me. I'd sooner make a cup out of my hands rather than blur the boundaries between the glass that held the light of my ancestor's soul one day and Tropicana from the Dairy Barn the next. They could go into the new dishwater everyday on the hottest germ-killing cycle, but there was no washing off death.

When my mother broke dishes, she sometimes said in Yiddish, "*Zol es zain a kappara*"—"let it be an atonement." She prayed that this broken dish would stand as the substitute for something far more cherished that might otherwise have been broken, like a person's ankle. Sometimes she shouted, "*Mazal tov*," as though she were at a wedding. She'd wish that all who were in hearing distance would pray about something good that might happen rather than dwell upon her clumsiness or upon what we had lost. For emphasis, sometimes she'd add, "It's just a thing."

In Lloyd Neck, my future mother-in-law concluded her plea for registering for china by pointing to the dishes arranged in her dining room hutch, gesturing as if she were a docent at the Met about to lecture on the Ming dynasty: "This is my china, my bone china." She then intoned British terms I was unfamiliar with: "Lenox, Royal Doulton, Wedgwood." You would think our tour of faience had turned a corner and we had landed in the "Eighteenth-Century British" wing. She concluded, repeating facts I already knew by now: "My daughter Janet married," pausing here to accumulate gravitas, "at the Hotel Pierre. She registered for china." True, but . . . her daughter's marriage had been falling apart for years, and Mrs. Ochs foretold that her older son's, soon to be celebrated, was bound for breakage even before his wedding day. If china was supposed to inoculate, it hardly seemed foolproof.

I had taken to studying Talmud and learned that the ancient rabbis knew that some situations in life called out turning to objects instead of prayer. The insight probably came from their womenfolk who kept their eyes ever open for the practical prayer of holy things, even if the practices came from the neighboring peoples they were supposed to avoid. They tested out what worked and passed it on. There was the *totefet*, a charm packet worn as a necklace to ward off the evil eye. For wearing or holding in one's hand, there were amulets of parchment written by proven experts and amulets of roots of herbs, knots of madder roots, spice bundles in packets, and preserving stones to heal or even prevent illness or miscarriage. The women were adamant that these objects worked, and rabbis inevitably declared they could be worn or carried even on the Sabbath, when such activity would otherwise be proscribed.

My favorite Talmudic object, a do-it-yourself project, counteracted the burden of a fever that wouldn't go away. The feverish sufferer was sent to sit at a crossroads and capture a large ant. The ant was then enclosed in a copper tube, and the tube was closed with lead. The tube was further sealed with sixty different types of seals, and the feverish person carried it about, shaking it and saying, "Your burden upon me, and my burden upon you," until the fever or its burden is gone. Rav Acha, imagining the possibility that the ant might have previously been seized and entombed by someone with an even worse affliction than persistent fever, improved upon the incantation. Better say: "My burden and your burden upon you." There was a locust's egg hung over one's ear for an earache, a live fox's tooth for drowsiness, a dead fox's tooth for insomnia, a nail from the gallows for swelling. Here was an inventory of objects one might want to have around just in case, like a first-aid kit, objects whose usefulness one might grow to understand and trust.

By this time I had already been married for twenty years and had two children. My mother-in-law (who had taken to me, always provisionally, despite my peasant ways) concluded I was never going to come round and understand the importance of china. I did take to accumulating other household objects. Multiple *hamsas*, protective amulets in the shape of hands, made of painted clay, stained glass, copper, silver and handmade paper hung throughout my house. Souvenirs from Israel, projects my daughters made, there wasn't a room without one. There were magic wands, one grandmother's rolling pin, and another's soup ladle that I deployed in crises. From the rococo abundance of amulets and ancestral protective mementos, you might think I had always been beguiled by the power of objects. In fact, I had gotten over shunning clothes, jewelry, and knickknacks lest I turn into one of my Papagallo-wearing classmates of suburban Jewish Long Island. Still, a revulsion for things could well up. On such days, I started giving something away. I'd let my arms levitate up a few inches, to celebrate being unburdened by the weight of things.

For my fortieth birthday, my mother-in-law bought me a set of dishes, service for twelve that appeared in the mail one day without warning. Not china, but a festive and multi-hued Lindt-Stymeist pattern from the '80s aptly called "Colorways," with rims of one color and centers of another, with every piece a different combination of shades: pink, green, apricot, cerulean blue, warm yellow. They are no longer manufactured, and for replacements, you have to keep up on eBay auctions and get lucky. She noticed that I had already gathered a few pieces on my own—actually, it was my mother who had found a few irregular dinner plates for me from a "Six Fifteen." There was one blue dinner plate with pink trim, and a pink plate with green trim. They were cunning, fit for a Mad Hatter's tea party, and having grown up with odd dishes, I had no trouble insinuating them into my own, admittedly motley *batterie de cuisine*.

By then, I was grown up enough to be touched by Mrs. Ochs' generosity; I did not feel intruded upon. Family life had grown more complex than I could handle; there were medical concerns, and I was commuting to New York to work and going to graduate school, too. Our tensions made home a hard-edged place. Mrs. Ochs' dishes made me feel understood, cared for, coddled, a little joyous at each dairy meal. They helped.

By then, our two mothers had become the most unlikely of best friends, keeping company by talking on the phone every single day. This didn't come about overnight. For years, my parents, who habitually argued with each other at my in-laws Passover table, had been barred as guests from their home. Their banishment ended after my father-in-law died and my parents, who believed in doing *mitzvah*s, good deeds in their book, made a point of looking after Mrs. Ochs. It turned out that having *machetunim* (in-laws) who cared about you trumped a lack of social grace.

Half of these colorful dishes we used everyday and they got chipped and broken. I didn't say *mazal tov* when breaking happened, but I nodded my head with respect toward my mother, who continues to pray a great deal for us in this manner. The other half of the dishes, as well as pieces my mother-in-law later found—a butter dish, a salt and pepper shaker, coffee and tea service and casseroles—were designated for "Best." They went un-used; I had just picked up a little hutch and installed them in it, and I looked at the lot of them thinking about how things given by people who love us have a way of holding us together. You could almost say that in this way, my mother-in-law nearly got me registered for china.

Which leads me to the night we were staying at the Hotel Providence for a little weekend get-away. I asked our waiter if he could box up the ar-tisanal cheeses we had ordered for dessert so that we might go upstairs to our room to watch the opening ceremonies of the Chinese Olympics on television.

"It's already started!" he said. "You just hurry on up and we'll bring it to you. We'd much prefer to serve it properly as room service." Soon enough, the cheese platter was delivered on a tray along with modern white plates and silverware tucked into thick green napkins. As Zhang Yimou's dazzling tribute to Chinese civilization unfolded in and over the Bird's Nest, we were having a lovely picnic in bed. Upon returning home, I planned to tell my mother-in-law about how much pleasure I took in our little elegant Chinese Olympics opening ceremonies feast. I would tell her about my new hutch, too, and I would point out how her genes were prevailing in my daughter, who, against my advice, had selected a pattern of china and put it on her wedding registry. My mother-in-law, in her late eighties, had been declining steadily and was in a nursing home. She was sporadically cogent and would not recall much, if anything, of what I said, but I still wanted her to hear.

As it happened, she passed away that very night. Her death was not unexpected. It was a summer weekend, and not a single one of the rabbis in her community was available to perform the funeral. My husband asked if I, a chronicler of Jewish ritual, could officiate. I told him, "Of course," as it seemed to be the right thing to say to a bereaved man. I had never performed a funeral, and my copy of a rabbi's manual, the one I used for research, was at home, as were any proper black clothes I would need to wear. I knew my daughters could lend me clothes and assumed that the funeral parlor would have some sort of a booklet that they handed out for Jewish funerals. From that and my memory of other funerals I had been to, surely I could piece together something persuasive.

There was no such booklet, just a card with the Twenty-third Psalm and the Mourner's *Kaddish*. When my sister pulled up at the funeral house parking lot, we went through her van and unearthed, under soccer balls and pretzel crumbs, a program from a memorial service she had attended. There was a poem about journeys and destinations and the "*El maleh rachamim*" prayer. I could use these.

Before the service began, the funeral director had me lead the immediate family into a small room. Both my husband's siblings were there with spouses of their second marriages. The funeral director handed me a little black object, and being nervous, I didn't know what it was at first. Fiddling with it, I saw it was some kind of fold-out razor-blade, and my first thought was, "If this were a *bris*, I couldn't fake it." My husband motioned that there were black ribbons for pinning on the mourners: *keriah*. What was the protocol: who pinned, who cut, who ripped? Muddling through, I acted as convincingly as I could, saying in "rabbinease," "Just as you tear these ribbons, so your hearts are torn." I pinned the ribbons on my husband, his brother and sister and made a cut with the knife. They each tore a little more, and now they looked like official mourners, ready to process out into the first row of the chapel.

My husband wore his torn black ribbon on his lapel throughout the *shiva*. He returned from that walk around the block you take on the last day, he returned to shaving and to work, but he couldn't part from that ribbon, an object that seemed to signal for him that he was not open to talking about this grief, not just yet, and maybe never. That was his business. The ribbon was eventually discarded, perhaps by me.

As of late, I've been giving something in my house away every single day, to pare my possessions down to the bare bones of necessity and beauty. My new thing, we'll see how long it lasts.

Even with this regime of a daily departure of objects, some things cannot be thrown out. Not as useful as my mother's *yahrzeit* glasses, yet once potent in my hand in opening up broken hearts just enough, I am still holding on to my knife.

2

On Raising a Son

One Mother's Search for Wisdom

HARA E. PERSON

One of them then said, "Rest assured that I will return to you at this time next year, and your wife Sarah shall have a son."

—GENESIS 18:10

M Y PARENTING STORY BEGINS with the biblical matriarchs. Like many of our matriarchs, I longed for a child, and after a short period of despair, was blessed with the birth of a daughter. Much to my amazement, two years later I was pregnant again. Whereas Abraham and Sarah were surprised by the promise of a son from a mysterious messenger, my prophecy came via ultrasound. The doctor was quick to confirm that it was definitely a boy. Sarah laughed; left alone in the examining room, I cried. Not unhappy tears, but tears of astonishment and, admittedly, also fear. I knew nothing about boys and felt completely unprepared to mother one.

I was raised in a strongly matriarchal family of mothers and daughters. Though my maternal great grandmother died when I was nine, her impact on me was formative. My maternal grandmother lived with us until I was ten, and helped raise me. Even after she moved out, she remained a major influence in my life well into adulthood. I had no other grandparents, only those two powerful women. I had only a sister, no brothers, and, inevitably, I had a daughter. While I did have a father, it was my mother who had managed the day-to-day life of our family while he went out into the world.

I *got* girls. I knew about girls and self-esteem, girls and body-image issues, girls and school performance. Boys, though, were foreign to me, even as someone who had dated and then married one. I didn't understand the way they were wired, how they saw the world, how they thought. I resented their historic privilege, their opportunities, the room they took up in the world by no virtue other than gender. So the news that I was having a boy terrified me, and not the least of my fears had to do with the fact that I could not now avoid the circumcision question, the first of many unavoidable issues related to gender that I would now have to deal with.

> When his son Isaac was eight days old, Abraham circumcised him, as God had commanded him. (Gen 21:4)

My son's *brit milah* provided one of the first lessons about boys. The imbalance of importance in Jewish tradition between the birth of a girl child and that of a boy child troubled me. Though of course I had already known about this disparity, when it became personal I struggled with the idea that there was a formal, ritualized covenant ceremony for him going back to the Torah while none existed, until modern days, for my daughter. Though we were committed to going through with the traditional covenantal *mitzvah* of *milah*, we downplayed it by not inviting anyone beyond our closest circle, and instead held a more public *Hachnasat Ben* (welcoming of a son) and naming ceremony one month after his birth. The morning of his *brit milah*, I looked around the room at the handful of men who were present and saw them grouped nervously around the *mohel*, their hands clasped protectively over their groins. Watching a group of grown men react so viscerally to the ancient ritual, I had a stunning realization that what lay behind the male privilege that I resented was male vulnerability. These men were not basking in their privilege, they were wincing in empathetic pain.

This parenting story may have begun with imagery borrowed from the epic struggles of our earliest ancestors, but my quest to understand what it meant to raise a son soon led me toward the early stories of our most heroic and complicated of male figures, David. It was in the David narrative that I began to look for insight and wisdom into the story my son and I would begin to create together, the story of this one particular mother and this one specific son.

> And the Lord said to Samuel, . . . "I am sending you to Jesse the Bethlehemite, for I have decided on one of his sons to be king." . . .

Then Samuel asked Jesse, "Are these all the boys you have?"

He replied, "There is still the youngest; he is tending the flock."

And Samuel said to Jesse, "Send someone to bring him . . . So they sent and brought him. He was ruddy-cheeked, bright-eyed, and handsome.

And the Lord said, "Rise and anoint him, for this is the one." (1 Sam 16:1, 11–12)

The biblical image of David as a boy presents an enchanting figure. He is young, powerless, artistic, and beautiful, at one with the natural world. Set apart from his older brothers who already occupy the male world of power and might, he lives a dreamy pre-pubescent existence. The arc of David's story goes from childhood to old-age, providing a rich source of material on the transformation of a boy into a man, and a man into a heroic, but flawed, leader. Like the familiar figure from fairy tales and legends, at the beginning David is the overlooked, underappreciated youngest son, the one least likely to succeed and the one with the most to prove, the one who has, unbeknownst to those around him, in fact been singled out for a unique destiny. The early stories of David contain universal archetypal elements found in the legends of emergent heroes such as King Arthur, Jack and the Beanstalk, and even in modern-day literature like the Harry Potter series. As Joseph Campbell writes, hero stories from around the world share the common motif of the ultimate triumph of a youngest son who is at the start "the despised one, or the handicapped: the abused younger son or daughter, the orphan, stepchild, ugly duckling, or the squire of low degree." The Torah, with its ongoing emphasis on the triumph of the younger son, offers plenty of other examples of this paradigm, from Isaac to Moses, but none are as richly nuanced as David.

From the start, my son exhibited behaviors that were unfamiliar to me. He was a new language I needed to learn, and quickly. As soon as he had the coordination to grasp objects, he was fascinated by anything with wheels. Before he could even crawl, he would lie on the floor and push cars and trucks back and forth. As he got a little older, strolls around the neighborhood could take an eternity, because he had to stop at every construction site, or look at every large and unusual vehicle. Amazingly, the world began to crack open a little wider as I experienced the universe through my son's eyes. Soon, along with him, I learned names of objects I'd never given a second thought to previously, things like backhoe loaders and scrapers and graders. My sense of the world around me enlarged as my eyes began to notice what I would have earlier simply edited out of view.

From construction equipment we moved on to dinosaurs, and I continued to learn along with him. Together we became fluent in brachiosaurus and triceratops and velociraptors. These taxonomies helped him shape the world into an understandable, approachable place in which categories created both meaning and safe boundaries. Like the midrashic Adam gaining dominion over the animals by naming them, the ability to label and categorize enabled him to gain mastery over the world and impose order over chaos.

My parents, stalwart adherents to the egalitarian values of '60s child-raising, had bought me blocks and trucks, and banned Barbie as bad for girls' self-image. My father, a Korean War vet (albeit one who spent his service within the United States), held deep anti-war beliefs. Toy guns, soldiers, or anything remotely related to war were taboo in our house. This was not a hardship as those held no interest for my sister and me, though there were times when I eyed my friends' GI Joes as a good way to expand the partner pool for my contraband Barbies. My toy life centered primarily around dolls and doll houses. I loved the blocks, those smooth pieces of blond wood, but with them I made neighborhoods of houses for the politically correct European doll house figures that spread across the living room.

My husband, the son of a veteran wounded in Sinai in '73 and an Israeli army veteran who intensely disliked his army experience, readily agreed to continue the toy philosophy I had grown up with. No war toys, no Barbies, and lots of gender neutral options. Legos and trucks and trains, blocks and balls and puzzles, and correctly proportioned dolls for both kids. My daughter loved the Legos and blocks, but like me, she built houses. Her play was about relationships between the personalities with which she infused her figures, the Lego people, and even an occasional wooden block. She had little interest in things with wheels, or balls, but truth be told, also little interest in baby dolls. For my son, though, it was all about power and height. Lego constructions fought with each other in pitched battles until one destroyed the other. Towers grew to staggering heights. Just as with dinosaurs or earthmovers, the bigger the better. Was this, like David's need to fight Goliath, a way to vanquish a feeling of powerlessness?

The insight into male vulnerability gleaned at his *brit milah* deepened as my son grew. Like many boys, he responded in a primal way to a range of heroic characters. Among his favorites were King Arthur, Captain Hook, and Batman. He didn't just worship the stories or the characters, he *was* the characters. From ages three to six, he routinely dressed as one of these heroes, complete with capes, cloaks, hooks, masks, or whatever was necessary for the persona he had adopted that day. And if he found himself in a situation with no costume on hand, a towel or sheet tied (loosely) around his neck as a cape would do just fine. But there would be no guns, no swords, no weaponry of any kind, until we finally admitted to ourselves that as much as we tried to protect him from knowledge of weapons and warfare, he was making Lego swords, and arming himself with branches picked up on walks in the park. Lacking the vocabulary for weaponry, he called them his "shooters" and happily, aggressively, pointed them at other children, dogs, and squirrels.

In fact anything could become a weapon—toy brooms, the cardboard from a roll of paper towels, a carrot. He was answering the call of an instinctive need to arm himself and no actual toy weapons were needed. He needed to protect himself and those around him. He collected miniature plastic swords (the kind used to spear sandwiches or place olives in martinis) and attached them to his beanie-babies with twist-ties, creating an army of weaponized stuffed creatures ready to defend the realm. And I began to understand that the urge to defend himself and his world was real to him. At one point we had to negotiate a classroom truce, in which he was forced to concede to disarming and leaving his weapons and other accouterments in the cubby before entering the classroom. He felt small and vulnerable, and being King Arthur or Captain Hook or Batman, sword and magic powers at the ready, helped him gain a sense of control. We swallowed our principles and got him a plastic sword—the best of all possible options.

> But Saul said to David, "You cannot go to that Philistine and fight him; you are only a boy, and he has been a warrior from his youth!"
>
> David replied to Saul, "Your servant has been tending his father's sheep, and if a lion or a bear came and carried off an animal from the flock, I would go after it and fight it and rescue it from its mouth. And if it attacked me, I would seize it by the beard and strike it down and kill it. Your servant has killed both lion and bear, and that uncircumcised Philistine shall end up like one of them, for he has defied the ranks of the living God." (1 Sam 17:33–36)

Scholars like Bruno Bettelheim and Jane Yolen write that every boy has to slay a dragon or kill a giant in order to leave boyhood behind and become who he is meant to be. Joseph Campbell sees these battles as "the hero-task" at the heart of his paradigmatic hero's journey, a necessary step in claiming his destiny. The dragon or the giant represent the fears that haunt the borders of childhood, and must be vanquished in order for the child to cross the threshold into fully functional adulthood.

David's story begins with the image of him as a youth, a shepherd and a musician whose music soothes the troubled spirit of Saul (1 Sam 16:23; 17:15). When he declares that he is prepared to fight Goliath, his proposal is met with disbelief. And it does seem to be an astounding act of either bravado or naiveté to imagine that he could possibly prevail. David's behavior is referred to by Bettelheim as the "symbolic struggle of personality integration against chaotic disintegration" in which two different aspects of his personality are in conflict—the compliant, obedient youth that he has been so far rewarded for being, versus the brave, heroic, and independent-thinking figure he wants to become. These two self-images battle against each other in the classic adolescent struggle toward the self-rule of adulthood.

David speaks to Saul of trials he has had to endure in trying to prove that he is up to the task of what will be the biggest test of all in his young life, the defeat of the Goliath. Campbell proposes that surviving a series of trials is both a common motif and necessary phase of the hero's journey in literature, milestones that mark the transformation of boys into mature men. For David, the successful culmination of these trials, peaking with the victory over Goliath, is a rite of passage into manhood. Internally, he has proven to himself that he has powers within that he can call upon, and externally, he shows that he has what it takes. It is only once he has done so that he earns the respect of the world of adult men, and is taken seriously as not only one of them, but a leader among them.

New lessons were learned as my son transformed from a boy into an adolescent, and then into a young man. It turned out that my son is tall and gained his height early on. Against the stereotype of boys maturing later, my son was just about his full adult height of six feet at his *bar mitzvah*, with a deep, bass voice. I was stunned to learn how the world saw, and reacted to, this tall little boy who looked like a teenager long before he could actually claim to be one. We live in a world in which teenage boys, when encountered loose on the street, are often feared. A tall teenage boy is perceived as even more of a threat, especially at night. There were several significant dragons my son had to battle as he made his way through adolescence; looking tall, mature, and thus threatening while still an unsure young boy was one of them. He had to be taught how to act in public so as not to pose a threat, and then when he got older and began to be out later with friends, not to call attention to himself from the police.

Much is gained in the transition from boy to man, yet I have come to see how much is also lost. My son has had to learn to be less trusting of authority figures. He has had to learn that in many situations the world rewards men for behaviors like bravery and bravado, and smiles less on displays of fear and self-doubt. Naturally, I would like to end the parallel to

David at a certain point in that narrative. Like all mothers, I would like to see my son emerge from the trials of youth as a respected leader among his peers. But of course I would like to see him steer clear of other aspects of David's later chapters.

As a feminist rabbi whose career has been spent in Jewish publishing, part of my work has involved giving voice to the silences of women in our texts, ensuring that women are written into the text and thus into the conversation. Through raising my son I have come to learn that there are ways and places where men's authentic voices are silenced as well. When men are expected to be strong and tough and solve problems and provide for those weaker than themselves, they have not been allowed to bring forward other parts of their beings. They have had to shut down/shut off their vulnerable sides and mask their feelings. To do otherwise is dangerous. It was only in the last years of my father's life, and due in large part to the experience of parenting my son, that I was able to understand how true this was for my father. Born into poverty and instability, he worked hard his whole life, creating a stable existence for his family. Though he loved musical theater and visual art, he was never able to give voice to those other sides of himself in a serious way, focusing instead on carrying the weight of protecting and caring for those around him through his work as a provider.

After joining Saul's army, David never again takes up music. He closes down that side of himself as he toughens up. As my son chooses which path he will take through life, I hope I can find a way to help him hold on to those aspects of himself that David gave up in order to become a great warrior.

> The man who kills him will be rewarded by the king with great riches; he will also give him his daughter in marriage . . .
> (1 Sam 17:25)

For David, as in the classic fairy tales, there is a tangible reward to being a brave warrior. Unable to understand how adults figure out how to create sustainable lives that involve jobs, homes, and long-term relationships, a child dreams of the one great act they can accomplish that will result in them being instantly gifted with the accouterments of adulthood, as well as earning the self-respect of their older brothers, fathers, and adult men in general. In mythology and fairy tales, the successful completion of the hero task has grand and tangible results. St. George slays the dragon and wins the hand of the princess. Jack the Giant Killer assassinates the giant Galligantua, rescuing the kingdom from the enchantment that has been upon it, and as a reward receives the king's daughter as his bride. Hercules rids the countryside of dangerous animals and in gratitude, the King of Thebes gave him his daughter's hand in marriage. The biblical story of David uses this same model of a great deed and reward.

The narrative of David's youth and ascendancy to power is so potent, in part because it is not just the story of one particular man, but it speaks in recognizable terms about growing up and realizing one's own potential. As Campbell writes, "The mighty hero of extraordinary powers . . . is each of us: not the physical self visibly in the mirror, but the king within." Royalty, as expressed in these classic stories, is a construct that enables children to come to terms with the temporary state in which they exist, a state in which they are subject to the rules and wishes of others. By seeing themselves as kings and queens in the making, they are able to imagine that one day they will be able to assume their rightful place as rulers over their own lives and choices. Bettelheim writes, "No child believes that one day he will become ruler over a kingdom other than the realm of his own life. . . . To the younger child, it may simply mean that then nobody will order him around, and that all his wishes will be fulfilled. To the older child, it will also include the obligation to rule—that is, to live and act wisely. But at any age a child interprets becoming king or queen as having gained mature adulthood." Once the great battle has been fought and won, sovereignty over oneself has been attained, and children can shape their own existence as mature adults.

My son eventually outgrew his need to face the world in costume, which is not to say that he doesn't still love the heroes of comic books, mythology, and Arthurian legend. His obsession with construction equipment and dinosaurs gave way to large-scale Lego installations for some time, until a passion for basketball, debate team, politics, theoretical physics, beer pong, and other more mature endeavors took over. With each twist and turn, I have continued to learn new vocabulary and absorb new information. As he grabs the world with two hands, makes it his own, and shares his experiences with me, my eyes learn to see people in new ways, my ears have become more attuned to a wider range of humor, and I have developed, if not a taste for, at least an appreciation of new forms of music. Having never willingly attended sporting events most of my life, I now log several basketball games a week during the season and can talk passably well about what is happening on the court.

This is a story about one mother and one son, not a reductivist tale about all boys. There are certainly many ways that my son, and my daughter, conform to gender expectations and stereotypes, and plenty of ways in which they each do not. I have come to understand that it is not always easy to have a mother who thinks and writes and talks about these issues. Now, as young adults, both my children are fluent in the language of gender and have the tools to analyze the world the around them in interesting and often surprisingly creative ways. But not every moment along the way has been smooth.

My son became *bar mitzvah* the day after I received an advance copy of *The Torah: A Women's Commentary,* a ground-breaking book I had devoted several years to shepherding through to completion. I thought that it would be very special for him to become the first student ever to receive it on the *bimah* as part of being called to the Torah. I was wrong. After I presented it to him on the *bimah* with great fanfare and much excitement from the *kahal,* his comment the next day, was "Mom, when you gave me *The Women's Commentary* on the *bimah,* it was like handing me a tampon in front of all my friends." Once again, he was my teacher, guiding me to see through his eyes.

My son is getting ready to leave home and find his way in the world. Some battles are behind him, but many are still to come. His various Sauls and Jonathans and Michals and Avigails await him, as do his Batshevas and all the other challenges of adult decision-making. May he have the strength to use his power judiciously, and may he rule his kingdom with gentleness, intelligence, and wisdom.

3

Between Sisters

Ellen M. Umansky

I AM THE MIDDLE OF three sisters. My older sister, Myrna, was thirteen when I was born; my younger sister, Amy, and I are less than seventeen months apart. Myrna left for college when I was four and got married soon after she graduated, while Amy and I grew up together as constant companions and best friends. We sang and danced around the house, putting on shows for our parents and close family friends; engaged in the same afterschool activities: piano, ballet, and religious school; were in the same carpools, and often hung out with one another's friends. In fact by the time we got to junior high school, we sometimes went on double dates, on one occasion with brothers. We went on vacation at least once a year with our parents, and in the first few summers following our father's death, took long road trips with our mother. From the time that I was nine and Amy seven, until I was fifteen and she thirteen, we also went to an eight-week summer sleep away camp together. As independent as I always felt, I don't think I would have gone away to camp had Amy not agreed to go with me. It was during those seven formative and memorable summers, away from our parents, that we forged an emotional connection that has endured for over half a century.

Yet Amy and I are very different from one another, both by nature and inclination. Indeed, as the two of us have often said, if we weren't sisters we probably wouldn't know each other. We were raised in a tightly-knit, extended family. Our paternal grandparents lived with us in New Rochelle, a suburb north of New York City, and our aunts and cousins, who lived nearby, came over for dinner at least once a week and more frequently stopped by to visit. Thus, my life and sense of self-identity became intertwined with Amy's at a very early age. Our mother dressed us alike when we were young, often in the same outfit but in different colors. In the 1960s, when Amy and I became teenagers, we listened to the same music, watched the same TV shows, and dressed in similar, hippie-style clothing. While my closest friends remembered that I had an older sister, although few of them ever met her, most of my school friends, when asking about Amy, would ask, as some still do today: "How's your sister?," not knowing or remembering that Amy isn't the only sister I have.

Amy and I have always been one another's best friend, yet our relationship is more complicated and emotionally charged than any relationship I've ever had, with the exception of my relationship with my older sister. Perhaps because Amy and I were so close in age, only a year apart in school, and so often together, we were constantly compared to one another. Our memories of the impact of these comparisons are highly selective and vastly different, primarily, I think, because by the time we were in elementary school our self-image and senses of self-esteem were already in place. Yet there is no denying that however unintentionally, the comparisons made by our father, and the consequent family roles that he assigned us, irrevocably shaped our lives.

The strong, charismatic patriarch of our family, our father frequently compared us, describing me privately or to others as "the smart one" and Amy as "the pretty one." Consequently, Amy came to see herself, and in many ways still sees herself, as physically attractive but intellectually inferior. I came to see myself, and still see myself, as bright but not particularly pretty. Although each of us cultivated those positive qualities with which we believed we were endowed—Amy still spends a good deal of time on her hair and makeup while I rarely go anywhere without something substantial to read—Amy grew up wanting to be as (book) smart as I was, while I wanted to be as beautiful as she. As close as we were, these desires were unspoken between us. In fact, it was less than ten years ago, that we openly acknowledged the lasting, painful impact that these childhood comparisons had on us both.

What prompted this acknowledgment was my re-reading and re-thinking the biblical stories of Rachel and Leah that I had heard and read many times before. I came to realize that in many ways, the biblical account of the relationship between these two women illuminates Amy's and my own complex relationship, a connection of love, friendship, envy, and eventual mutual acceptance. Like Amy, Rachel is "beautiful of form and of face" (Gen 29:17), physical attributes that particularly attract Jacob to her. In contrast, her sister Leah is described as weak-eyed, an ambiguous adjective that within the context of the story, suggests that she is not physically attractive. Like Leah, I am the older sister. Near-sighted from the age of nine if not earlier and needing to wear eyeglasses, I saw myself as weak-eyed. As much as I told myself that whether or not I was pretty didn't matter, I hated to wear my glasses, only putting them on, reluctantly, to read the blackboard, watch a movie, or after the age of sixteen, drive a car. When I didn't say hello to people in the hallways of my high school, Amy always came to my defense, truthfully telling people that it wasn't that I was unfriendly; it was just that I was near-sighted and couldn't see them. I came to her defense as well. From elementary school through high school, if our peers or teachers (some of whom had me as a student and Amy the following year), criticized what I took to be Amy's character or ability, I stood up to them with eloquence and passion. In fact, one such incident, in which I talked back to a teacher who suggested that Amy had lied about something she had witnessed, nearly got me suspended from fifth grade.

Perhaps it was because we loved, and still love, each other so fiercely that when we bickered or fought, as we sometimes did, we said words that were particularly hurtful and when we were young, threatened to beat the other up. In fact, we might well have done so had our mother not intervened. Even now, offhanded comments that we might brush off if said by someone else, are taken as personal criticisms that sometimes bring one or both of us to tears. At the same time, it pained and still pains us when the other is upset or unhappy. There have been, and still are, times when we're annoyed or angry with one another. Yet we both know that should either of us truly need the other, she would be there, not just emotionally but physically as well. In the biblical narrative, such is not the case with Rachel and Leah. Their mutual envy seems to hinder whatever friendship they might have had before Jacob arrived.

Although the biblical stories of Rachel and Leah primarily center on the relationship that each has with Jacob and their ensuing rivalry with one another, there is, as Lori Hope Lefkovitz writes, a "story beneath this story." In this narrative, "Leah and Rachel love each other and each other's children." Worrying far less about Jacob than he worries about them, "their feelings [for one another] are complex and strong and various." Christian theologian Elisabeth Schüssler Fiorenza has described this inquiry as feminist critical hermeneutics. As Schüssler Fiorenza makes clear, this interpretative method necessitates moving beyond the Bible's androcentrism by reading between the lines, filling in the blanks, and when necessary, inventing new stories, recognizing that texts that solely focus on men's experiences "must not be mistaken as trustworthy evidence of human history, culture, and religion."

The rabbis also knew that there was a story behind the story. Honoring Leah and Rachel as mothers of Israel, they created stories that describe empathy and love between the sisters. In one midrash, Rachel and Jacob come to believe that since Laban is a deceiver, he might well substitute Leah for Rachel at the very public marriage celebration that he has arranged and thus agree upon a sign to give one another under the *chuppah*. When Rachel sees that her father indeed intends to make the substitution, she imagines Leah's embarrassment and humiliation should Jacob decide not to go through with the wedding. Out of compassion for her sister, she sacrifices her own happiness and tells Leah the mutually agreed upon sign so that Jacob, thinking that the veiled Leah is Rachel, will marry her (BT *Baba Batra* 123a; see too *Eicha Rabbah* 24). In an even more inventive telling, in Rachel's voice, the rabbis write, "I went beneath the bed upon which he lay with my sister; and when he spoke to her she remained silent and I made all the replies in order that he should not recognize my sisters' voice. I did her a kindness, was not jealous of her, and did not expose her to shame" (*Eicha Rabbah* 24). In yet another rabbinic midrash, Leah is pregnant with her seventh son. Able to discern the will of God, Leah knows that Jacob is destined to have twelve sons who will be the progenitors of the twelve tribes of Israel. He already has ten (six by her; two by her handmaid Zilpah and two by Rachel's handmaid Bilhah). Additionally discerning that the fetus inside of her is a boy and wanting to spare her sister the shame of giving Jacob fewer sons than either of their maids, Leah prays to God to transform the fetus into a girl. Willingly sacrificing some of her own communal honor (and perhaps, Jacob's increased attention) in order to augment her sister's happiness and historical significance as a "mother of Israel," Leah consequently gives birth to her daughter, Dina, while Rachel later bears Joseph and Benjamin, who, because of Jacob's great love for her, become his favorite sons (BT *Berachot* 60a).

The mutual love and compassion that Rachel and Leah possess in the rabbinic tradition reveals a great deal about the kinds of complex relationships that frequently exist between sisters. As with Rachel and Leah, the words that Amy and I have said and the actions that we have taken, or failed to take, on behalf of one another most often have had familial repercussions. So have feelings of hurt or anger caused, however unintentionally, by something that one or both of us has said or done. The truth is, despite our closeness, we have not always been there for one another in the past.

When we were in our twenties, we married men with very different ideas of family life and connection. I married someone who, perhaps because his maternal grandparents lived nearby and regularly visited, embraced the concept and reality of an extended family. Amy's husband, however, wanted their marriage to replicate the kind of nuclear family in which he was raised.

Consequently, Amy and I no longer went on vacations together, requests to go out with Amy and her husband in celebration of Amy's birthday were politely but firmly declined, and I and everyone else in what my brother-in-law referred to as "the family" were not invited to attend their sons' visiting days at sleep away camp, even though we expressed a desire to be there. When Amy and her husband went out for dinner, they went out with their "friends," a term that my brother-in-law made clear didn't include my husband and me. My husband, on the other hand, was always happy to include Amy. She came to visit as often as she could and made it a point of attending all of my sons' birthday parties (alone, I recall) and being with us (usually without her husband) for my husband's or my birthday celebrations. Yet as the tension between my husband and me increased and our marriage began to deteriorate, Amy understandably didn't enjoy being around us as she once had. She began to feel that my husband primarily wanted her around as a "buffer," someone he could talk to or do things with instead of talking to or being with me.

For a number of years, we were also geographically separated. But our life circumstances and choices created greater distances. I missed our connection, and wondered how to bridge the space between us. Too often, our communication deteriorated into hurtful exchanges. I thought about Rachel and Leah, sisters who seem to overcome considerable obstacles to preserve their connection. Like them, there is so much that ties us together; it is inconceivable that one of us would ever walk away from the other. Like Rachel, whom the rabbis describe as asking God to subjugate God's jealousy towards the Israelites for worshipping idols just as she subjugated her jealousy towards Leah for marrying Jacob seven years before her (*Eicha Rabbah* 24), so we have learned to suppress words of disappointment or anger for the sake of our friendship.

What strikes me most about the biblical and rabbinic narratives of Leah and Rachel is that through their relationship, they come to accept one another and ultimately, themselves. Initially, each of them wants what the other has. Rachel longs to be as fertile as Leah, while Leah longs for Jacob's love. Leah and Rachel begin to put aside their rivalry after Leah's son Reuben brings her mandrakes that he found in the field. Leah believes that these fruits, commonly seen as aphrodisiacs, will end what apparently was a period of infertility (Gen 29:35), and she does in fact later bear Jacob three more children. Rachel also believes in the mandrakes' power and thus approaches Leah and asks for some of them so that she too might bear a child. Leah, however, is still pained from Jacob's emotional and physical rejection and retorts: "Isn't it enough that you took my husband?" (Gen 30:15). To this, Rachel offers a practical solution. If Leah gives her some of the mandrakes she will let Leah sleep with Jacob that evening in her stead. Leah readily accepts. These events prove to be a turning point in their relationship, for as a result of this agreement, the sisters begin to develop greater understanding and compassion towards one another.

Leah comes to realize that no matter how much Jacob loves her sister, what matters most to Rachel is bearing children. Hence, when Rachel finally bears a child, she says that God has finally removed her disgrace. She names him Joseph (meaning "God will add on") as an expression of her hope that God will grant her another son (Gen 30:23–24). Perhaps on some level she already knew that. Yet Rachel's willingness to let Leah have sex with Jacob and possibly conceive again (which, in fact, Leah does) reveals to Leah her sister's sense of desperation. Similarly, Leah's wanting to sleep with Jacob even though he has no desire to be with her reveals to Rachel how much Leah craves his love. Leah knows that even if she has sex with him, Jacob will not love her or necessarily want to be with her again. This is evident when she meets him in the field and forthrightly says "I am the one you will bed [tonight], for I have bought you with my son's mandrakes" (Gen 30:16).

Rachel discerns that as much as Leah would like to have more children, what she really seeks is Jacob's affection. Thus, when Leah bears a sixth son, she names him Zebulun ("dwelling of honor"), saying that she hopes that now that she has given birth to six sons, her husband will finally give her the wedding gift that is due her, namely a place of honor in his home and heart (Gen 30:20).

Over the years, Amy and I have similarly come to better understand, accept, and appreciate one another. There wasn't one event or moment that triggered this; there have been many. I remember that for Amy and me, my high school graduation was bittersweet. As much as we knew that I was ready to leave high school, we fully realized that my going to college meant that for the first time we would be physically separated from one another. As Amy wrote in my high school yearbook the night before I left: "Even though I'll probably never admit it, you know that I'll miss you. . . . Always remember the fun we've had and the fights too! . . . Whether I cry or not tomorrow [when you leave] . . . won't matter because I'm crying now. . . . Know that I love you. Take care and write. Love always, your little sister, Amy." I still have the graduation gift that she gave me. It sits on a bookshelf across from my desk in my home office. In fact, I've kept in on a bookshelf near my desk in every place I've lived since college. It is a six-inch white statue made out of hard rubber, of a girl wearing a robe and black graduation cap and tassel, displaying a diploma that she's holding in her hands. The girl's deep black eyes (my eyes are dark brown) are staring ahead and she's smiling, as if imagining all of the wonderful things that lie in store. Printed in clear capital letters at the base are the words: "World's Greatest Student."

I treasured this gift, and continue to treasure it, as an expression of how proud Amy was, and still is, of my academic achievements. I too am, and have long been, proud of her. Despite her deep-seated intellectual insecurities, she has been a first grade teacher for many years. A few years ago, I spent a day in her classroom, where I witnessed the great extent to which she brings her knowledge, musical and artistic talents, and patience (something she always possessed in far greater abundance than I) into the classroom. I also have come to appreciate and learn from Amy's attention to skin care and physical beauty. Over thirty years ago, just before I got married, she asked me whether she could apply my makeup for the wedding. I said yes, probably because I sensed that helping me look pretty on my wedding day meant a great deal to her. When I saw how pretty the makeup made me look, I realized that I didn't just look pretty. I *felt* pretty as well.

While the biblical Rachel becomes a mother and Leah shares moments of physical intimacy with Jacob, the fact remains that Rachel does not become as fertile as her sister and Leah never wins Jacob's heart. Similarly, I will never feel that I am as pretty as Amy, nor will she love intellectual debate and discussion as much as I. Still, through our relationship, she and I—like the biblical Rachel and Leah—have come to accept not just one another, but ourselves. Today, when progressive Jews pray, we include the names of these foremothers. For me, their presence in every prayer service is a reminder of the power and the challenge of relationships between sisters. Amy and I continue to stand together—literally and figuratively—not letting our insecurities or differences tear our friendship apart.

Now divorced with our children grown, Amy and I are making up for lost time. We see each other at least once a month, usually more, meeting in New York City for dinner and a Broadway musical (as we did with our parents), celebrating birthdays and holidays, visiting relatives, shopping at craft fairs. Once a year, the two of us visit our parents' graves. Recently, the two of us went on a two-week vacation in celebration of Amy's 60th birthday. Taking a river cruise from Brussels to Amsterdam, two cities that Amy has always wanted to visit, we laughed and cried and dreamt of future trips together.

4

The Face under the *Huppah*

Relating to My Closest Stranger

NANCY FUCHS KREIMER

I LOOK ACROSS THE FRONT seat of the car at my husband and wonder: Did I see *that* face under the marriage canopy? I once heard a rabbi instruct a couple arriving under the *huppah* to gaze into each other's eyes. "Just as the Torah has seventy faces," he explained, "so does each person. At this time—for a fleeting moment—if you look carefully, you can see all seventy of each other's faces" (*Bamidbar Rabbah* 13:15).

I am quite sure now. I definitely did *not* see that face under the *huppah* almost forty years ago. Sitting next to me is the person with whom I have slept for over half my life. But at this moment I do not recognize him at all.

We are on our way to a much-needed vacation after a stressful and spiritually arid fall. We got a late start, the weather report warns of snow and ice in Connecticut, and the Friday afternoon traffic on the New Jersey Turnpike is already beginning to build. We have been on the road just an hour when my husband announces, in that voice that makes me feel like an incorrigible child, that—given the circumstances—this time *he* will be determining our route. Alone.

There are several ways to drive from our home in Philadelphia to Boston. We have travelled them all together many times, over many years. Early in our marriage, we realized that we each favor a different plan. Both involve a bridge. Mine is the shortest route by miles; his sometimes involves less traffic. We both believe, with perfect faith, that our chosen path is likely to be the fastest, although in all those years we have never been able to establish conclusively who is right. On any given day, either plan might turn out better. The truth is: he detests idling on the highway, while I am offended by the idea of a detour. Once, we decided to "compromise" by going through Scranton, a choice that took an hour longer than either of our routes, but had the virtue of making us both equally unhappy.

On sunny days, or if just one of us is centered, we handle this difference between us with grace. I hear the voice of the family therapist we saw years ago: "You can either be right or be in relationship." Or he remembers the refrigerator magnet that we took home from a couples' workshop that said, simply, "Different minds!" I remind myself that I have made a career of listening to people who think differently than I about matters far more fundamental than driving directions. When we are lucky, one of us catches the humor, indeed absurdity, in our battle of wills, turns to the other and says "I don't like the sound of my voice." We *can* be grown-ups sometimes.

But not always. When we are struggling with core issues, or just too many peripheral ones that have piled up for too long, crossing the Hudson River is nothing compared to bridging the gap between my mind and his. "Between the closest people, infinite distances exist," wrote Rilke. He went on to speak of the "marvelous living side by side" that can grow up when that is recognized and valorized. It is true. But on occasions like this one, it does not feel marvelous. Perhaps the issue is not really traffic delays. The event is not small, just miniature. Being trapped in one car together for hours, condemned to live with the consequences of whatever is decided, stands in for the larger spiritual challenge of a long-term committed relationship.

I sputter and then begin to seethe. I try to remember the command: "Love your neighbor as yourself." At moments like this, the word "love" calls to mind the little heart icons people insert in email messages along with smiling faces. In a rant against the love commandment that helped earn his reputation as a critic of religion, Freud observed that "men are not gentle creatures. . . . Civilized society is perpetually threatened with disintegration." That speaks to me, as our little society of two feels rather shaky right now. Freud did not want to rely upon love. As a Jew in Europe, he saw Christian civilization promoting this commandment with a stunningly poor success record. I think Freud was right: I don't love myself nearly well enough to keep me civilized by loving others as myself.

Back in the first century, a rabbi named Ben Azzai beat Freud to this insight. Ben Azzai challenged his famous colleague Rabbi Akiba who claimed that the "*klal gadol b'torah,*" the great law of the Torah, was "love your neighbor as yourself." Ben Azzai had a different idea. He believed that the great law of the Torah is not a law at all but simply the information that

God creates humanity in God's own image. Ben Azzai saw the weakness in basing ethics on feelings. "If I am willing to be cursed and shamed, perhaps the other fellow is too." On the other hand, knowing God makes us in God's likeness requires people to treat one another with dignity and honor, Ben Azzai reasoned. "Look whom you are cursing and shaming! The image of God," (*Bereshit Rabbah* 24:6).

Before I had ever heard of Ben Azzai, his "great law of the Torah" was my way to begin to understand God. It all started with the story of the coins. It was the coins that helped me live into a conundrum from childhood, a conundrum related to the problem I am facing right now as I sit beside someone I actually do love. As the aging pastor in Marilynne Robinson's novel *Gilead* puts it, "There is nothing more astonishing than a human face."

As a child, I spent hours fascinated by a book in my home called *The Family of Man*, a "photo history of the human race." As the author intended, I felt a deep kinship with the faces in that book. But how to make sense of this sameness along with the estrangement of being in my own head? How could I be a member of a family and also so lonely? More than mere wonder, this aspect of human life filled me with bewilderment, a bewilderment that had an element of the uncanny. The mystery of separateness and connection was not just intellectually interesting; it was incandescent: was one of those profound early experiences I only later learned to call "holy."

Then I heard about the coins. As a teenager sitting in Hebrew school class one late afternoon, I learned the Mishnah in which the rabbis report how they admonished witnesses in capital cases. "An earthly king stamps his image on a coin and they all look the same. But the King of Kings puts his image on every human being, and every one is different"(m. *Sanhedrin* 4:5).

I imagine some of my classmates heard that Mishnah and thought "That makes no sense. How can people of every different nationality all look like God?" But for me, it made perfect sense. I realized that I truly did believe that human beings are created in the image of God. I was very clear about that, although until that moment I had not been at all clear if I believed in God. But now I guessed that I did. I believed in a soul, a sacred part of me that was of the same essence as every other person, even as each of us looked, thought, and experienced the world in a unique way.

It seems altogether reasonable that some people, knowing how different we are, one from another, imagine a world in which the ultimate source and power is also plural—multiple deities, gods and goddesses—ones to look out for each tribe, each nation, even each of us ourselves. But, no! Some of us intuit—although we cannot prove it—that the world is a "blooming, buzzing confusion," but that there is just one Source.

This theology spoke to me, gave a religious grounding to my emerging political awareness and blended well with the humanistic and progressive worldview of my time and place.

In rabbinical school, I learned that the "image of God" is a way of speaking about human beings that appears only three times in the Hebrew Bible—all in the first nine chapters of Genesis. In Akkadian, the word for statue is *tsalamu*, the word for king, *tsalam ili* (image of God)—God's representative on earth. The creation story in Genesis asserts that all human beings are *tzelem elohim*, Alas, as Genesis tells it, God's representatives on earth fail in their role. Human society comes close to the disintegration Freud saw lurking. God brings a great flood, after which God again asserts—perhaps surprisingly—that human beings are still the very image of God.

The charge in Gen 9:6 is a heavy one. Human life is godly, therefore sacred and inviolable. Humans can take animal life, but no one, not a human nor an animal, can take human life with impunity. Over the centuries, that paradoxical verse has served as an argument in favor of capital punishment and war as well as an argument for their abolition. For the rest of the Hebrew Bible, human beings are *nefesh hayyah* (a designation they share with animals) and possessors of *kavod* (a term they share with God) . . . but not again referred to as the "image and likeness" of God.

During the Greco-Roman period the rabbis, the New Testament authors, and later Christian writers developed "God's image" as a key theological concept, one that spoke to the world in which they lived. Those societies put great stock in the statues of their emperors. They had rules concerning the care of the statues. The first century Rabbi Hillel referenced this when claiming that he was going to the bath house to fulfill a command of God. "If we wash the statues of the king, how much more should I wash my own body!" (*Vayikra Rabbah* 34:3).

The *tzelem elohim,* then, was not merely the soul, the spark, the intangible essence of a person—it was everything. One is not permitted to leave the body of a criminal exposed overnight as that would be mocking God's *tzelem.* Jewish tradition imagines the ethereal "soul" to have a physical embodiment. It is called the "*luz* bone," and is located at the top of the spine, exactly at the point where the mind connects with the body. It is said to be the only part of us that does not turn into dust in the grave. It is from the *luz* bone that our bodies will be rebuilt at the time of the resurrection of the dead (*Bereshit Rabbah* 28:3; Zohar I, 69a and 137a; II 28b).

The name comes from the story of Jacob who famously dreamt of a ladder between heaven and earth. He named the place Beth El, but its name, according to Genesis, was *Luz* (Gen 28:19). The *luz,* then, is God's home inside us, the inner manifestation of that ladder of divine-human connection.

In an essay, Israeli novelist David Grossman calls the *luz* bone the "spark of uniqueness," or the "core of the soul." In his novel, *Be My Knife*, Grossman has his hero say, "I . . . gave my *luz* up for lost until . . . the sweet and crazy notion came to me that maybe my *luz* isn't in me at all, but in someone else."

Perhaps Grossman's character was on to something. Neuroscientists have begun talking about circuits in the brain they call "mirror neurons." A mirror neuron is a neuron that fires both when an animal acts and when the animal observes the same action performed by another. If indeed our brains have, in their very neuronal structure, the capacity to know others' brains, feel others' pain, catch others' joy, then we are connected to one another not only because we make up rules (as Freud suggested), but because, along with the instinct for self-preservation, there is the reality of connection. That, too, is part of our evolved selves; our *luz* bone *is* in an other. The sense that we all are images of the same One captures that connection.

But back in the car, we are approaching New York at rush hour and neither Akiba nor ben Azzai is having much luck with me. Akiba's rule of love is surely not helping traverse this trivial spat. Freud was right. My emotions are too complicated, too mired in ambivalence, to count on them to keep me good. And Ben Azzai's theological dictum also fails to impress. My God-self may want to resonate with the God-self of the other, but there is another part of me that just wants to take care of me. I know what the image of the coins tells me: that the other is me and not me. That he is *not* me leaves me full of judgment. That he *is* me should bring compassion.

A belief that others are images of God—even the other with whom I am angry—is a belief hard to access in the moment. As Hillel knew in taking *himself* to the bath, these fine ideas about humanity, God, and others have to start with something real and embodied. And they have to start with ourselves. Right now, I feel, as the writer Emile Cioran described it, like "mud God never laid a hand on." And the more I fail to live up to the God image, the muddier I feel.

Which is why the Jewish spiritual-ethical practice called *Mussar* that I have been studying these last few years spends little time on a theology of godliness. Rather, it talks about our evil inclination, the *yetzer ha ra*. That is the inclination that right this minute is in full throttle in me. The *yetzer ha ra* is ego, but not in the healthy sense of Hillel taking himself to the bath or someone standing their ground with self-awareness and integrity. It is ego that is out of whack, on over-drive, whining and simpering: I want us to go to Boston *my* way. I want what I want when I want it. My *yetzer ha ra* is always ready to fight for my life when nothing momentous is actually at stake. Into this perfectly natural human moment, Reb Simcha Zissel of Chelm, whom my *Mussar* teacher Rabbi Ira Stone channels to great effect, throws in a curve ball, more like a dart than a ball: Crush that *yetzer*! You think this is all about you. But you are here on earth to bear the burden of the other.

The other?!? The guy who thinks he is so smart and knows what he is doing even when he is wrong? *Oiy*. *Mussar* suggests a reframe of our therapeutic culture. We can view the burden of the other as our spiritual challenge. Reb Simcha's advice is not always appropriate. If someone is abusive, we should leave. But otherwise, forget finding God in a sunset or a melting moment of connection with the oneness of it all. Can I see the command in that face, the face I can't even recognize right now, the command to bear his burden? That is where God is.

There is the rub. I often find I do not even know what the burden of the other is. What about this other, the one sitting in the car with me? What *is* his burden? Torah, in a commandment even more radical than "love your neighbor" tells us to "Love the stranger" (Lev 19:34) and more improbably still, that "we know the heart of the stranger." Fortunately, it goes on to tell us in commandment after commandment (some say thirty-five more in all) that what Torah is really after is not love or heart-knowing, but treating the stranger well.

So there is no rub, after all. I do not have to know the other's burden, just bear it. This helps me as I think about the stranger who is my closest other. The great contemporary Jewish philosopher Emmanuel Levinas, whom Rabbi Stone also regularly channels, speaks about "the strangeness of the Other, his irreducibility to my thoughts and my possession." It is just that otherness that "calls into question my spontaneity." There is a name for that calling into question, Levinas says. It is "ethics."

The *Mussar* tradition challenges us to arrange our lives around this idea. How is the other's burden my spiritual opportunity? For me, God is a name for the Mystery. If I want to pay attention to the mystery we call God, what better place to look than right here in the depths of what cannot be known, which happens to be right inside the other with whom I share my life? The spiritual opportunity is to acknowledge the "not knowing" and to accept that it includes myself.

For the mystery is also inside me. One of Freud's most important contributions, the unconscious, turns out to be, if anything, an understatement. In neuroscience circles, Freud—long relegated to the humanities by the sciences—is now receiving belated recognition on this point. Brain scientists are saying that our conscious brains are truly the tip of the iceberg. While Freud thought that this was about repression of unacceptable emotions, the neuroscientists see it more as a matter of efficiency. Our brains simply cannot handle most of what we have to do minute to minute; the majority takes place under the radar screen. In other words, more often than we realize, we act for reasons that we do not know, and we make up stories after the fact so that our behavior is meaningful to us. We are, as the title of one book on this subject puts it, *Strangers to Ourselves*.

Which brings me back to God. The God of the Bible offended Maimonides as much as he offends the "new atheists" of today by being imagined as a human being, an unpredictable one at that. But what better way to point to the unknown? That makes sense to me. The God who is seen as a person is a God of mystery. God as the unknowable is imaged in human form for good reason. We enigmatic creatures, barely able to comprehend our own selves, are the most astonishing mystery of all. The best way to revere God is to honor the strangers across the globe, the strangers I live with in my home, the stranger I am to myself.

None of this matters if it cannot become real in the moment, on the New Jersey Turnpike. And what I want to know is simply this: How will we leave this narrow place, this stupid, weary marital fight, no less burdensome for being so familiar? When will we get over ourselves and step into a broader space?

Since this is an old play, I recall some of the satisfying endings in the past. Once we saw an accident on the side of the road that instantly brought our own life into scale. Sometimes it takes getting out of the car at a rest stop and seeing it all against an immense sky.

At times, what lifts us from our funk is remembering our parents' marriages, both now ended only by death. Between them, those two couples logged almost one hundred years of compromises, basing it all on mutual respect, trust, and bromides taught them by their own parents. "In judging a person, consider his batting average."

Lately, we have begun the practice of chanting Hebrew verses together from the Bible to tunes written by Rabbi Shefa Gold. Shefa taught us her chant to Gen 2:10—"and a river went out from Eden and watered the garden." In times of discord, stopping to chant those words can remind us of the river of blessing that is ever flowing in the background of our lives. If we can quiet down, we can hear the river nurturing us.

We are told that humans share 97 percent of our DNA with chimps. But we are the only animals who make up stories about a God who creates people in God's image, places our soul-bones in others, and is forever sending out a river from the Garden of Eden. We tell these stories in order to transcend the messiness of our lives and to capture the wonder. Perhaps if we could find the "story teller" in our brain we would indeed find our souls. That would be the place where the seventy faces get woven together into one. The place where we engage in our own most amazing act of *imitatio dei,* creating our "selves."

That is how I understand my religious commitment: to stay in conversation with Jewish stories. It is the meaning, for me, of "covenant." It is how I leave my flat reality and return with transformed eyes.

Transformed eyes are just what I need today as we drive on into Connecticut. Need and do not quite achieve. But if God is the power that makes for renewal, that belief in change may turn out to be real, as real as the twenty billion synapses of our brains, ever firing in new configurations, forging new connections, literally birthing new neurons. The scientists call it neurogenesis, the ability of the adult brain to grow in astonishing new ways.

As we get out of the car, we are grumpy and exhausted, annoyed with each other and most of all with ourselves. There has been no heart melting, no rainbows. The redemptive moment still lies in the future. Sometimes we have to make the journey in less than the ideal way, and all we can say at the end is that we completed the trip.

But suddenly I am awash in gratitude. Transformation may yet happen. God renews creation daily; my neurons are still growing. And for us, there is the blessing of time, the gift of the covenant we signed up for almost forty years ago. And even though I know full well that this, too, is just a story among others, it is our story. We will get other chances to do this better. There is always the ride home.

5

Loving Our Mothers

Vivian Mayer

Y EARS AGO WHEN MY son was five years old, I had a visit from *Rivkah Imeinu*, our Mother Rebecca.

I was chaperoning his class on a school trip to the neighborhood library. I was standing off to the side of the large room, two classes worth of kindergarten children sitting cross-legged along the floor. The librarian was holding up a book and asking, "And what do trucks carry for us?" The children's hands all shot up, and the librarian began taking inventory: Bread! Toys! Milk! Fruit! Garbage!

My sweet, dreamy David was in the back of the group. His hand was also up in the air. I could hear him eagerly lisping his answer as he waited for the librarian to call on him. "Eggs! Eggs!" he was trying to add. The room was filled with children and just as many items to load onto this make-believe truck.

At a certain point, his hand still raised, his lips still mouthing "eggs, eggs," David was distracted toward the window. He turned away from the librarian and stared up and out at the sky. It was during those very moments that the librarian's sweep of the room reached his corner.

"Yes, you in the back."

No response.

"The boy with the stripes," she tried again.

My eyes were on my son. I, too, was feeling his anticipation to say "eggs!" Now the librarian was finally calling on him but he was looking away! How could she possibly get his attention when she didn't know his name!? All I had to do was say "David!" and he would have his moment.

35

My heart beat in urgency for my son who clearly needed rescuing—my sweet child who, one day, had gone to school with new pants and came home pouting because his teacher hadn't noticed them; my little boy who could lie on his back for hours playing out a battle between a corkscrew and a nutcracker; this earnest child who obeyed instructions so meticulously that he once did not eat his lunch because his teacher had cautioned the class not to eat anything before their sandwich—and his lunchbox had no sandwich that day; my little dreamy *luftmensch* looking out the window wanting to say "eggs" and not knowing that he was being called on at that very moment. I could intervene and call his name. "David!" was all I had to say. "She's calling on you! It's your turn!"

In those disproportionately long split seconds of inaction, I became aware of *Rivkah Imeinu*, our Mother Rebecca. I recognized the urge inside of me as her urge. This same frantic beating in my chest must have been what drove her to push her mild mannered Jacob forward for fear that he would not succeed without her intervention. I suddenly understood her vigilant listening at the edge of conversations for the cues that her *tam yo-sheiv ohalim*—her uninitiated sheltered boy—might be missing. The anxious desperation overwhelming me in the library reflected the desperation that had compelled Rebecca to cross the lines of trust so that her Jacob would get what she knew he deserved.

At the same time that I recognized Rebecca inside my own urges, I was also painfully aware of her from the outsider's view. I was privy to the ultimate unfolding of her story: she would lose both of her sons as a result of her interference—Esau enraged and likely more estranged from his mother than ever, Jacob forced to flee to another land, never to see his mother again.

According to the sympathetic traditional reading of this tale of family-genesis, Rebecca was a hero who made a sacrifice. Well aware of the consequences, she relinquished her sons in order to set right the line of inheritance as she knew it must be set. We might imagine that though she regretted her losses, she never regretted the ruse that clinched the dynasty's throne to its rightful heir, Jacob. The *midrash* embellishes upon the righteousness of Jacob and the depravity of Esau. It affirms Rebecca's designs as the only way to ensure that the ultimate inheritance of Torah reach the one who was to be named Israel.

However, looking at this narrative through a modern Freudian lens, as Dr. Lori Lefkovitz does in her book, *In Scripture: The First Stories of Jewish Sexual Identities*, Rebecca's tale becomes less a tribal coup d'etat and more a poignant family saga. Jacob is the homebody, smooth and soft and bonded with his mother. Esau, his foil, is the huntsman, hairy and rugged and bonded with his father. In this binary, symbolic reading Jacob is the emasculated male who is both saved and exiled by his mother's actions. Rebecca is the controlling Jewish mother whose doubt in her own child's power is the very force that ensures his weakness. In this particular light Rebecca's valor fades and her character loses some appeal.

Back in the neighborhood library, I cringed as I recognized our mother Rebecca inside myself. I held my impulse under guard. I did not say, "David! She's calling on you!" Instead, I watched the librarian decide that she would move on to the next person. I watched David's attention return to the happenings of the room, his unrelenting hand-waving and lisping of "eggs," and his eventual recognition that the answer-fest had ended even though he hadn't gotten to share. And, yes, the congenial nature of his acceptance of the situation did reassure me that I had not ruined his life that afternoon.

That class trip to the library was a turning point for me. It was a proud moment of mothering. I had successfully made space for my son and trusted in his own capacities. I had distinguished between my own anxiety and actual harm. Rebecca's "appearance" would continue to guide me toward cultivating a specific type of self-restraint. The Genesis matriarchs and patriarchs bequeath the Jewish people a heavy legacy of trial and error in child-rearing, and I had now been inducted as an active participant in its evolution.

But this successful restraint of my potentially crippling impulses came with a tinge of bitterness. My ancient Mother had come to me as a negative model. "Do not do as I did," was her ultimate message. I had deep aversion to Rebecca's *modus operandum*. And though this worked well for my parenting, it was actually not so good for the relationship between me and my Jewish Mothers.

As a young girl, I had found the stories of these good wives and mothers romantically appealing—Sarah's miracle birth, Rebecca's generosity, Rachel's beauty, and, with some pity, Leah's fecundity. In Yeshiva Day School, criticisms regarding the behavior of these righteous women were countered with the classical, traditional spin. Our mothers were prescient. They were fulfilling the Divine plan; Sarah by banishing Ishmael, Rebecca by favoring Jacob, Rachel and Leah by competing to bear sons. Each, through her actions, was building the family of Israel as it was meant to be.

But as I became a young woman, I moved from a child's innocent view of our heroines to a more psychological, critical reading. This was in step with the culture that I eagerly belonged to that encouraged us to look honestly at our own faults without averting our eyes. We wanted to know our Jewish ancestors as the flawed and fully human beings that they surely must have been. We were not interested in saint-stories.

This enterprise of honest examination brought everything into question. As I became more and more connected to the negativity of these narratives, I found the archetypes frightening. I remember hearing a talk that examined the story of Rebecca drawing water from the well for Abraham's manservant. The Torah describes her as running back and forth, fetching and pouring until the stranger and his camels have been watered. Connecting this depiction of young Rebecca to her later role as a mother, the rabbi mused whether this earlier, solicitous generosity might be another face of the very anxiety that compels over-functioners to manage other people's lives. Was young Rebecca manifesting the excessive care-taking that is characteristic of co-dependency? Even overflowing kindness becomes suspect in the eye of the savvy daughter who wants to be nothing like her mother. Was there anything I could value about this matriarch?

I found no solace in the characters of my other Mothers either: blue-blooded Sarah, beating down her pregnant handmaid for imagining herself her equal. Disappointed Rachel, blaming her husband, "Give me children or I will die!" who, when she finally does give birth, names her son Joseph "*Yosef li ben aher*" meaning "let the Lord give me yet another son!" And dowdy Leah, the un-chosen, measured against the beauties, embarrassingly eager for her husband's love and attention, finding her self-worth only through her children.

Each of these women had become a big "Do Not Enter!" sign: the Jewish Status Queen, the Jewish Manipulating Mother, the Jewish Frustrated Bitch, and the Jewish Desperate Frump. I had no compassion for how fiercely they had fought for their accomplishments and only a little compassion for their pain. And yet, God help me, I knew each one of these mothers from the inside out. I could easily beat my breast in confession: "I have sought to control, I have blamed in bitterness, I have looked down on others, I have used my disappointment as a weapon, I have resented beauty and wished for it at the same time." It became clear to me that if I was going to be forever on guard against my Mothers, I would be forever on guard against myself.

I have since learned to identify this type of harsh judgment as "internalized oppression." This is the phenomenon of looking at ourselves through outside eyes and recoiling as we recognize the very stereotypes that we are desperately seeking to avoid. The only escape from such harshness of judgment is compassion, and yet, it is nearly impossible to be compassionate when we are filled with aversion. It sometimes happens, though, that there is a moment of expansion, an *et ratzon*, where for no identifiable reason, aversion makes way for open-heartedness, and judgment steps aside for kindness. I experienced such a moment of grace and blessing during a certain episode of personal struggle some years ago. Through no clear action of my own, this moment of expansion showed me a new path toward my mothers and, simultaneously, toward my own self as a Jewish woman, mother, and wife.

In telling the story I'm about to tell, allow me please to be purpose-fully vague and to say simply that once upon a time, back when I believed that I might actually live into the ideals of a feminist utopia, I had been benevolently welcoming to someone whose presence I soon grew to resent and despise. Though I never dared voice any of this aloud, my mind flashed with hourly bursts of indignation to the tune of "who does she think she is!" and "how dare she!" I wished I could be generous to this person who had in fact done me no harm. I was too ashamed of my limited capacity for sharing to tell anyone how I was feeling. I didn't know which was causing me more suffering—my furious jealousy or my self-disdain for ever having imagined that I might have been wide-hearted enough to share in the first place.

One day at the height of these consuming feelings, I stood to say the *Minchah* afternoon prayer hoping for just a moment of stillness in the midst of my internal storm. I opened in usual form with the customary salutation, bowing low to position myself before "our God and God of our ancestors." I named each mother and father with the phrase "God of" attached to their respective names, "God of Abraham, God of Isaac, God of Jacob, God of Sarah, God of Rebecca, God of Rachel, and God of Leah . . ."

This peculiarly repetitive formulation of the Divine name suggests a complex theological prospect: that while we do assert that God is one and singular, we equally assert that the identity of God alters within each specific human-Divine relationship. God of Abraham is not, in fact, the manifested God of Isaac, and the God of Isaac is not exactly the God of Jacob. In this ep-ithet, which God offers to Moses at the burning bush, each of our patriarchs' names serves to define a different human-Divine possibility. Abraham hears the voice of God that calls "Go forth!" while Isaac hears the message "Stay in your place." Jacob hears God reassuring him, "Do not be afraid." Each of these men is directed, through his God, to specific challenges and specific pledges that belong to him alone.

Now that the matriarchs are also mentioned in the feminist emenda-tions of our liturgy, God's identity expands to include even more faces. The One who chooses Sarah for motherhood. The One who reveals the cause of internal conflict to Rebecca—"The Lord said unto her: 'Two nations are in thy womb . . .'" (Gen 25:23). The One who shows compassion to the neglected—"And the Lord saw that Leah was hated and opened her womb" (Gen 29:31).

So did I stand on this particular afternoon, naming my ancestors one by one, each name giving shape to the God I was about to address. "Blessed are You, our God and God of our Ancestors, God of Abraham"—the man who is inextricably linked with the attribute of *Hessed*, generosity that knows no bounds—"God of Sarah," the grudging woman whose very life is the foil to this generosity. The words "*Elohei* Sarah, God of Sarah" arrested me, first in aversion, then in pain. The resentful turmoil that I had been feeling in my heart found a mirror in Mother Sarah, bitch and princess, who had castigated the handmaid Hagar for encroaching on her domain after she herself had invited her in.

Until this moment I had, ever so righteously, found it easier to ally with the runaway Hagar than the offending Sarah. Nachmanides' thirteenth-century commentary on the passage in Gen 16:6 refers to Sarah's debasement of Hagar as a grievous sin and the origin of the enmity between her own children (the people of Israel) and Hagar's (the people of Ishmael, the Arab nations). Nachmanides' bold comment had served well as handy ammunition against the apologetics commonly used to justify Sarah's harshness.

But on this day, I did not condemn Sarah. Instead I wondered what it must have been like for her to have her spiritual life so linked to that of the ever-so-tolerant Abraham. How was Sarah's own relationship with God affected or defined by her husband's utter devotion to God? I wondered—when poor Sarah had first offered her handmaid to Abraham as a surrogate mother, had she beheld herself through her husband's noble eyes, imagining that she would be able to handle the challenge of the new relationship? Had she, like me, reached for her magnanimous heart only to be ambushed by her limitations?

A pin-hole of compassion opened.

The openness and generosity that I had been reaching for (and whose mark I was sorely missing) was based on the perfect vision and spiritual abilities of other people, not my own. Abraham is known in the Jewish tradition for his welcoming tent. He hears his God telling him to push his giving nature to its edge. He remains astonishingly able to let go, even regarding his sons, miraculous gifts of his old age. I too had placed myself among idealistic Abrahams of a sort. It had been tempting to think that I might be just as benevolent and selfless. But now I could empathize with Sarah. As her resentment grew she must have scolded herself for being less tolerant than Abraham would have been. I imagine her shoving down her bitterness until it finally burst out in a rage directed at her husband, "Do something to put this handmaid in her place!" Abraham refuses to take this on and, instead, hands it back to her. Sarah treats Hagar cruelly, and Hagar flees.

Looking at Sarah through my own suffering, I did a double-take. She had sinned because she had overstretched. She had been listening to the God of her husband and not to her own God. Nachmanides, in his admonishing comment, was not teaching us to vilify our Mother Sarah; he was simply teaching us that the moral mistakes of archetypal models have enormous and lasting consequences. Standing in prayer, I felt myself standing in the presence of that compassionate Truth, *Elohei* Sarah, the God of Sarah. "Dear Child," the benevolent voice said to us both, "You are good. You have borne a tremendous amount. For everyone's sake, don't take on more than you can bear." I began to cry. Through this filter of God's voice I discovered a deep compassion for Sarah where I had none. And I discovered that in that deep source there was some compassion available for me, as well.

Recognizing my God and my people's God as the God of Sarah reminds me that my Mother Sarah had never been banished from the Divine embrace of love and guidance. It was I myself who had banished her. Naming God through Mother Sarah brought Sarah herself back from across the line and into my heart.

God's relationship with Sarah Our Mother is, and has always been, a deep part of the Jewish consciousness. The fact that it is now included in many official liturgies as an explicit name of the Divine brings this relationship closer to the forefront, but it is not a new conception by any means. All our Mothers are revered and appreciated. I come full circle to the pietistic reverence that, as a younger person, I disdained. I stand now in full eagerness to honor my Mothers and their bequests to me, daughter of Sarah, daughter of Rebecca, daughter of Rachel, daughter of Leah.

From that first, startling moment of discovering compassion for Sarah through the name *Elohei* Sarah I challenged myself to ask, who is the God of Rebecca who loves her still though she is beset with worry, afraid that her children will not take the path that she wants for them? Who is the God of Rachel who loves her still through her desperation? If I can imagine that love I can feel the presence of that very force who will love me, too, when I am feeling worried or territorial or disappointed.

Our ancient Mothers are our royal pedigree, fascinating characters, psychological archetypes, and constructs of our people's earliest memories. But they are also portals to Divine compassion.

I do not always have compassion for all parts of myself. I still sometimes recoil at the actions of our Mothers and my own. But I now have a mechanism in the words of my daily prayers that helps me to remember that the very name of the Divine is manifested through the names of my imperfect, struggling ancestors. The opening of every silent standing *Amidah* reaches the consciousness of the Jewish people and reminds us that God knew our Mothers and Fathers and that our Mothers and Fathers sought God. As part of this legacy, I courageously inch forward, too, seeking the Divine. Seeking the always-possible love in any way it avails itself to us.

6

Portals to Sacred Family Life

JULIE GREENBERG

"Torah is not high up in the heavens."

—DEUTERONOMY 30:12

THE FAMILY AGENDA FOR the day included soccer practice and a birthday party, an orthodontist appointment and getting the bird's wings clipped. As we were each mobilizing to leave for the day, I turned to D, and said, "We need diapers."

"I can't get them, I'm busy all day."

"I'm busy all day too."

We continued to bicker about whose turn it was to buy diapers and who was more overwhelmed with busy-ness. I listened to us and I thought, "This isn't the way I want to have a conversation with my partner and this isn't how I want to discuss our baby's needs."

I left for class. My mind gripped the situation, hashing over it like gears cranking in a car. I thought, "Men don't like women to ask them to do things because it reminds them of their mothers." I thought, "We are bumping up against the incompatibility of men and women," and "Relationships are impossible." Spinning through one psychological analysis after another, I was working myself into a tight, stuck place.

"Take it to prayer." My spiritual director colleagues and I had been encouraging one another to "take it to prayer." I had become plenty good at guiding others, but ironically, while I enjoyed communal prayer at times for the sense of community and some sense of spiritual nurturance, traditional prayer had never been a transformative process for me. This was new territory. "Take it to prayer." I decided to listen.

Deep breaths relaxed my clenched hands on the steering wheel and I chanted Rabbi Shefa Gold's interpretation of the Talmudic phrase "You are the Source of life for all that is and Your blessing flows through me." I made some quiet space and as I did so I felt God welling up, filling the space. Flowing through the space. Flowing through me.

When I reached my destination I went directly to a phone, called D and said, "I'm sorry." I bought the diapers later in the day.

Prayer gives me hope whereas getting stuck causes such despair and hopelessness. I came home from work to find that D had cleaned the house. The kitchen was sparkling, the toys had been picked up, there were purple tulips on the table. Our acts of generosity are redemptive. My heart opened once again to him.

The next week when we ran out of diapers, with no discussion, he bought the diapers. The diaper dilemma, which at first felt tense and impossible, opened a door to a greater spiritual practice that uplifted our situation.

These small interactions, calling for spiritual practice, are the building blocks of the quest to love well. I think this endeavor to be in holy relationship is the most important spiritual work we can do. It has taken D and me over ten years to even begin to be caring, productive parents together with a minimum of attack and defense. Getting there tapped every psychological, spiritual, and material resource either of us could possibly muster. And on this adventure, a further dose of trust, understanding, and compassion is always valuable. Our partnership evolved in a non-traditional way, but many of the challenges we have faced are universal.

Partnering never seemed to me to be a pre-requisite to parenting. The sequence of falling in love, deciding to be mates, getting married, raising a family, never compelled me. That particular order of events seemed arbitrary. For instance, I knew I was ready to mother without any aspirations towards marriage. Thus, I was the happy solo parent of Rosi, Raffi, Zoe, ages ten, eight, and six, when an unexpected partner joined the journey.

The same week that I was bringing home my fourth baby, Joey, D rented a room in my home. D shared with me that he longed for a family; I was open to sharing my family. I passionately loved parenting and appreciated adult companionship while doing it. Over the next few years we evolved into a "parenting partnership"—building a friendship that allowed us to parent together even though we were never lovers and only lived together the first year.

D arrived on the family scene at a time when I, Solo Mom to three young children and a new baby, held the priority of integrating my newly adopted fourth child into the web of family relationships. I wanted to attend to each of my four young children as the family grew. My priority was not the dishes, the toys, the laundry on the floor.

I would do the laundry with efficiency honed by a decade of single parenting, and dump it in a clean heap from which each child transferred their own belongings into a heap in their own area. The kids and I didn't fold or sort or put clothes in drawers or closets. These happy heaps of clothes were certainly functional if not traditional. Everyone had clean clothes to wear every day. What felt like joyful family building to me, looked like physical chaos to my new friend.

Sitting amidst a mound of scraggly unsorted laundry, he complained "I get so angry about the socks. I'm just not that evolved. It's the heap of mismatched socks that gets me."

"It's just you and me, each of us fragile and vulnerable doing the best we can. I'm not any more evolved than you."

"You're not. Uh-oh."

"That's why the Torah teaches that the teaching is not out there in the heavens or far away across the sea. It's right here in our mouths, in our hands. It's in the socks." I want the Torah to be a shared resource for both of us, but he just thinks I'm preaching to him. We are stuck with the mismatched socks.

The daily-ness of what we encounter, like those socks, can be a portal to a holy journey. Those socks could point us to inner work and to outer dialogue, just as Jewish ritual objects such as the *shofar*, the *lulav*, the *matzah* point to meaning beyond themselves. The *shofar*, on a physical level is simply a ram's horn, and yet it calls us to wake up to the need of the world and to the still voice inside. The *lulav* is four species of plant bound in a branch, designed to be waved during the festival of *Sukkot*, and yet it also reminds us to attend to the four corners of the earth and to all the strands of self internally. The *matzah*, dry unleavened bread on its most basic level, is a call to freedom, freedom for all those living under oppression in the world and freedom of consciousness within.

Similarly, those socks could lead to inner reflection on each parent's values about housework and children, on relationship dynamics in household leadership, on whatever blocks there are to creative problem solving about the socks. The socks could lead to connection between us exploring how to partner around these issues despite different backgrounds and expectations.

These portals appear all the time in family life. Many times I bump up against them with no consciousness and the conflict around them feels annoying and frustrating. Every now and then, when I'm able to bring a spiritual awareness to the issue, the "thing" opens a door to what is beyond.

Caring for a baby together was an astonishingly intimate experience for me. Never had anyone other than me taken one of my kids to a doctor's appointment. Having another adult cook dinner for us in our own home was remarkable. The act of passing the baby bottle back and forth as we handed over the child felt wondrous to me. The wonder had to do with this other adult, who was not being paid and who had no formal reason for being there, joining me in the care of this precious new family member.

When Joey was four, baby Mozelle joined the family and D became "Daddy" to the younger two and a "Dad-like-figure," to the older three. He ended up living a few blocks away in his own home, with the kids walking freely back and forth. We danced a dance of early partnering without stopping to talk about it. We were two very different people who didn't know each other or our own selves well enough and we were trying to forge a new kind of relationship. We had completely different assumptions but didn't even realize how different our expectations and perceptions were. We lacked a common language. His was a language of deeds. "Who else's kitchen floor would I wash? Of course I'm committed." I craved a language of words, "How can we co-create a life together if we never discuss it?"

All partnered people are engaged in a cross-cultural endeavor. Each has their own experience, expectations, assumptions, desires about what it means to be in relationship. In any successful union the rules of relationship are co-created, negotiated, either consciously or unconsciously, by the people living it. We were sometimes able to step through a portal of disagreement into cooperative connection.

We literally had to learn to feed each other. In the early years, he would cook food that seemed odd or incongruous to the family. He'd put tofu in the chili, serve potato chips as the vegetable. I couldn't feed him either. I knew he was a vegetarian but had no idea that meat on the table grievously offended him. It took him years of silent suffering before he let me know how he felt. I also couldn't tell him what I liked or wanted because he was so insecure feeding a whole family that he'd melt down. Maybe he got more confident as a parent, maybe I got more sensitive in talking to him. Somehow we learned how to feed each other, which resulted in years of delicious, pleasing family meals.

One day D and I walked through the Wissahickon woods in the full glory of its fall foliage.

He said, "I was really upset by the belt buckle Joey was wearing. Where did that come from?" Even after thirteen years, I can rarely predict what will upset this dear man.

My mind raced to scan the buckle our young adolescent son was wearing. It was something Joey had asked me for permission to order on-line, using money he had earned.

I vaguely recalled that the buckle showed a coin slot with the words, "Five Cents: Insert coin, unzip, shake well, Guaranteed action, internal use only." In retrospect, the message did seem pretty sleazy. At the time I had only followed my inclination to say Yes to my kids' interests barring any glaring reason to object.

D continued, "I think this is a kid who needs really firm limits and a really strong sense of judgment about what's appropriate. I want to tell him never to wear that buckle in public. I am offended that you approved it, and we need a better system for making these decisions."

"You know, to tell the truth, I didn't even think about it that much. It just seemed like some idiotic thing that would tickle a thirteen-year-old's fancy."

"You weren't thinking about how other people would see it. He needs to learn how other people react to him."

"You're saying you'd like me to think about how other people are gonna see it before approving this kind of thing."

"Yes."

"I can try to be more aware of that. And I want to ask you something too. Instead of confronting Joey and putting him into an oppositional position, I think it's important to walk through the thinking process with him. He needs to create neural pathways for thinking and making decisions about this kind of thing."

"What do you mean?"

"Like say to him 'now that you have this buckle, where do you think is a good place to wear it? What would your teachers think of it? How about your grandparents? Which of your friends would enjoy it?' Let him do the work of coming to these realizations."

"Okay," he concurred. "I'll try that."

Mundane objects, like tofu or the belt buckle, can become handles beckoning toward transcendence: they point towards the work of transformation that needs to happen to create a flow of shared power, communication, and empathy. On the journey of love, things that might not seem to have much significance can be major stumbling blocks unless they are approached as portals to greater understanding. These things become momentary "sancta," items that point beyond themselves to a bigger world.

As D and I strengthened our partnering, two steps forward, one step back, our drama that felt so intense internally, played out against a backdrop of meticulous daily care for kids. No one ever missed a dentist appointment or forgot the carpool. School forms were sent in on time and play dates were planned. Skinned knees got tended, bedtime tucks provided, fears calmed, jokes shared. Academic and athletic efforts were championed. Animated conversations about politics, ethics, social issues flew around the dinner table every night. The stakes were high, calling D and me to attend to our relationship with one another because the intricate, intimate heart strings of five children were tightly intertwined with our progress. Family building was a sacred process.

With Jewish sancta, or ritual objects, generations of experience form an expectation that the thing means more than the thing itself. For instance, the *shofar* resonates with the ram in the bush at the Binding of Isaac. It resonates with the blast that will precede *mashiach*. It reminds us of countless High Holy Days where we create new beginnings again and again.

The sancta of our own lives might be more of a surprise; without a community embracing and cherishing a particular item, you might not expect that it will vibrate with potential. Often the momentary, ordinary sancta of our lives become apparent as the epicenter of conflict. The first hint of possibility that there is something more there than the thing itself might be your own resistance, reactivity, or distress. Why are socks so upsetting? Because there is something greater to be learned about your Self and about the Other. It isn't just about the socks or the house keys, the toothpaste cap, the damp towels.

Society has moved beyond the old days when families were created from economic need and material necessity. We now create families based on love. This is a promising development because love is good for the world. But we're fledglings at the spiritual path of love. The momentous God-work we do in relationships requires such courage, dedication, and luck. I sometimes feel brave as I navigate these rewarding and yet treacherous relational pathways. Torah reassures me when it says that it isn't too puzzling, that it is very close to us. We can open our eyes to everyday sancta and rise to the challenge of entering the door that is opened.

In my experience, relational excellence can encompass various kinds of connections. Men and women, women and women, men and men, beyond gendered relationships, each of us and the earth, parents and children, teachers and students, humans and animals, vertically with older and younger generations, horizontally with peers.

The way I see it, for God to be One, it is this multiplicity of "others," these diverse expressions of God's particularity, who need to be in compassionate communion. But how to get from here to there? How to make love work? I embed my own small attempts at loving partnership, which have sometimes gone well and sometimes not at all well, in the Big Story of the human race trying to learn to love. Maybe small items such as the diapers have a key role to play in this huge endeavor.

My prayer is for the holy alchemy that transforms our encounters with diapers, socks, tofu and the belt buckle, into the holiness of sacred family life. Bringing curiosity to a conversation about a belt buckle, allowing tofu to be a gateway into emotional as well as physical nourishment, seeing socks as more than trouble heaped on the floor, these are ways of saying "Torah is right here in our hands."

> [Torah] is not too puzzling for you, nor too far away. It is not something high up in the heavens, so that you might say: Who shall go up to the sky for us, and bring it to us and make us hear it so that we might do it? It is not beyond the ocean, so that you might say: Who shall cross the ocean for us, and bring it to us and make us hear it so that we might do it! But rather this teaching is very close to you, upon your mouth and in your heart—it can be done! (Deut 30:11–14)

II

From the Narrow Places
(Psalm 118:5)

7

"Sing, O Barren One!"

Ambushed by a Hysterectomy at Age Twenty-Six

ELLEN FRANKEL

WOMEN AND CHILDBIRTH. From their first appearance in the Torah, women are associated with biology, specifically, their capacity to give birth. God, irremediably gendered male in Hebrew, creates the entire universe through his mouth, speaking it into material existence, and then forms human beings from the earth, doing so without hands, without sex, without pain or bodily peril. The first man, Adam, is first characterized as a doer, commanded to work and steward the earth. When he disobeys God and eats of the forbidden fruit, he is condemned to live out his activist nature in suffering and with difficulty, "by the sweat of your brow shall you get bread to eat," until he returns to his source, the earth from which he came.

The first woman, in contrast, is presented as derivative and incomplete from the outset, created to fill a deficit—"it is not good for man to be alone"—and creating a new deficit by depriving Adam of a piece of himself. And when Eve disobeys God, she too is condemned to live out her quintessential incompleteness in suffering and difficulty: "in pain shall you bear children. Yet your urge shall be for your husband, and he shall rule over you." Woman's role, like man's, is to feel forever uncompleted until she fills this deficit with an other; but she must then create a new absence, surrendering up a piece of herself, a child, bone of her bone, flesh of her flesh, returning Adam's rib, as it were.

—————

When I was a girl and then a young woman, it never dawned on me that I would not be able to bear children when the time came. When I got my period at thirteen, I knew that meant that I was normal; it never occurred to me that pregnancy would be beyond my reach. In fact, I spent my twenties worrying about an unwanted pregnancy, getting myself on the pill in college and then switching over to an IUD after I was married. Ironically, I switched to an IUD because I feared that the pill was too dangerous for someone like me who had been exposed to DES (diethylstilbestrol) in utero. At that time, the early '70s, the copper T was considered a far safer means of birth control.

My new father-in-law, a physician in general practice, agreed. So he asked his best friend, a gynecologist, to implant the copper T in me as a personal favor, at no charge. And that is how I became yet another victim of the law of unintended consequences.

My husband and I delayed our honeymoon for two years so we could finish our graduate school coursework at Princeton and so he could finish his dissertation and get a teaching job. And so, in the summer of 1977, we headed for Paris and the British Isles for ten weeks on a literary pilgrimage, armed with a BritRail pass and a small inheritance from my grandfather.

Near the end of our trip, I began to experience sharp pains in my groin, which steadily worsened each day. But since I didn't want to end up in a foreign hospital, I grit my teeth and soldiered on, willing myself to stay well enough to make it home to trustworthy American medicine. Unfortunately, we had scheduled ourselves to leave Princeton the day after we returned home, packing up our grad school apartment and relocating to Lancaster, Pennsylvania, where Herb was to start as an Assistant Professor of English that fall. When I went to the Princeton Hospital soon after we arrived home, the surgeon I consulted took an X-ray, assured me that the IUD was still securely in place, and urged me to see a doctor as soon as I settled into my new home in Lancaster. I spent that last night in Princeton in the bathroom, sick to my stomach, scared and miserable, but determined to push on to the next stage of our move.

In Lancaster the next day, a new neighbor in university housing referred me to her gynecologist. When I described my symptoms to the doctor's receptionist, they scheduled me for an appointment that day. As soon as Dr. Grant examined me, he yanked out the IUD and told me he was admitting me to the hospital. For the next week, I was injected three times a day with antibiotics, and then Dr. Grant told me that he would have to operate. I had pelvic inflammatory disease; my ovaries and fallopian tubes were abscessed, and if we didn't act now, I stood the risk of developing peritonitis, a potentially fatal condition.

The day before surgery I was asked to sign a hospital release form. Although much of what happened next is a blur, this particular moment remains with me to this day in crystalline clarity: The form I was to sign specified that the planned procedure would involve "definite removal of one ovary and fallopian tube, probable removal of both ovaries and fallopian tubes, and possible complete pelvic clearance." Complete pelvic clearance. The phrase sounded so clinical, like something at a construction site. But I signed the release form. I didn't consult anyone, not even my husband. I trusted my doctor, although I had only known him for a week. From the acuteness of the pain, I knew that my condition was deadly serious. And looking back now, I think I was probably in too much shock, denial, and shame to consider alternatives. I just wanted the whole thing over with.

I remember waking up afterwards in my bed, still foggy from the anesthetics, seeing Dr. Grant, a good-looking, kindly Scotsman, looking down at me, and asking him, "What did you do?" He tried to put me off, telling me we would talk later when I felt more alert, but I persisted. I wanted to know now.

He told me gravely, "We had to take everything out. Ovaries, tubes and uterus. You might have died if the abscesses had ruptured."

I remember muttering in my dopey fog, "Tough luck," then falling back to sleep.

No tears, no screams, no flailing arms. I played the *shtarke*. Just as I had resolved in England when I first got sick, I was determined to keep toughing it out. Even now.

The first stories I learned in Hebrew School were about the patriarchs and matriarchs, Abraham and Sarah, Isaac and Rebecca, Jacob and his four wives. A common theme running through all these stories was barrenness. Sarah, Rebecca, and Rachel all had trouble conceiving, and it was a source of great trouble for all of them as well as for their husbands. Sarah's pregnancy at age ninety required divine intervention, and resulted in Ishmael's expulsion from the family. Rebecca's pregnancy, also facilitated by God, culminated in the birth of bitter sibling rivals, Jacob and Esau. And Rachel's two pregnancies proved disastrous: provoked by jealousy of Joseph, the only son of Jacob's favorite wife, Joseph's brothers broke their father's heart and sold their brother into slavery; and Rachel's second son Benjamin killed his mother in childbirth, which is why she died naming him Ben-oni, the "son of my affliction."

I can't imagine that my Hebrew school teachers explained to us at the time that the biblical trope of barrenness served to single out these ancestral women for a special role in the Divine Comedy of the Jewish People, that their trials triggered divine intercession, which only comes to the meritorious few. No, I took the infertility of Sarah, Rebecca, and Rachel simply at face value: these women had trouble getting pregnant, and they were lucky that God helped them out. I read no existential significance into their stories nor did I see any theological point to them. Bad things sometimes just happened to good people.

Obviously, after my hysterectomy, my interpretation of these biblical stories changed. But by then I had learned to "read" all literary texts in an intricately nuanced way. After all, I was getting a PhD in Comparative Literature! I had come to appreciate the way that authors can inject irony, ambiguity, and unreliability into their texts. (It was only later that I would learn about the "hermeneutics of suspicion," i.e., reading a text, especially as a woman, with a jaundiced eye.) From my continuing informal Jewish study, I had also learned about *PaRDeS*, the four levels of reading traditional texts in rabbinic biblical interpretation. So I was already "reading between the lines" whenever I opened the Bible.

But now that I had myself become a barren woman, I had a different relationship to these scriptural stories. I was not so much focused on the narrative voice of the text as I was on the characters themselves, whether they were imagined by some ancient author or whether they were recorded from real life. In fact, it was the Hebrew word itself, *akara*, barren, that pierced me each time I read, heard, or chanted it. Unfortunately, that was very often. Every year we read the stories of the first biblical families as we follow the annual cycle of the Torah readings. In the *Hallel* service, recited on holidays, we read Psalm 113: "[God] sets the childless woman among her household as a happy mother of children." The line at the beginning of the book of Isaiah, "Sing, O Barren One!" (54:1), appears in three different *haftarot*—in the prophetic portions that accompany the Torah portions *Noakh, Ki Tetze*, and as the fifth *Haftarah* of Consolation following Tisha B'Av. Every Rosh Hashanah, we read the story of Hannah, who fervently prayed for an end to her barrenness, and then in gratitude for having her wish granted, sent this miracle child away after weaning him to serve out his days in the Temple.

I wasn't alone in these visceral reactions in synagogue. The year after my hysterectomy, my father-in-law chanted the *haftarah* on the First Day of Rosh Hashanah, the story of Hannah, as he always did but was unable to complete it. When he froze in the middle of his recitation, he was taken by ambulance to the hospital, initially diagnosed with a heart attack. Luckily, the fear proved false. But that was the last time he chanted that *haftarah*.

The funny thing about the Hebrew word, *akara*, is that it's one of those odd words called a contronym, a word that is an antonym of itself, like the English word "cleave." The root of *akara* means "core," but similar to its English translation, it can mean either "root" or "uproot." When we core an apple, we take its heart out. So *akara* means essence but also absence, lack, emptiness. A barren woman is thus hollow at the pit of her being.

Besides all the written texts reminding me of the new fact of my barrenness, there were all the visual texts constantly confronting me: my young married friends were becoming pregnant with their first children. There were invitations to baby showers, *brises*, and namings. As I recuperated from my surgery in late August of 1977, I became aware of all the bulging bellies of the scantily clad women surrounding me—at the mall, the swim club, the supermarket, fast food restaurants, department store changing rooms. Had there always been so many pregnant women in view? Why had I never noticed them before?

I became the veritable embodiment of envy. "Why me?" I asked myself. "Why not me?" How could I be happy for others when I had lost everything? I was only twenty-six, for God's sake! We had only been married for two years. Why had we waited before having children—until it was too late? How could all those unwed teenagers get pregnant, not even wanting their children, and I, who would be such a fit mother, be barren?

I wondered whether these feelings of loss, jealousy, bitterness, and grief would ever go away. Even if we adopted children, would I ever feel whole again?

There's one emotion associated with these events that I've never really talked about, and I wonder whether it eats away at me unconsciously even now. That emotion is shame. Although never using this term, the Bible intimates that all its barren women were consumed with shame. When Sarah despairs of giving her husband an heir, she gives Abraham her handmaid Hagar as a surrogate; but once Hagar becomes pregnant, Sarah cannot abide having her nearby, "for I was despised in her eyes" (Gen 16:5). When the childless Rachel compares herself to her fertile sister, Leah, she complains to Jacob, "Give me children, or else I die" (Gen 30:1). The barren Hannah explains to her husband that she is so distraught because his fertile second wife has taunted her due to her inability to give him children; she tells the priest Eli that she is "in anguish and distress" because she cannot conceive a child. In the eyes of a traditional society, a childless married woman brings shame upon herself and her husband; not that much has changed in the three millennia since then. According to current Orthodox law, a Jewish man whose wife has failed to bear a child after ten years of marriage can divorce her.

The day after my hysterectomy, I felt covered in shame. I didn't want to see anyone, especially not my parents or in-laws. Clearly, I had failed them all utterly. I would never produce a biological grandchild to carry on their genetic line. Although my husband and I each had a married sibling, neither of them had any children; it seemed unlikely that either would. Typically, my mother showed no emotion when she visited me after my operation, telling me only later that she had cried for three days when hearing of its outcome. I remember when my husband's parents came to see me, so different from my own parents, their eyes filled with tears of sympathy and comfort, but I misinterpreted their distress as disappointment and blame.

My husband's first words on seeing me were "So we won't have children," which only deepened my shame. I had failed him as well. Like most newly married couples, we had never discussed what we would do if we couldn't have biological children. I had already decided that we would adopt. But he had summarily crossed off this option. How could our marriage survive such a fundamental disagreement?

But the worst moment came when my roommate at the hospital, a young cognitively impaired woman who had just given birth out of wedlock, sat with her mother to decide what to do about the baby. It was clear from their conversation that the hospital social worker had counseled the new mother to place the baby for adoption.

"Even a dog keeps its young!" the mother of this young woman now barked at her bewildered daughter, so clearly incapable of taking care of a child by herself. Later that day, the rest of the family dropped by, echoing the mother's sentiments.

I sank lower in my bed, embarrassed to be overhearing this outlandish conversation and even more ashamed of my new sterility. Even dogs give birth, I thought to myself, even girls with Down's syndrome. But not me. Of what use is a PhD if I can't have a child?

Had I shared these feelings with my husband, with my parents and in-laws, with my close friends, or with a therapist, they certainly would have protested that I had nothing to be ashamed of. I hadn't caused my hysterectomy. It wasn't my fault. But shame is a locked door. It doesn't want to let anyone in. A person overwhelmed by shame imagines that letting in the light will only makes things worse. When just the opposite is true.

To overcome my shame, I became an Iron Maiden, tough, determined, unstoppable. While others wept over my loss, I transcended it. While others told me they couldn't imagine how I felt, I told them I was OK. With stitches still in my abdomen, I taught several sections of Freshman Comp that fall in my living room. I wrote my doctoral dissertation in four months. I pushed on, aggressively pursuing adoption (my husband quickly changed his mind after his first impulsive declaration), taking adjunct teaching jobs, writing books, volunteering for Jewish organizations, making a life in spite of being an *akara*.

But the truth was that I was in profound mourning. Denying that fact only made the grief last longer.

Over the thirty-five years since my hysterectomy, I have learned that time does heal most wounds, even ones that are at first denied. My life has been remarkably fruitful, even though my womb has not. The two children we adopted, a daughter and a son, are now grown and married, and our daughter has three children of her own. Although we've had our share of troubles with our kids, we are full of gratitude for the exceptional people they have become. We've learned the same hard-won lessons of parenthood that biological parents learn. While I might occasionally envy my friends whose children have inherited their brains and talents, I've also come to value the inborn strengths of our own children, and come to appreciate the wisdom of not looking for our own images in our children. And the exclusion I used to feel when my friends shared stories of their pregnancies, labor, childbirth, or difficulties with breast-feeding no longer ambushes me.

In the end we all must come to terms with barrenness. Like Adam, we all must surrender pieces of ourselves. Like Eve, we all must own up to being incomplete, unfinished. Whether we give birth to children or adopt them, we must ultimately let them go. That's the truth contained in the paradox of *akara*. We are both full and empty at our core. The secret of happiness is learning to embrace this paradox instead of denying it.

8

El Na Refa Na La

Please, God, Heal My Daughter!

AMY EILBERG

IT WAS APRIL OF my daughter's freshman year at Oberlin College. Her father Howie and I, in different cities, were on the line together for the fateful conference call with the dean of students. I remember it as one of those heart-stopping, nightmare moments, time out of time, never to be forgotten. The dean kindly but firmly delivered the message that Penina could not stay at school any longer. After several weeks of monitoring, our daughter's weight had continued to fall dramatically. It was not safe for her to stay on campus till the end of the semester. She needed to come home immediately for medical treatment.

Penina had always been a beautiful, gifted, loving, and all-around wonderful child. Obviously smart, musical, and kind from a very early age, she was irresistibly lovable to all her knew her. To say that I adored her is an understatement.

Penina's father and I had divorced when she was five years old. She had listened tearfully as the three of us sat on her bed and we told her about the separation. She cried a little, asked a few questions, then went back to her play, unaware of how the course of her childhood had been forever changed. With only occasional protests about a favorite piece of clothing left at the wrong house, she was a remarkably good sport about the rhythm of joint custody—half the week at her dad's house, the other half at mine—that defined the rest of her childhood. She seemed to love the one she was with, slipping into the rules of dad's house when at dad's, and the rules of mom's house when at mine. I sometimes wondered what she did with the feelings evoked by her bi-located life and the barely concealed tensions between her father and me.

I vividly remember her visit home the Thanksgiving of her freshman year at Oberlin. She was the same wonderful girl but more so. She was dramatically more mature, more sure of herself intellectually, full of fascinating observations on society and on her studies. It was thrilling to watch her blossoming. My maternal heart leapt with joy.

Her father noticed her weight loss before I did, on occasional visits home that winter and early spring of freshman year. I could see that she looked a little different, but chalked it up to a change in her personal style, suited to the counter-cultural milieu on campus. (Later a friend soothed my guilt about my own cluelessness. "You just didn't consider the possibility that she was starving herself!") But Howie recognized it, and we began to collaborate closely, trying to negotiate with her unnamed eating disorder, while engaging the help of campus health providers. Still, her weight continued to drop.

After the dean delivered her sober message, I zoomed into action. First, I dashed off a quick e-mail to my close friend and *hevruta*/study partner, since I had to cancel our study appointment to talk to the dean. Only later did I realize that I had written out the whole story not only to my friend but to the mailing list of 150 Jewish spiritual directors all over the country. No time to be mortified at my inadvertent breach of Penina's privacy. I was busy trying to save her life.

Then, moving into crisis gear, I called experts all over the country to seek their advice about what kind of treatment would be most helpful. I frantically researched and interviewed multiple eating disorders treatment centers, determined to find the very best help for my child. Too panicked to stop and feel, I raced through the research and networking calls.

Surprisingly, the best treatment center was not in the San Francisco Bay Area where she had grown up, but in Minneapolis/St. Paul, where I had moved with my husband Louis after Penina left home for college. I flew to Oberlin to help her notify her teachers, pack up her things, and say goodbye to her friends, then to bring her home to Minnesota for treatment.

I found her still beautiful, but gaunt. As we sat at lunch at an off-campus cafe with her boyfriend, the conversation was fascinating, astute, and at times light-hearted. But Penina could not eat. With a great deal of urging, after two hours of sitting over a tiny lunch, she had taken a few tortured bites. What had happened to my child, that she seemed to think that food was poison? It was like watching an otherwise healthy loved one suddenly delusional about a single subject: she could no longer understand that starving herself was bad for her.

I brought her home to Minnesota, where Howie met us tearfully at the airport, having come from California to help take care of her. More torturous meal times followed, as we watched her unable to eat even small amounts of the strange foods she suddenly claimed to prefer. A medical work-up produced a diagnosis of anorexia nervosa and a strong recommendation for inpatient treatment. She was almost sick enough to be admitted to an internal medicine unit of the hospital for malnutrition, but it was best to try to get her into an eating disorders unit. The doctor said that she was reasonably stable, but that at this low weight the metabolic balance in her body could shift precipitously at any time. If she appeared to get sicker, the doctor instructed calmly, we should take her to the emergency room.

There was no available bed in the dedicated eating disorders unit. Our best hope was that the unit would move Penina to the top of the long waiting list because she was so sick. In the meantime, it was days before Passover, usually filled with joyous preparations for lavish meals. I went through the motions of preparing the kitchen for Passover and cooking for a much smaller crowd than usual. When Penina left the room, I wondered if she was purging in the bathroom. Occasionally, I imagined that her heart had suddenly stopped and I would find her unconscious on the floor. As often as possible, we'd invite doctor friends to unobtrusively come by to visit to help us decide whether in fact she was reaching the point where we should take her to the ER. (Howie once asked frantically, "Take a look at her fingernails. Aren't they getting bluer?")

I wept upstairs in my bedroom, asking my husband to be ready to take over leading the *seder* for me if I seemed unable to continue. How on earth could I recite the *Shehecheyanu* prayer, thanking God for the gift of this time of life? How could I celebrate the festival of liberation when my daughter was imprisoned by this mysterious and tyrannical illness?

Penina, emaciated but still beautiful, was delightful and captivating as ever, making insightful comments throughout the *seder*, trying to pretend that we were not all staring at her unnaturally thin body. A childhood friend who had come from her own college campus to be with us for the holiday entered the nightmare with us, as Penina playfully picked at the carrots on her friend's plate. Penina had essentially stopped eating.

In one of many inversions of ordinary logic, we were thrilled when we got the call on the second day of Passover that Penina could check into the hospital. Good news and bad news: a bed had become available on the unit. Since Penina was the most urgently ill patient on the waiting list, she was to be admitted to the hospital on the second day of Passover.

It felt like checking her into a prison, as the intake nurse reviewed the long list of convoluted rules on the unit, the inverse of the bizarre rules within the brain afflicted with an eating disorder. No long, wide sleeves (in which food could be hidden). No cutting one's food into tiny pieces or pushing food around the plate (to make it appear that she had eaten when she had not). No using the bathroom without supervision (until tendencies to purging could be ruled out). No internet access, to prevent patients from accessing diet websites. Even visitors were caught in the web of strange policies: no large glasses of water or carbonated beverages. (These were forbidden to patients who could drink to make themselves feel full, so visitors could not indulge either.) No packages of any kind could be sent into the unit (God knows what they imagined family or friends might send in).

Suddenly the nurse whisked Penina off to lunch while we waited. Are you kidding? I thought. This girl is going to eat lunch? Through the miracle of what they called milieu therapy (i.e., strict rules, close staff supervision, and peer pressure), we later learned that she had eaten lunch that day. I cried in gratitude.

For the first time in weeks, there was nothing for me to do: no networking or researching, no coordinating with Howie or doctors, no endless shopping in the fruitless search for something that Penina might eat. I went home and collapsed on the floor of my bedroom, weeping.

In the ensuing weeks and months, I was often inconsolable. My husband's strong and gentle embrace, a call from a close friend across the country, or a hug from someone at synagogue brought brief moments of comfort. But sometimes nothing helped. In retrospect, though, there were a number of things that allowed me to walk through this dark time. They were prayer, friends and community, the cultivation of trust and patience, an acceptance of brokenness, and a commitment to rigorous truth-telling.

Prayer. During the terrible days of crisis and panic, I was utterly unable to pray. I was too busy networking, strategizing, and coordinating. Truly, I could not bear to stop and feel the excruciating emotions overwhelming me. But now Penina was in the hospital, safe and cared for, and needing privacy to begin her healing journey. My days were suddenly endlessly long, as I tried to get through the day, waiting for visiting hours to come. A mixture of feelings began to rise, a blend of intense fear, horror, confusion, and grief. I still could not pray, but I could ask others to pray for Penina.

My "mistake" of sending the news to the Jewish spiritual directors' listserv turned into a blessing. This group of deeply kind and prayerful people knew of Penina's illness and my suffering. I wrote them, asking them to treat the information I had inadvertently revealed as confidential, and to pray for Penina. Emails began to flow in, one more beautiful than the next, containing tender words of prayer for Penina's health and my aching heart. A group of my spiritual direction students wrote, "Together, let us hold *Penina Tova bat Hana ve-Hayim* in a white healing light. May it bring wholeness, vitality and shalom to her body and her spirit. Let the light surround, cradle and sanctify her, restoring health, strength and joy." I wept over their prayer. I printed it out and had it framed, placing it in various places around the house, wherever I might need to breathe in prayers for my daughter's healing.

One day, my spiritual director reframed my confusion about being unable to pray. She said that the weeping itself was prayer—like the words of the Psalms, prayers of lament, misery, and desperate longing for help. It helped me to be able to accept the cries and the silent ache in my chest as a reaching out to God. Occasionally a single word of prayer emerged from my depths: "Please." "Please." It was, perhaps, something like Moses' terse, impassioned plea for his sister Miriam's leprosy, "*El na, refa na la.*" "Please, God, heal her please," (Num 12:13).

Community. Seeking comfort from loving friends and community, a primary source of support for me during other painful experiences of my life, was complicated this time. I would have found comfort in revealing our family's trauma to our friends and synagogue community, to invite the flow of prayer and compassion that would surely come in response. But I needed to restrain my extroverted impulse in order to follow Penina's lead about how much privacy she needed. Eventually we found a balance and agreed that I would tell just my inner circle of loved ones. These people loved me, held me, cried and prayed for Penina's healing. Above all, my husband's constant, rock-solid love and attentiveness were precious beyond measure.

Trust. In retrospect, I remember my practice in those days—sometimes consciously, sometimes not—as a prayer to God to deepen my faith and trust. I had no choice but to trust in God, in Spirit, in Life, and the force of healing in the universe, for the alternative was unbearable. I had cultivated these qualities in my prayer life for many years, so these prayers had well-worn lyrics engraved in my mind. "O God, Who is my Help, I will trust in You and not be afraid," (Isa 12:2). And from a translation of the prayer *Adon Olam* that I especially love: "In God's kind hand I place my soul, when I sleep, again to wake; and with my soul, this body, here. God's love is mine; I shall not fear." As I had often coached other people in pain to do, I recited over and over again the words of the *Shema*, "Hear O Israel, *Adonai* our God, *Adonai* is One," synchronized with my breathing. These sacred words served as an anchor for my tortured mind and heart as I tried to calm myself after a visit to the hospital or as I lay awake at night.

Patience. Honestly, I did not want to be patient. I have always loved the authentically urgent language of the *Mi Shebeirach*, the traditional Jewish prayer for healing, that concludes with no less than three requests for a complete and speedy healing ("May it come now, quickly, and soon"). I wanted my daughter to be out of danger immediately and to rapidly do the inner work needed to get out of the grips of the eating disorder. But such work does not proceed quickly. The healing journey would take as long as it would take, and I needed to live with the uncertainty of when and how fully my daughter would get well. And I needed to respect her own space and timing. I desperately wanted to help her, but needed to learn to step back and wait for her to ask. I had no choice but to pray for patience. Again, beloved sacred texts moved in me. "I wait for you, O God; my soul waits," (Ps 130:5). "O God, I wait for your help," (Gen 49:18).

Embracing Brokenness. Part of the healing process for me was a fuller embrace of brokenness as a part of our lives. I needed to accept that Penina was not a perfect child, if by "perfect" I meant a distorted image of a happy-go-lucky, feel-no-pain kind of human being. In my own inner work I had long since recognized places of brokenness in my life, and come to understand that suffering is an inevitable part of the human condition. Yet for my daughter, I was attached to an illusory image that she would waltz through life, enveloped entirely in joy and possibility.

I had to own up to the foolishness of that image, let it go, and grieve my cherished vision of the blissful life she would lead. I could not prevent my child from feeling the pain that had generated this illness, nor could I offer easy wisdom that would readily take the hurt away.

It was a deep confrontation with the suffering at the heart of human life, in tension with my primal maternal wish that my child be forever spared any significant pain. Very gradually, the Jewish wisdom that pain is a part of life that I had so often taught and reflected on sank in, leaving me with sorrow but not horror at my child's anguish. After all, do we not hear the sound of shattering glass at the climax of the wedding, a couple's day of consummate joy? Do we not recite the *Yizkor*/memorial prayer in the midst of the most joyous days of the Jewish year, a reminder of the necessary interweaving of joy and sorrow in every human life?

Occasionally, I could take a moment of comfort from the rabbinic image of the first set of tablets, shattered by Moses when he descended Mount Sinai only to see his beloved people in the throes of apostasy. The Rabbis teach that the shards of the first set of tablets, broken in rage, were not discarded in shame. Rather, they were gathered together and treasured, carried in the ark throughout the Israelites' journey (BT *Baba Batra* 14b). So, too, are we to honor the broken pieces of our lives as our life journeys unfold.

Lurianic Kabbalah imagines that the process of the creation of the universe included a cosmic shattering of vessels needed to hold divine light brought to earth. According to this mythic image, the vessels are scattered throughout the universe, and the purpose of human life is to perform acts of sanctity, through which the shards, one by one, are gathered and returned to their source. This profound image suggests that experiences of shattering lay at the very heart of existence. They are neither a mistake nor an anomaly in the scheme of life, rather an invitation to live with more wisdom and compassion. Of course, most of the time, watching my daughter so ill was excruciating. But occasionally I would have glimmers of awareness that this time of suffering might eventually bring blessing in its wake.

Truth-telling. Another sacred presence in my life during this dark time was a commitment to rigorous truth-telling. We all knew that the path to healing lay not in denying the seriousness of her illness, but in the determined exploration of the many dynamics that may have contributed to it. Penina's willingness to examine her own personal history and her inner life in a whole new way was clearly a major reason why she got well as quickly and as fully as she did. But there is nothing easy about such honest soul-searching, neither in her own personal work nor in the renegotiation of relationships that continued for years into her recovery.

Here too, a sacred image guided and supported me. I had learned many years earlier in my life that the path of healing and holiness is always to be found in heart-wrenching and heart-opening honesty. As the Psalmist puts it, "God is near to all who call, to all who call upon God in truth" (Ps 145:18). That is, we have most access to sacred sources of comfort and meaning when we face reality as it is, grapple with the hard issues, and engage in the difficult conversations. The pain of this honest grappling is the agony of excavating a wound or ripping away diseased skin: it tears us apart, but only through this tearing can healing come.

———

Penina spent two weeks in the inpatient unit of the eating disorders clinic, five weeks in "partial," a step-down program requiring forty hours per week at the clinic, and two months of outpatient treatment, ten hours per week at the clinic, while adjusting to living in a healthy way on her own. The staff had told us that recovery from eating disorders is a years-long, uneven road, and that we should expect that she would slip and need hospitalization again.

But Penina, an all-A student with a strong will, had turned her energy from learning how to eat as little as possible to learning how to get well. She engaged in the healing process with inspiring courage, focus, and rigorous honesty. She continued to live with disordered thoughts about food for years, but she gradually learned to work with the deeper feelings that had given rise to the addictive behavior of restricting her food intake. By the time she graduated from college, her active eating disorder had become a manageable challenge in her life.

Why did this happen to our daughter? I certainly wonder about dynamics in Jewish culture that may predispose some individuals to eating disorders. So many Jewish families, our own included, associate food with love and particularly lavish meals with joyful times. At the same time, many women stand at the buffet table, spread with delectable foods, chatting about their diets and the caloric content of every thing they pile onto their plates. Combine this crazy-making dynamic with a powerful stream of perfectionism in our culture, and there is no question but that eating disorders find fertile ground in the Jewish community.

As my friend had said, I had never imagined that my daughter would fall prey to anorexia. After all, the strong feminist consciousness that was the air my daughter breathed would surely prevent her from feeling critical of her own lovely body. But this was an illusion. Pernicious messages about the desirability of thinness are ubiquitous in American culture, so that no one is immune to the danger. While the news media are today more focused than ever on the health risks of obesity, eating disorders are a life-threatening epidemic among American girls and young women.

Were there issues in our family that had pushed Penina to want to take up less space in the world? Without a doubt. Yet somehow I was blessed with calm about this toxic question, a question that could have compounded the suffering in my aching heart. Perhaps it was the fruit of many years of therapy and mindfulness practice, but those self-blaming thoughts simply did not plague me. Our family was who it was. There was no changing the history and no point in torturing myself with reductionist, self-blaming theories about why this had happened to Penina. This was the challenge before us, and we needed to use our energy to support Penina in her healing work.

I am boundlessly grateful that my daughter is thriving in her mid-twenties, building a rich interpersonal and professional life. The eating disorder is in our past, though the traumatic memory can easily be reawakened in me when I see any young woman dieting unreasonably. I so want to spare others the pain we all experienced.

People occasionally ask what I would say to someone in the grips of an eating disorder. Of course, every illness is unique. But I know that I want for every woman and every man to be guided by the wisdom of the early blessings in our morning service. I want everyone to know in their bones the truth of the blessing recited upon using the bathroom, *"Baruch ata . . .*

asher yatsar et ha'adam bechochmah," "Blessed are You, O God . . . who created the human being with wisdom." This body that you have been given is a creation of the divine, a vessel of infinite beauty, shaped with ultimate understanding. Barring medical reasons that require weight loss, you do not need to diet to be true to the body that God created for you.

So, too, I want for everyone to fully embody the affirmation in another early-morning blessing, *"Elohai neshama shenatata bi . . . ,"* "The soul You have given me, O God, is pure." Your body and soul are perfect just as they are, requiring no adornment or adjustment. The messages that you hear every day in news media, advertisements, television, and radio are horribly, dangerously wrong. You are perfectly, infinitely beautiful just as you are. This is what I wish for Penina, for all the children, for all the families threatened by an eating disorder. I wish for all of us to live more fully into our tradition's teaching that we are sacred, beautiful, and endowed with wisdom, just as we are.

Penina Eilberg-Schwartz Responds:

I don't know what God has to do with it, but I am the daughter, and I was healed.

The story my mother told about my illness has many similarities to the one I tell. But here, as with so many histories, there are different versions at play. My mother's story is one of the personal and the divine. Mine, at least the one I tell myself most frequently, is of the political.

America taught me to eat, and transmitted a broken relationship with food—one driven by guilt. This culture of guilt was deeply woven into my consciousness, despite being raised by feminists and knowing intellectually to remain critical of the emaciated women on billboards. The hysteria about eating healthily, especially when it's expressed in extremes (i.e., eat only this; this food is good and this food is bad) feeds eating disorders. It fed mine.

It is hard to escape all this. On my college campus, I found myself in a community of people occupied with the pursuit of social justice, a community that continues to tell itself that it's immune to the sexism and phony solutions of the wider society. I learned that food was inextricably linked to justice issues. I learned, in this community, to recognize the horror of the American industrialized food system—the mistreatment of animals, the unsustainable use of land, and the unequal access to quality food. I learned to recognize the sexism inherent in the messaging that our society sells to us, but I also learned that something is wrong with the way we eat.

How can we eat normally when the world is so broken? I bought into the dichotomous ways of eating around me, the social justice community's answer to all this, that I should be thin and delicate (read: weak) while men should be muscular and broad (read: strong).

I decided to eat just "what I needed." I internalized the messages around me of what was good eating, and I just took it farther—very little bread, no meat, no sugar, and very small plates of food. I didn't want to be strong anymore if others couldn't be, if I couldn't do anything to change what I saw was wrong in the world. I was disgusted with myself for not doing more, and so I punished myself.

I don't know what advice to give you, if God forbid, someone you love ends up where I did. But I know we all have a part in it, that when we are worrying about our weight or how we eat, someone may well be watching, someone who is already sick and could be triggered by what we're saying and doing, or someone who's not sick yet, but on their way. We need to opt out of all of the dramatic solutions to the problems with our eating and food systems, as legitimate as some of them may seem. None of this is so simple, and there is already too much illness in the world for us to create more of it.

Ima, if there's a God, I think she wants us to eat and be full.

Also, *Ima*, I'm so sorry.

9

Facing Pain, Facing My Fears

Ruth H. Sohn

IT WAS OUR SIXTH ER visit in three weeks. This time Reuven, my hus-band, had awakened me at five in the morning, shaking uncontrollably with pain, the bottom of one of his feet covered with purple blotches. I had never seen him like this. Reuven had an unusually high tolerance for pain, but even multiple doses of Vicodin had failed to register any effect. "I wanted to wait until nine so we could see my own doctor but I don't think I can wait any longer," Reuven said, speaking with visible effort.

We quickly dressed and I helped Reuven up and out to the car. Luckily, the hospital was only minutes from our home. The doctor who examined Reuven in the ER happened to be the same doctor who had seen him on one of our previous visits, and he immediately moved to have Reuven admitted. "I don't know what is going on here, but these purple blotches look like some kind of clots, and it is clear there's something serious happening. I'm calling your cardiologist to come in."

Reuven was admitted and it was decided almost immediately that he would need open heart surgery to clarify and repair whatever the current problem was. We were both deeply shaken. We knew the risks of this sur-gery and the difficult recovery that would follow. Just seven months ear-lier Reuven had suffered an acute aortic dissection—a condition that often proves fatal—and doctors in Israel had saved his life with emergency open heart surgery in which they replaced part of his aorta with a Dacron graft. Reuven's father had died on the operating table of the same condition thirty years earlier at the age of fifty-three. Reuven was forty-nine and our three children were fifteen, twelve, and seven years old.

Thankfully, the surgery in Israel proved a huge success and we were all overwhelmed with gratitude. Reuven proclaimed the date of the surgery as his "re-birthday" and we talked about celebrating it regularly in the years ahead.

Now seven months later, after a series of complications, the doctors concluded that some kind of problem had developed in the area of the Dacron graft in Reuven's aorta and that a second operation would be required to repair it. But the exact nature of the problem was still unknown. It took another two weeks for the doctors to learn that Reuven had developed a serious systemic infection that needed to be stabilized before he could have surgery, while at the same time, he faced the risk of a stroke that only the surgery could remove.

The doctors started Reuven on strong IV antibiotics to clear up the infection, and debated between themselves whether it was more urgent for Reuven to have the surgery or to get the infection under control.

During these tense weeks of waiting, we had a lot of support. The day Reuven was admitted to the hospital, when I returned home in the late afternoon, a tray of cooked lasagna was sitting by the front door. For the next three and a half weeks, I did not cook a single meal—our *minyan* community took care of providing dinners the entire time Reuven was in the hospital. My parents were in Los Angeles for the winter and they helped out with the kids, and our three children also stepped up to the plate. Perhaps most important, Reuven's surgeon came by daily to examine him and he was always ready to turn off his cell phone and sit with us and, in an unhurried way, explain what was happening and answer our questions as best he could.

But even with all of this, the weeks of waiting were among the most difficult I had ever experienced. I tried to be with Reuven at the hospital as much as I could, between teaching my classes at the Jewish high school where I taught and also attending to our three children. I became adept at writing lesson plans on the fly and grading papers sitting by Reuven's bed. But as busy as I was, with as little time alone to think as I currently had, there was no escaping the desperate fear of what lay ahead that would overtake me at night after I fell into bed, exhausted.

You might have thought that the prospect of Reuven undergoing such serious surgery would be easier the second time around, at least for me. But it wasn't. I now knew how complex the surgery was, and how painful the recovery from this surgery would probably be for Reuven, even without complications. I also knew that serious complications might hamper Reuven's recovery as had happened the first time around. Even before this latest series of incidents had landed Reuven back in the hospital, his six-month CT had indicated that his aorta had not healed as anticipated, and that his condition was actually quite precarious. Now, the seriousness of these new complications and the need for Reuven to undergo a repeat of such radical surgery had me struggling with moments of overwhelming fear. I desperately did not want to lose him. I did not want him to have to suffer more pain. And there was very little I could do about either fear.

My regular morning practice of meditation and prayer helped to some extent. I also took comfort knowing we were in many other people's prayers. But I was struggling with the fear that overtook me at night and sometimes during the day.

My spiritual mentor and friend, Sylvia Boorstein, a well-known and gifted teacher of both Buddhist and Jewish mindfulness practice, gently suggested I might want to experiment with bringing my fear into my meditation practice. First settle in and sit with your breath, she suggested. "Then invite your fear, and just sit with it. Notice where you feel it in your body, and what it feels like, and see what happens."

A few days later I decided to try. I had gotten the kids off to school and had some time before I needed to go to school myself. I decided this would be a good morning to take some extra time with my meditation. I settled into a comfortable sitting position on a chair in our bedroom, as I did every morning, and focused on the flow of my breath. Breathing in . . . breathing out . . . feeling the breath in my body, feeling my body filling and emptying. I sat for a few minutes this way, allowing my awareness to be filled with the steady flow of my breath, noticing the way my body calmed to the steady flow of my breath.

I felt ready. I invited into my awareness my love for Reuven and my fears for him, our children, and for me . . . I allowed myself to open to my fear, and I felt my chest immediately constrict with heaviness, choking off my breath. I tried to open again to my breath, and then to the feelings. Feel your breath . . . feel the fear, I said to myself . . . feel the pain . . .

Generally, I don't entertain dream-like images in my meditation practice. Notice and return to the breath, was my usual process. But opening up to the fear and to the pain I had been carrying and thought I knew, but in reality had been holding at bay, I now found myself taken down deeper, opening up to the feelings themselves . . . and then I was standing before a large pool of water, surrounded by people of all different ethnicities and ages, all of us walking slowly to the pool, and squatting down, reaching into the pool of water with our hands, and bringing the water to our mouths to drink. We were all drinking from the universal pool of pain, I realized with a start. All of us. All of humanity. Some people were coming and some were going . . . we weren't there all at once, but in time, all of us would drink from this pool. I was so moved by the slow and steady movement of the people around me, by their unsmiling but accepting faces, by the inevitability of each of us coming to drink from this pool. I drank in and allowed myself to open to the pool of pain—my pain and the shared pool of pain, no longer just my own. Something shifted inside and in the next breath I felt myself filled . . . and realized that the pool of pain was no longer just that, but had transformed into something different. It had become a pool of compassion.

Like water, like breath, I felt the flow of compassion coursing through me, around me, over and underneath me, opening my heart even more, and connecting me to all the other people drinking from this shared pool of pain, now a shared pool of compassion. I felt my heart expanding, opening to the flow of the waters of pain and compassion, of healing and love. Life-giving waters that only a truly open heart can know.

I felt so deeply connected, so deeply alive, in touch with the pulse of life connecting us all. And I felt my heart still expanding, opening to this flow, even more deeply. It was infinite. It could hold us all, now and forever, in life and even in death.

In the days and weeks ahead, the meditation experience stayed with me. There was no assurance that everything would be ok. That is not what I was looking for, or expected. But I felt calmer, because I trusted that I could be with the truth of whatever was happening, however difficult, and I would not be consumed by it. If I could continue to be open to what was happening, however difficult or painful, with an open heart, I trusted that I would again and again find access to the even deeper flow of life-giving energy of compassion and love.

I also came away from the meditation strengthened in my belief that acts of kindness and love could provide others with healing and comfort and a deeper connection to life itself. Isn't this what life is really all about, I thought to myself—learning to open our hearts so we can give and receive love more deeply? Offering a person kindness and loving care and an open ear and heart—these acts are among the most simple and profound ways in which we connect with each other.

I did not talk about the meditation with Reuven, but I trusted more in the power of my love and caring for him to come through, even when unspoken. And instead of my love and concern for Reuven leading to the clutching fear of what might lie ahead, the meditation helped me trust in the value of being fully with Reuven with what was happening right now. "All we really have is this moment." I had first heard these words as a mindfulness practice teaching, but they came to mind now with new power. I hoped that Reuven would be able to sense and draw comfort and strength from my ability to be more open and calmly present to him and what was happening day to day.

Sometimes, a line from the liturgy or the Hebrew Bible that we have known and even recited for years will suddenly light up with new meaning. This happened for me some time during that week, after the meditation experience. Psalm 118:5, which we often sing as part of *Hallel*, psalms of gratitude and praise to God—*Min hametzar karati Yah, anani vamerkhav-Yah*—is usually translated as "Out of distress I called out to God; God answered me by setting me free." A translation that is closer to the actual meaning of the Hebrew is: "From the narrow place I called out to God; God answered me with expansiveness." *Hametzar*, like *Mitzrayim*, the Hebrew word for "Egypt," is based on the Hebrew word *tzar*, or "narrow," and suggests "the narrow place." *Merkhav* builds on the Hebrew root *rakhav*, which means wide, expansive, or spacious. The movement from a narrow, constricting place to a wide expansiveness is dramatic. We can feel it. I found that connecting this more literal meaning of the Hebrew with the emotional states being described was powerful and insightful. This was another way for me to be with the worry and anxiety that I sometimes fought against.

The experience of distress can indeed be a narrow place of constriction. What do we usually do when we are worried or frightened? We shrink into ourselves like a turtle retreating into its shell—our neck and shoulders contract, we tense up and our breath constricts. When we need them most, we clutch in fear and close ourselves off to our greatest sources of comfort and calm—our very breath and our connection with other people and with the holy. Our vision is constricted and our sense of what is possible collapses into itself. We may find ourselves sinking fast into panic or despair. What can help us now?

It is from this narrow place of constriction that the psalmist cries out to God, with the simple name for God, "Yah," inviting the speaker to open her heart along with her mouth in the very utterance of her cry.

The verse reminds us that when we find ourselves in a difficult narrow place—whether that be fear or pain, anger, sadness, or worry—that we too can call out to God from where we are. The verse invites us to trust that if we do, we, like the psalmist, may experience a response to our heart's deepest need, in ways we cannot anticipate. The very act of crying out to God requires us to open our hearts, the single most important step for opening to God's wider presence that fills every place in which we find ourselves. And suddenly, the energy of our emotions, instead of being uncomfortably squeezed, has enough room to simply flow through us. No longer stuck, we may in fact find ourselves energized by the feelings we were dreading, energized to see new possibilities, and able to respond to our situation with new-felt emotion or clarity of purpose.

I tried to notice when I was starting to feel myself sinking into the narrow place of worry and fear, and I turned to this verse from Psalm 118 to help me open to my fear and speak the prayers I most needed to ask. I asked for healing for Reuven and for strength and courage for myself. I asked God's help to stay present to what was happening now, and not get overwhelmed by the uncertainty of what lay ahead.

A week later, Reuven experienced new TIAs, fleeting stroke-like symptoms that indicated a rising risk of an actual stroke and the doctors decided they had to go ahead with Reuven's surgery, even with the systemic infection still far from being under control. The next morning I arrived at the hospital early to be with Reuven before he went into surgery. He was in his usual good spirits and made a few jokes as he gave me his wedding ring and we expressed loving reassurances to each other. And then he was wheeled away. While the nurse had suggested Reuven give me his ring in case he experienced any swelling during or after the surgery, I welcomed the idea of having something tangible to hold onto while Reuven was in surgery, symbol of our love for each other that he had worn on his finger for the last eighteen years.

The next few hours were extremely difficult. I went home and got the kids off to school. I stayed home and prayed on and off, holding Reuven's wedding ring in my hand, and in between tried to keep busy. Finally the phone rang and the doctor gave me the news for which we had been hoping and praying: the surgery had gone smoothly and had been successful. Reuven was in recovery. I cried in relief and gratitude. Later, back at the hospital, Reuven came out of recovery, and though he had a lot of pain and discomfort, he was alive and fully conscious and aware.

> Thank you, God, for our lives that are in Your hand and our souls that are in Your keeping, and for Your miracles that sustain us daily, morning, noon, and night . . . (Daily liturgy).

The next day, Reuven was still in considerable pain and discomfort but we were all amazed at the complete change in his appearance: overnight he seemed to have gone from black and white to color. We had not even realized how gray his face had gone over the past months. Five days later, a thinner, weaker, but still pink-cheeked Reuven came home.

For the next two months, Reuven recuperated at home and received strong antibiotics intravenously. He continued to make an excellent recovery and today, ten years later, Reuven runs ten miles or more several times a week and travels all over the world attending conferences and giving lectures. He and I both continue not to take anything for granted, but to have enormous gratitude for every day.

While my worries and fears for Reuven eased over the years, the power of my meditation experience stayed with me and continued to inform my understanding of how to live in the world. I have come to a deeper acceptance of the inevitability of pain and loss as part of life and a deeper appreciation of the healing potential in our learning to be open to all of our feelings and the fullness of our experiences. Over the years, other family members and friends, including two of my closest friends, have faced life-threatening illness and some have died. It has been profoundly important for me to be able to walk with them on their journeys, even through the narrow places. As a result, it continues to be a priority for me to do the work I need to do to be emotionally present and available to myself and others in difficult times.

However, it is not just the big challenges, but the small ones too, as we navigate our way through the complexities of life and our relationships, that can find us struggling. We have a natural tendency to try and avoid pain and discomfort, and we live in a culture that encourages us to do so. To live more and more from the grounded place of an open heart—open to everything that is unfolding in and around us—has become one of my guiding aspirations.

Over the years my prayer practice has deepened around these normal challenges of life. I have had to learn that praying from the depths of my heart can be an intentional practice, not only an occasional spontaneous act aroused in certain moments. Again and again, I have found that when I can open to the full truth of where I am at the moment and pray to God from this place, my prayers are most powerful and often allow some internal shift or insight to emerge. Sometimes what emerges is a clearer sense of what I really need to ask help with: to see what I need to see and hear what I need to hear; perhaps strength or courage, compassion or patience; the ability to listen and not have to offer anything to fix; the ability to be open to my own pain, so I can be present to others.

I recently came across a text from the Zohar that describes the experience I have found in this sort of prayer:

> What is the meaning of Out of the depths I call You, *Adonai*? So it has been taught: Whoever offers his prayer before the Blessed Holy One should convey his request and pray from the depth of his heart, so that his heart may be completely with the Blessed Holy One . . . to draw blessings from the depth of the well, so that it will gush blessings from the spring of all. And what is that? The place from which the river issues and derives, as is written: A river issues from Eden (Gen. 2:10). . . . This is called out of the depths—depth of all, depth of the well, springs issuing

and flowing, blessing all. This is the beginning of drawing blessings from above to below.

When we can pray from the depths of our heart, our hearts are able to open to God's even deeper and wider presence, and we can find ourselves drawing blessing from the well, the spring of all, the source of the river of Eden that the Zohar speaks of so often, that sustains all of life. Indeed, this teaching suggests that our prayer—our opening our hearts to God—can activate the drawing forth of blessing, opening the flow of blessing for ourselves and others.

The imagery of this text mirrored my earlier meditation experience of opening to the depths of my own fear and pain and discovering the shared pool of pain of all human beings that can, when we open to it, become a pool of compassion. The repetition of the word "blessing," or *berachah*, in the Zohar passage reminded me that the word for "pool," *bereicha*, is essentially the same word in Hebrew. The image of a pool of water filling from another source—a deeper well or spring, or perhaps a waterfall flowing down from above—and overflowing with the bounty of these waters is a moving picture of the dynamic flow of blessing and of divine life-giving energy in the world. We can experience this divine flow of blessing in one moment as compassion, in another as healing, and in another as patience or wisdom.

Praying for healing for loved ones continues to be a learning process. Increasingly, I find myself praying for *refuat hanefesh*, the healing of the soul, as fervently as for *refuat haguf*, the healing of the body, and I sometimes feel that the healing of the soul is the more critical need. I often pray that the person who is ill find the capacity to open to the love of the others in his or her life more fully, and that in the face of the present challenges, each of these loved ones can be there for each other. Heart opening remains my most basic prayer, for myself and others.

As these experiences taught me, and as I am often reminded when the more modest challenges of day to day life trip me up, it is only when we stop running from our pain and our fear and face it head on, that we have a chance to move forward. Often this path brings more than mere survival, and we discover unexpected gifts along the way. The Torah offers us this lesson too, perhaps most dramatically with the narrative about our forefather, Jacob, when he anticipates seeing his brother Esau for the first time in twenty years and is overwhelmed with fear that his brother may still want to kill him for having stolen his blessing and birthright twenty years earlier. This is one of my favorite passages in the Torah, and recently, when I revisited the text, I realized that it presents us with an inspiring example of what can happen when we face and engage our fears.

Jacob is so terrified at the prospect of seeing Esau that he desperately grasps at several different possible sources of protection simultaneously. He sends ahead to Esau multiple ingratiating messages and an impressive array of gifts, prays fervently to God for protection, and separates his family into two groups to increase the odds that at least some of them will survive. But it is only when Jacob has sent both groups ahead and is left alone at night, that Jacob finally has the experience that enables him to cross the river and move forward on his life journey, to meet his brother face to face the next day.

What happened that night when Jacob was left alone? The Torah tells us that a man wrestled with Jacob until the break of day. The thirteenth-century commentator, Rabbi Hezekiah ben Manoah Hizkuni, suggests that the man was an angel sent by God in order to prevent Jacob from running away. According to this view, Jacob was so overcome by his own fear that he was about to run away, leaving his family to face Esau alone. The angel forced Jacob to face himself and his fear and guilt toward his brother. It was through this intense wrestling that Jacob came to merit a true blessing—the name Israel—and the assurance that he could survive his encounter with Esau. No longer would Jacob be constrained by his old pattern of deceit and trickery associated with the name Jacob. Now, the new name Israel celebrated his proven ability to directly confront and wrestle with both the deepest fears holding him back and the intimations of the divine calling him forward. Now, having faced his fear and his own inner demons, Jacob could go on to meet his brother with an open heart and embrace. Finally he was even able to offer his brother a blessing of his own, far beyond the material gifts he had sent ahead. "Seeing your face is like seeing the face of God," said Jacob to Esau.

Facing our fears and being willing to be with our own pain and the pain of others turns out again and again to be a path to blessing, opening us to the truth of our experience, and to the even deeper flow of compassion and love for ourselves and each other. From there we can discover more honest, loving, and authentic ways of being with each other, and moving forward in our life journey, one step at a time. It all begins with our ability to be fully present and open to what is happening now, in this moment. We will inevitably forget, but with every breath, we have the chance to remember and begin again.

10

My Mother as a Ruined City

Insights from the Book of Lamentations

RACHEL ADLER

August 1999

Rabbi Jacob said: This world is like a corridor before the world
to come. Prepare yourself in the corridor so you may enter the
banquet hall. (*Pirkei Avot* 4:16, in some eds. 4:21)

*M*Y MOTHER IS WAITING *in the corridor. She wanders continu-
ally, agitated and shaking. She is trying to get home, she says. This
condo apartment in which she has lived for twenty-five years is not home.
Everything is strange. If only she could get home, she says. There is something important she has forgotten to do, but she cannot remember what it
is. There are people who loved her whom she has hurt. "I am so ashamed,"
my mother says, and she weeps. I try to comfort her and she says haltingly,
grasping for the words that no longer come, "you are very kind, but I wish—
if I could only be with someone from my own family."*

*My mother does not know me. My mother does not know what "daugh-
ter" means. She does not know if she has eaten or taken a walk five minutes
ago. She does not know the day, the season, the year, the weather, her phone
number, her address. The dignified woman with the graduate degree cannot
read even a children's book or watch a children's movie. The day is a succession*

of agonizing seconds we try to fill for her with walks and music and the flicker-
ing images on the TV, to whom she talks. These are normal manifestations of
advanced dementia, two geriatricians have assured us.

Another woman with a mother in approximately the same condition
said to me, "I wish I could say the memorial prayer, Yizkor, for my mother.
I want to remember the person she was who is gone." Our mothers cannot
remember, and we cannot remember them. Even God cannot be asked to re-
member them, lost as they are in some limbo between heaven and earth. We
are waiting in the corridor.

2001

My mother can no longer speak, but something is very wrong. My mother is
rocking back and forth. She claps her hands. She cries "Why, why, why?" but
it sounds to me like "Vai, vai, vai," the ancient Hebrew for woe, alas. She does
not respond to requests to show us where it hurts. It occurs to me that maybe
there is no physical locus for her pain, that what I am seeing is the classical
expression of lamentation, the hands clapping, the body anguished, the mouth
mixing words and cries of pain. The words of the biblical book of Lamenta-
tions rise in my mind: O Mother, "How can I express your devastation? Your
ruin is as vast as the sea: who can heal you?" (Lam 2:13). It is the first time
words to God have fit the horror I am witnessing. The analogy is powerful
for me: My mother is a ruined city. The lights are blinking out, the streets are
empty. "Lonely sits the city /Once great with people!"(Lam 1:1). Like despoiled
Jerusalem, my mother is all alone.

It may seem strange that the book of Lamentations is my touchstone
for my mother's dementia, a book read only on the fast of the Ninth of Av
to a diminished congregation sitting on the floor in a disordered sanctuary,
a book chanted with the saddest, most haunting melody in the world. A lot
of people avoid the Ninth of Av, when we act out our sense that God has
abandoned us and read this painful book. Similarly, a lot of people avoided
my demented mother. The demented are abandoned by droves of friends,
acquaintances, even family. Let me explain a little more why this book became important to me during my mother's plunge into darkness.

The book of Lamentations is a series of laments over the destruction
of Jerusalem in 586 BCE. There are already conventions by this time about
how one laments the destruction of a great city. The first such laments were
written in Mesopotamia 4,000 years ago. But Jerusalem is not just a great
city. It is the center of a nomos, a universe of meanings that people inhabit.
In 586 BCE those meanings had to do with the sacrificial cult and the great

Temple where God dwelt among the people Israel, protected them from their enemies, and heard their requests. Jerusalem is also the center of the monarchy and of its messianic hopes for continuity; it is the City of David. Lamentations records the destruction of this nomos, the destruction of the meanings within which the people Israel situated themselves and made sense of their world.

1998

My mother's nomos is destroyed by dementia. She can no longer situate her-self, no longer make sense of her world, no longer touch the meanings that sustained her. A whiteboard hanging in the kitchen and a litter of notes and notepads from 1997 to 1999 attest to her attempts to hang on. There are lists of what to do when she gets up in the morning, lists of the phone numbers of the man she loves and her children, attempts to sign her name, practice for writing checks, all of them failures. Untouched nutritious food in the freezer and cabinets is replaced by cans of Ensure, which by 2001 is all she can take in.

Some time in 1998 she says to me, "You're the one who knows it all. So why?" I answer her half joking, "Because it's really hard to be human, but I don't know any other choices." She looks amused. Later she begins to talk, instructing a classroom of children only she can see. Words come out wrong. There are no sentences. Later all the words go except for "why" and "help." And I can't.

The book of Lamentations both bewails and remakes this shattered nomos quite explicitly by reconstituting the broken alphabet of creation. Four of its five chapters are alphabetical acrostics. Chapter 3 is a triple al-phabetical acrostic. Chapter 5 is not an acrostic but has the same number of verses as there are alphabet letters. The alphabet represents the total-ity of language, and the acrostic thus represents the gamut of catastrophic experiences and the gamut of human reactions that can be represented in language. The structure of the book, its strict, alphabetical sequence of verses, barely serves to contain the wildly disordered content. The poet and the two speakers, the woman Zion and the man who has known affliction, pour out a torrent of personal and collective woe: physical torment, humili-ation, pity, self-blame, accusations hurled at a violent and predatory God, dreadful tableaux of jeering enemies, starving children, cannibal mothers, slave laborers, slaughtered bodies, pleas for mercy, pleas for bloody revenge. This torrent of complaint strikes the listener as confused, because lament is without rational sequence. In the first two chapters a refrain surfaces several times: *Ain menachem lah*, "no one comforts her." No one comforts the forsaken Zion in her anguish.

2000

For my mother too, there is no comfort. The web of relationships in which all social beings are held is for her a broken web. The filaments that connected her to relatives, friends, caregivers, dangle free without reaching her. No one can reach her to comfort her, not with words, not with music, not with touch. The words and images of the book of Lamentations come thick and fast. Everywhere there is destruction. Everywhere the enemy has triumphed. Everywhere where there was once beauty and order, there is the rubble of what was a person, a home, a life.

The scholar Tod Linafelt says that on several levels, Lamentations is survivor literature. The reader has to work out how to survive its harsh and agonizing content, but also Linafelt sees it as literature written by survivors and focused on the all-important question of the survival of Zion's children. Its genre, lament, has an unsavory reputation among many Bible scholars, who seem to regard lamenting as unnecessary negativism by people who should properly be shouldering their guilt, repenting, and being hopeful. I embraced the book of Lamentations precisely because it gave voice to the feelings that were not cheery, that did not look on the bright side. It permitted me to be angry with God about my mother's dementia, instead of joining with other family members in murmuring, "You have to admit, she is wonderfully taken care of. In a nursing home, she would have been dead long ago."

While I was reading to make sense of my mother's anguish (and mine, and my sister's) I came across the work of the cultural critic Elaine Scarry, who writes about physical pain and its effects on the universe of the sufferer. Intolerable pain, says Scarry, unmakes the universe, expunging thought and feeling, self and world, "all that gives rise to and is in turn made possible by language." In severe torment, the sufferer is utterly isolated, unable to experience relatedness, unable to defend her values from a torturer's insistence that she betray them, or to give or withhold consent to a medical procedure, unable to attend to her surroundings, unable to speak—for language is displaced by gasps, moans, and screams. In contrast, Scarry observes, "to be present when the person in pain rediscovers speech is almost to be present at the birth or rebirth of language."

I want to argue that emotional and spiritual pain can also leave us tormented and bereft. And to be present when the sufferer re-achieves relational speech is to be present at the rebirth of redemption. My mother never regained relational speech. I am the survivor of my mother's disintegration, and I am the one who re-approaches language. I recover language first in the form of lament, the form in which the book of Lamentation is written. It is not comfortable language, but it comforts me.

Concerning Lamentations, Kathleen O'Connor writes:

> It serves as a witness, a knowing, a form of seeing, wherein readers recognize their lives, symbolically or more literally, and in that recognition they are no longer alone in their pain. . . . Within its poetry, we can say, "Yes, that resembles my life," Now or in the past or perhaps in the future. Curiously, perhaps paradoxically, by focusing on suffering, by bringing it into the open, and reflecting it back to readers, Lamentations offers solace. Nearly bereft of comfort itself, the book is immensely comforting.

The Hebrew name of the biblical book is not Lamentations but *Eikha*, literally, "How." Three of the five chapters begin with this word. Is it "How?" with a question mark? How did this happen to us? Or is it "How!" with an exclamation point? How changed everything is! How unlike the way it was before! We cannot comprehend how far down we have come—all the way down to death. Hence, Lamentations begins with a dirge as if the female figure Zion were already dead. I could have used a good dirge to sing, while my mother was sitting all day in frozen immobility and unbreakable silence.

Women were prominent among the first lamenters, I learned. Lament-singing women accompanied by flutes and other instruments sang the dead to their final rest, and led the communal singing on such occasions in biblical Israel, and in Palestine and Babylonia of the rabbinic period. Lament was considered a women's genre, and it was an art. Women composed the poetry orally and formed repertoires that they adapted to individual deaths. Why women? After all, women nursed the sick, and in the days before communal burial societies, washed and shrouded and laid out the dead. It made sense that they also lamented at the burials. They were experts in destruction and loss.

In two of the five chapters of the book of Lamentations, the speaker is a lamenting woman, Zion, the personification of the ruined city, the bereaved mother of its people. The poet cries out to her, "Arise, cry out in the night / At the beginning of the watches, / Pour out your heart like water / In the presence of *Adonai*," (Lamentations 2:19).

1998

I am asleep on the living room couch when suddenly the lights go on. I sit up. Mother is fully dressed getting coffee. I look at my watch: Three AM. "Mother, why are you up in the middle of the night?" "It's time to get up," she says flatly. "It's three AM!" I argue. "That's wake-up time," she says. I realize that three AM is meaningless to Mother. I take her to the window. "See how dark it is? Everyone is sleeping because it is night. In the morning, the sun will shine and everyone will get up." "I'm up now," she says. "Well, I'm going back to sleep," I tell her. I lie rigid on the couch until she drifts back to bed, but I am pouring out my heart like water.

The outrageousness of pain forms the core of Zion's complaint. She keeps presenting to God the palpable, soul-shattering reality of suffering and death as simply unjustifiable as punishment. She accuses God not of injustice but of compassionlessness. "*Re'eh v'habita,*" "See and look hard," are words that recur along with words for pain, suffering, torment, agony. Zion interrupts the poet-narrator in 1:9 to say, "See *Adonai,* my misery; How the enemy triumphs." And in 1:11: "See *Adonai,* look hard at how abject I have become." She calls on witnesses to her ordeal: "May it never befall you—All who pass along the road / Look about and see: / Is there any agony like mine / which was meted out to me / when *Adonai* made me suffer / on the day of His wrath" (1:12).

2002

The outrageousness of pain is what got to me, her pain, my pain, my sister's pain. Our devastation by dementia. My mother is still there. My mother is still not there. The wheeled geriatric chair sits in its same spot in the living room it has occupied since September 2000, when a Parkinson's-like syndrome abruptly paralyzed her legs and stiffened her arms. For three years now they have dressed her only in hospital gowns, since her limbs will not bend enough to make clothing convenient. Glasses of Ensure are poured down her throat, a towel preserving the hospital gown from drips or from the times when she simply opens her mouth and lets the life sustaining fluid flow out. (Testing proved this behavior to be volitional—indeed the only volitional act left in her repertoire. Is it a protest against the prolongation of her dying?)

My mother and the large artificial potted shrub do not move, do not speak. It is like visiting Sleeping Beauty's castle. The '70s furniture provided by a decorator at enormous cost waits silently for its hideous upholstery to shred and crumble. The CD player plays the same collections of "Classics You Know and Love." Sleeping Beauty sleeps, but the machine keeps going; the blood pumping inexorably at the ideal pressure, the flawless lungs inhaling and exhaling, the skin, unmarked by sores, slightly tacky from countless applications of lotion, like the rubbery doll a little girl grasps on a sweaty Chicago summer day. Sleeping Beauty is no beauty any longer; hair grey and sparse, missing teeth that abruptly dropped like autumn leaves, a face emptied of charm and intelligence. Shrunken and bony, she waits not for the kiss of life but for the kiss of death which does not come, does not come. Is it the day of God's wrath? Or is God also sleeping?

It is wrath, says the man who has known affliction, who speaks in Lamentations chapters 3 and 4. "He has made me dwell in darkness / like those long dead / He has walled me in and I cannot break out, / and when I cry and plead / He shuts out my prayer," (Lamentations 3:6–8). The man who has known affliction sees the violence in his situation. He sees God as violent, and maybe I do too. "He is a lurking bear to me, / a lion in hiding: / He has forced me off my way and mangled me, / He has left me numb," (Lamentations 3:10–11). But maybe it is not divine wrath. For all I know it is something in the environment or her diet or some virus, some miniscule denizen of the God-created universe, just trying to make a living, triggering some inexorable physical law that God will not countermand. These are the rules. But was this the best universe God could create, this place of pain and madness and slow death?

Reconciliation 2003–2012

Despite all efforts to keep her alive, my mother slipped away October 31, 2003. I discovered that despite the conversation we had when I insisted that I wanted simply to be a mourning daughter at her funeral, she had left instructions that I am to do the service. I pull everyone in. I speak, my sister speaks, my son speaks. We sing the Twenty-third Psalm. I have created a psalm mosaic of verses about waiting for God, about stigma, about the bird extricating itself from the snare, flying away, escaping. But at the funeral, we are all angry. My mother's beloved points out all the friends and relatives who didn't visit when she was alive. We did our mourning alone with no community to comfort us. Now it feels like mourning someone who has been dead for years.

Mother's beloved died within six months of her demise. Her finished taxes were stacked on his table. So few of us left to remember her, to remember him.

We try to recover Mother the way she was when she was well, but it is so hard not to keep seeing her frozen and unresponsive in a geriatric wheeled chair. Now occasionally, I get flashes of her and Aunt Lil giggling and sharing desserts, toasting one another on New Year's Eve with Alexanders made with whipped cream and crème de cacao but no brandy. Mother playing Scrabble or Rummykub, Mother as a guidance counselor, as an entertainer writing comic song lyrics for someone's party, industriously hooking rather horrible rugs from a kit (handicrafts was not her strong suit). I can remember Mother in graduate school ("I only know how to get an A or flunk," she confides), Mother young in a turquoise dress with a black velvet stole, smelling of Arpege and younger than that, a Mother I know only from photos, a framed picture of a smiling bride carrying gardenias, a solemn child with bobbed hair. Dementia ravaged her for eleven years after seventy-five relatively happy, productive years. Why should the dreadful end dominate our memories?

We do not end the chanting of Lamentations with the last verse. The rabbis have a rule that any public reading must end on a hopeful note. So after the despairing last verse, we repeat the penultimate verse, "Take us back to you, *Adonai*, and we will turn back. Renew our days as of old." After lament, we are saying, let there come renewal.

> Like a bird escaped from the fowler's trap;
> the trap broke and we escaped.(*Ps* 124:7)

> Adonai is the healer of broken hearts,
> the binder up of wounds.(Ps 147:3).

11

Wrestling with God and Evil

Judith Plaskow

I AM CERTAIN THAT I was born a theologian. From as early as I can remember, I have been fascinated by the question of the existence of God and other theological puzzles. The problem of evil in particular has always been an especially urgent topic for me. I was twelve when one of my closest friends and I began reading and talking about the Holocaust. We devoured *The Diary of Anne Frank*, spent hours discussing it, and also read a number of other books that we seem to have picked up haphazardly. Although I cannot remember any titles other than *The Diary*, I know that this reading inducted me into the mystery of human evil.

In college, I discovered the works of Elie Wiesel. Reading *Night*, and then over time, his early novels—*The Accident, Dawn, Town beyond the Wall*, and *Gates of the Forest*—brought together the themes of God's existence and the riddle of evil that I had spent much time contemplating in high school. Wiesel's anger at a God from whom he was unable to disconnect himself shaped my own understanding for many years. I loved the integrity and deep irony of his story in *Gates of the Forest* of three rabbis in Auschwitz who put God on trial for the Holocaust and find him guilty only to be chosen for extermination the next day. I can no longer reconstruct exactly when I read each book or when certain constellations of ideas began to come together for me, but the notion of holding God accountable for Jewish suffering resonated deeply with a theme that I had always loved in Jewish tradition: the idea that the covenant entails mutual obligations and that, just as God can hold the Jewish people responsible for their sins, so God is also bound by God's covenantal promises.

In the mid-1970s, I gave a *d'var Torah* (talk on the Torah) on the second day of Rosh Hashanah on the story of the binding of Isaac. I argued that God's command to Abraham to sacrifice his son illustrated "the amoral sovereignty of God"—an important Jewish theme, from Isaiah's "I form light and create darkness, I make weal and create woe" (Isaiah 45:7) to Wiesel's sad, angry, and ironic tales. Though this was some years after college, it expressed an understanding of God that had been percolating in me for a long time—since my first encounter with Wiesel. My favorite line from Albert Camus's *The Plague*, another novel that spoke to me deeply during my college years, also captured this understanding. Explaining his response to the plague to a comrade in struggle, the protagonist Dr. Rieux says, "Since the order of the world is shaped by death, mightn't it be better for God if we refuse to believe in him and struggle with all our might against death, without lifting our eyes to heaven where he sits in silence?"

I spent my junior year at the University of Edinburgh and, in a biblical studies class, had the opportunity to study the *Book of Job* in some depth. I had previously encountered *Job* in high school when we were reading *The Bridge of San Luis Rey*, and my English teacher asked me to look at *Job* and talk about its relationship to Wilder. I distinctly remember coming into class completely puzzled about what God's answer to Job had to do with the rest of the book and expecting the teacher to explain what I had obviously missed. When I studied *Job* in Edinburgh, however, I realized that my earlier confusion actually embodied an important insight: God's speeches don't have anything to do with the question Job was asking. Job, like Elie Wiesel, was a man profoundly connected to God through his overpowering anger. Job undergoes a moral education in the course of the book, moving from raging about his own personal undeserved suffering to recognizing larger patterns of injustice and the absence of any link between people's behavior and reward and punishment. God overwhelms Job with God's might in answering him out of the whirlwind but completely ignores the issue of justice that Job so eloquently raises. I saw God as a great bully saying, in effect, it's my game; if you don't like it, take your marbles and go home. My immersion in the *Book of Job* fed my fascination with the problem of evil as well as my understanding of God as responsible for evil along with good.

As a graduate student at Yale, I wrote three of my four required doctoral comprehensives on the problem of evil. I did my historical theology exam on the doctrine of original sin, my philosophical theology exam on the problem of evil in analytic philosophy, and my special exam on Holocaust theology. I no longer have a copy of my philosophical theology paper, but I remember ending it by allying myself with Ivan Karamazov's desire to "give back his ticket" in protest against a world in which innocent children have to suffer. Wiesel's anger at a God who cannot be disconnected from the Holocaust and Rieux's refusal to believe in a God who remained silent in the face of plague continued to speak to me very deeply. I finished my graduate education still believing in a God with whom it was appropriate to be angry. As the classical formulation of the problem of evil puts it, either God could not prevent evil or God would not, and the "would not" was much more compelling to me than the idea of God's powerlessness.

It was several years before I consciously relinquished this understanding of God, but my feminism had already begun to undermine it in a quiet way. Through several feminist groups in which I participated from my graduate years onward, I experienced a new kind of agency, a sense of participation in a larger social and even cosmic project, a conviction that women working together could remake the world. In the summer of 1972, I had the privilege of attending the Women Exploring Theology Conference at Grailville, an amazing event at which sixty women came together not just to express our pain and anger at our marginalization within our various communities, but also to initiate new modes of thinking and acting as religiously committed women. The conference was a life-changing experience for me, a week during which I made formative friendships and witnessed the power of women working together to transform our respective traditions.

The center of the conference consisted of morning groups organized around particular themes that met throughout our time together, and I was part of a group of four that decided to focus on consciousness-raising (one of the essential tools of early feminist organizing) as a religious experience. We spent an extraordinary week both immersing ourselves in and analyzing our prior experiences in consciousness-raising groups and recreating those experiences through the power of our conversations. At the end of the week, I suggested that we use the rabbinic story of Lilith as a vehicle for communicating both our process and our insights into the religious dimension of consciousness-raising. I went back to my room to try to compose a story, and "The Coming of Lilith" came pouring through me.

When all the groups reported out on the last evening, there was a sense of tremendous excitement and jubilation as group after group offered new paradigms and images for thinking about God, self, sexuality, singleness and community, politics and tradition. My Lilith story ended with Eve and Lilith returning to the garden together, eager not only to transform their world but sensing that their connection would mean changes in the very nature of God. Independently, the group on Singleness and Community had decided that traditional names for God were no longer adequate. They had made a list of words that meant God to them: changing, creating, extending me beyond myself, enabling, connecting, challenging, loving, nurturing, confronting, and numerous others. Their non-objectifying process words expressed through many "ing" endings captured the energy of my Lilith story and of the conference as a whole and conveyed a sense of what Mary Daly would call "God the verb" in her *Beyond God the Father* published a year later. Initially unperceived by me, the edifice of my prior beliefs was giving way—not with a mighty crash but quietly, hardly noticeably, before the power of an alternative understanding.

It was at my mother's funeral in April 1979 that I discovered I had left behind my earlier understanding of God. My mother died of a malignant brain tumor that robbed her of her intellect and personality and left her in a persistent vegetative state for six months. She was fifty-eight when she died her cruel and lingering death. Her illness and loss could easily have provided me with a splendid new opportunity to be angry at the God who had evaded Job's questions about mercy and remained silent during the Holocaust. But quite to my surprise, I found I was angry not at God but at the colossal irrelevance of the Reform funeral service. I simply did not want to hear about God the Lord and King, mercy and judgment. I wanted to be told that people are born and die, that God gives and takes away, that the moon waxes and wanes, that tides move in and out, that nothing really dies, that everything is taken up in our memories and in the ecology of the planet.

My mind floated to Nelle Morton's article "The Goddess as Metaphoric Image" in which she discusses her fear of flying and her irritating habit of pleading with the powerful male deity in the sky whenever a plane hit turbulence. She describes an occasion on which she told herself to stop behaving like a child and to see what would happen if she invoked the Goddess. Morton discovered that the Goddess was not mistress of the skies and wind but was in the clouds and air currents, and she relaxed her tightened limbs and even enjoyed the rhythm of the plane's movements. This was the God/dess that I wanted to hear about at my mother's funeral—a God/dess who is the cycles of life and death, who gives birth to myriad life forms as the ocean gives rise to waves, and who sustains us in life and also in sorrow. The transcendent and omnipotent God of my girlhood and young adulthood, who had betrayed his (sic) promises to the Jewish people and who could have prevented a brain tumor if he so willed it, had simply vanished. I no longer looked to a God enthroned above me in the sky but God/dess all around and in me, in the firm ground beneath my feet that allowed me to walk upright. Without my conscious awareness of the steps in the process, my feminist insights and commitments had brought me to an understanding of God that I could happily embrace.

Given this profound shift in my understanding of God, it is perhaps not surprising that I scarcely addressed the problem of evil in my book-length exploration of Jewish feminist theology, *Standing Again at Sinai*. I did not plan to avoid the issue and, in fact, I was rather startled and a bit nonplused when I finished the book and realized that I had not dealt with it. There was a time when I would have picked up any Jewish theology that did not discuss the Holocaust and flung it across the room in disgust. But God's responsibility for evil had simply ceased to be a problem for me. I no longer thought of God as the omnipotent Lord of history with the power and responsibility to intervene in creation. God, the ground and wellspring of life, could act only through the world, not upon it from outside. The enterprise of theodicy—the effort to justify God's goodness and power given the existence of evil—had become much less interesting to me than the ways in which our language about God supports social, political, and religious inequalities of power.

Yet, while I thus understood my failure to deal with God's relationship to evil, in the aftermath of writing *Standing Again at Sinai*, I came to see the omission as a serious one. Whether or not God should be blamed for the evils in the world, evil is still a reality that demands exploration. Where was the place in my irenic theology for the recognition that as women become effective in the world in new ways, we also gain new power to hurt and destroy others? Hadn't I learned that the fact of being oppressed offers no guarantees that one won't in turn oppress others? Wasn't there a deep connection between the amorality of the creativity at work in the cosmos and the human capacity to use our own creativity for great good, for great evil, and for everything in between? The anger at God I had nursed for many years now transformed itself into the insistence that an inclusive monotheism must embrace the complexities and ambiguities of existence as part of the nature of God. A concept of God that provides a map of the universe that does not leave out its terrors was far more satisfying to me, I realized, than one that expresses and crystallizes ideals. My life-long wrestling with human and divine evil had changed along with my concept of God. But I was not ready to relinquish the question of God and evil.

Two experiences I had in 1991 contributed to my interest in rethinking God's relationship to the ambiguous forces at work in the universe and ourselves. In the summer of that year, my partner and I visited Iguassu Falls and spent three days in the Amazon. Iguassu is one of the largest series of waterfalls in the world and lies on the border of Brazil and Argentina. I expected to find the falls beautiful; we had been told that they were not to be missed, but I did not expect to be utterly mesmerized by them, to feel as if I could stand and look at them forever, and to weep when we had to leave after three days. When we visited the "Devil's Throat," a spot where it is possible to stand on a platform over the roiling waters at the bottom of the largest waterfall, I felt that I was gazing at the wellspring of life in all its terror and sublimity. On the one hand, the energy, potency, and beauty of the water were incredibly energizing and empowering. It seemed to me that if human beings could only tap into the electricity of the current and allow it to flow through us, we could indeed "let justice well up like water, / Righteousness like an unfailing stream" (Amos 5:24). On the other hand, the waters knew no moral purpose; they could as easily overwhelm and destroy as nourish and vivify. They seemed to transcend the distinction between "power with" and "power over" that had been so central to feminist theology; they could lift up and sustain or engulf and annihilate. I had seen the face of God, and it brought home to me the complex and multi-faceted nature of all creativity, human and divine.

A week later, we spent three days at a hotel in the Amazon at the juncture of the Rio Negro and the Ariau River. We arrived at night, in pitch blackness, after a long boat ride up the Rio Negro to be directed to a room with only screens for the outer wall, filled with sounds of frogs and crickets. I awoke in great excitement at 3:30 in the morning, feeling like a child who has gotten up too early on Christmas morning and can't wait for the day to dawn. Two hours later, we were startled by what sounded like the whole river being drained by a huge vacuum, a terrifying noise that we afterward discovered was howler monkeys calling to each other. We dressed hurriedly, went outside, and accompanied by a black spider and a howler monkey, climbed a tall wooden tower to see the sunrise. I have a phobia of heights and normally would not think of ascending an open and rickety-looking wooden structure, but in this case my excitement overpowered my fear.

The sun rose as it had set the previous evening, a giant red ball, ascending into the sky with amazing rapidity. As it rose, the whole world came to life. The egrets we had seen on the river the previous evening flying to their trees at sunset took off again, as did flocks of flycatchers. The macaws that lived at the hotel began to squawk and squirrel monkeys swung from tree to tree. The vast panoply of sights and sounds made us feel as if we were present at the moment of creation. Our time in the Amazon was both magical and unnerving, rich and overwhelming: the density and tangledness of the vegetation; the strange sounds; the snakes, monkeys and other animals that might appear at any moment and that were still wild even when they lived at the hotel; the vultures feasting on the carcass of a crocodile; the hordes of ants; the piranhas lurking in the river. I experienced a deep sense of reverence for the astoundingly intricate and complex universe of which I was part. "This is not the Lord of history at work here," I wrote in my journal of the trip, "but the infinitely fertile and inventive source of life."

These experiences reinforced the understanding of God that had been growing in me since my mother's funeral. God is the creative energy that underlies, animates, and sustains all existence, the Ground of Being, the source of all that is, the power of life, death, and regeneration in the universe. God's presence fills all of creation, and creation simultaneously dwells in God. In theological language, I am a panentheist: I believe in a God who is present in everything and yet at the same time is not identical with all that is. In my concept of God, wholeness or inclusiveness carries more theological weight than goodness. The world as we know it has little use for human plans and aspirations. We can be stunned by the beauty of the raging waters of the sea and an instant later, find ourselves and the things we love annihilated by them. We can be astounded by the care, altruism, and intricate interdependence found everywhere in nature and also by its predation and violence.

When we look at ourselves, we find the same, often ambiguous, mixture of motives and effects. Most people are capable of great kindness and also of cruelty. Human beings have imagined remarkable ways to care for the most vulnerable among us and have also used our ingenuity to torture and kill. Moreover, there is not a straightforward relationship between our intentions and their outcomes. Things we mean for the good frequently have unforeseen negative consequences just as we can mean something for ill and yet good can come of it. To deny God's presence in all this, to see God only in good, seems to me to leave huge aspects of reality outside of God. Where then do they come from? How are they able to continue to exist? How can we not see that the same amazing inventiveness that allows us to establish systems of justice, feed the hungry and find cures for many diseases is present when we develop new weapons or build crematoria?

Recently, I asked myself whether I can still find meaning in my once-loved *Book of Job*, given how thoroughly my concept of God has changed. Are there parts of the book that continue to resonate for me as for the girl I once was, and what might I read differently? I find that I am no less moved than was my young self by Job's anger at the injustices of the world and by his gradually dawning, if incomplete, realization that others besides him suffer without reason. "People remove boundary-stones; / They carry off flocks and pasture them; / They lead away the donkeys of the fatherless, / And seize the widow's bull as a pledge," (24:2–3). *Job's* vivid descriptions of the disconnection between human behavior and its just rewards appear to me no less breathtakingly brave or devastatingly accurate than when I first read them.

But when I turn to God's reply to Job, I find myself less angered by its evasiveness than struck by its extraordinary beauty and power. Here, in a more sustained way than anywhere else in the Bible, we find a description of the intrinsic value of nature apart from human purposes, a paean to the wonders of a strange and mysterious creation that preexists human beings and that has its own order and meaning. The natural world of God's reply to Job, like the waters of Iguassu, is unrestrained, turbulent, powerful, joyous, and beautiful. While I had always been aware of this dimension of *Job*, I had dismissed it as irrelevant to the book's central problematic. I was never able to hold together my indignation at God's refusal to answer Job's question about justice and my love for the language of the "morning stars [singing] together" (38:7), the horse quivering "like locusts, his majestic snorting [spreading] terror" (39:20), and the Behemoth, made as God made us, eating "grass, like the cattle" (40:15).

But now it occurs to me that, much as Job may not want to hear it, this is God's answer to his question. Right, the author of the speeches imagines God as saying to Job, the order of the universe is not founded on justice. It is not about you or your human standards. The world is about other things entirely: creativity, beauty, diversity, power, energy. It's about the amazing panorama of creation, the springs of the sea and the dwelling of light, the storehouses of snow and hail, the ostrich leaving her eggs on the ground to be trampled and the eagle making its home "in the fastness of a jutting rock" (39:28). This is a different reading from saying, as many have argued, that God's perspective is broader than ours, that if only we could see the world from God's point of view, we would understand the fairness of Job's suffering. The truth is that God's speeches show no concern for fairness, and, in any event, there is no such thing as justice that leaves its comprehensible meanings behind.

But God doesn't stop there. The speeches are followed by the puzzling epilogue in which God turns to the "friends" who, throughout the book, have berated Job and told him he must have done something to deserve his misery. God says to them, "You have not spoken the truth about Me, as My servant Job has" (42:7). What can this mean when God has seemingly been rebuking Job for the previous four chapters? It strikes me now that the apparent contradiction between the thrust of God's speeches and this surprising conclusion may hold the key to the book.

God, the wellspring of life and creative energy that dwells within all that exists, is unconcerned with justice; indeed, the very word "concern" unduly personalizes the Ground of Being that sustains and enlivens all that is, good, bad, and indifferent. But it is our job to be concerned with justice. Job has spoken well of God for two reasons: first of all, unlike the friends, he tells the truth. Lambasted by his supposed comforters, hemmed in on all sides, he still refuses to say what he knows to be false—that the good are rewarded and the wicked punished. Second, Job refuses to relinquish the yearning for the justice he fails to see in the world. Finding set before him life and death, first blessing and then curse, he chooses life in the form of speaking truth and demanding justice. This is our task as human beings in the face of an all-embracing God: to affirm the ties that bind us to each other and creation, and to be the justice required for creation to flourish.

III

Opening the Gates
(Psalm 118:19)

12

In the Right Time

Reflections on an Abortion

SUE LEVI ELWELL

IN MANY JEWISH COMMUNITIES across the world, when one learns of a pregnancy, the response is *b'sha'ah tova*, "may it happen in a good hour, in the right time." In June 1970, I was a twenty-two-year-old unmarried woman about to graduate from college. I was pregnant. I did not know this phrase, but I was clear that this was not a good time, or the right time, for me to become a mother. It was not the right time for me to begin a family.

Will you join me on a walk? It's Shabbat *afternoon, and I'm too restless for a nap. I've been wanting to speak about this for a long time. But I have not been able to find the words. I think of Etty Hillesum's musing, which has lodged in my heart since I first encountered it: "Everyone seeks a home, a refuge. And I am always in search of a few words."*

I want to speak about shame. My shame. A couple of months ago, I attended a training program to update clergy who volunteer at our local Planned Parenthood clinic. For decades, on and off, I've volunteered as an intake worker and, for the past few years, as a pastoral caregiver, listening to the spiritual concerns of women who have come to terminate unintended pregnancies. The program began: a step-by-step slide presentation to help refresh those of us who provide client support. Viewing a slide that listed possible manifestations of clients' shame and ambivalence about the procedure they are about to undergo, I was ambushed by a piercing memory. In

1970, I came to Planned Parenthood seeking an abortion. I listened to the remainder of the presentation with a different, altered sensibility. In spite of years of volunteering, this image catapulted me back forty years. I had been that client who did not know the words to acknowledge her shame.

We are walking through the woods, following trees marked with red splotches of paint about four or five feet from the ground. The sun is high in the afternoon sky. The tall trees are dense with late summer foliage, and wind-blown leaves create a shimmering carpet beneath our feet.

In 1970, I was an intense, curious, driven young woman passionate about my studies and looking forward to graduate school. If I had known *Shir haShirim*, I would have quoted it to the young man with whom I was in love. I now know that we lived in the midst of what is now called the sexual revolution. But I was no revolutionary, and indeed, was just beginning to evolve as a woman and as an intentional agent of my own fate. I loved shyly, without sharing my delight with even my closest friends. My circle of friends talked about ideas and about many aspects of our lives, but we did not share intimacies with one another. Somehow, I knew to contain my joy, to stifle my amazement at the pleasure I shared with my lover. In my small Midwestern college town, love did not speak; it whispered.

I went to Planned Parenthood initially to obtain birth control, clear that my sexual behavior was not an expression, at that time, of my wish to begin a family. But our careful use of foam and condoms failed. When I returned to Planned Parenthood, just weeks before graduation from college, my pregnancy was confirmed. I was headed to the University of Washington for the summer to study Hebrew as the recipient of a coveted government grant. And then I was moving to the east coast to pursue graduate work in Jewish Studies. This was not the right time to be pregnant. When I met with the Planned Parenthood counselor, I requested a referral that would help me secure an abortion.

I was seeking a medical procedure that was illegal in most states. In 1970, New York, Alaska, Hawaii, and Washington were the only states in which an abortion requested by a woman and her physician was automatically available. But I could not go home to Buffalo, where my family lived. I had visions of running into someone I knew in the airport, and could not imagine going to any of our family physicians. And I didn't know how to begin to find an abortion provider in any other city in New York, or in Washington, even though I was headed to Seattle in just a few weeks.

So I called the local Protestant minister who had identified himself to Planned Parenthood as a member of a national network of clergy who helped women connect with safe abortion providers. We met in his church study. He asked me, "Is the father of your baby white?" I was stunned by his question.

My affirmative answer was met by another question: "would you prefer to speak with a rabbi?" I asked whether any rabbis in the area were equipped to help me. When he said no, we continued our conversation, but I remember my anger and resentment that I needed to go through this gatekeeper to gain access to what I understood to be a simple medical procedure. He provided me with a phone number of a clinic and wished me luck.

When I called the clinic, hundreds of miles away, I was offered an appointment for a consultation in six weeks. I needed to pursue other options. I could not wait that long.

I did not know then that less than one hundred miles away, in Chicago, a network of abortion counselors and providers called Jane was working with thousands of women every month to procure safe abortions. I had actually met Rabbi Daniel and Dr. Myra Leifer, active members of this courageous group of clergy and health-care professionals who helped women safely terminate unintended pregnancies. From 1969 to 1973, more than 11,000 women secured illegal but safe abortions thanks to Jane, officially known as "The Abortion Counseling Service of the Chicago Women's Liberation Union." But I did not know about Jane. And this was two years before the heralded publication of the inaugural issue of *Ms. Magazine*, which included a petition entitled, "We Have Had Abortions," signed by fifty well-known women, including Gloria Steinem, Lee Grant, Lillian Hellman, Anaïs Nin, and Billie Jean King.

A friend lived close to the clinic I had called. I thought, if I go to this clinic and show up in person, maybe they'll take me, sooner than six weeks. My heart pounding, I dialed her number. "I want to come and visit you, but . . . I need your help. I'm pregnant." There was a long silence on the other end of the line. My friend answered: "I know a doctor who can help you. I had an abortion last fall." I can't remember if I laughed or cried—probably both.

Two weeks later, my parents and siblings drove across the country to attend my college graduation. The next day, after kissing them goodbye, I boarded a plane not for Seattle, as they thought, but towards the east coast destination where I had already secured an appointment with my friend's physician. My friend recommended that I present myself as a local college student. We then went to the local public library to secure a library card in case my residency was questioned.

The OB/GYN examined me and sneered as he told his nurse to make an appointment for a D&C, dilation and curettage, a common procedure for surgical abortion, in three days. However, before he would perform the outpatient surgery, I had to provide evidence that I was eligible for the procedure. Between 1967 and 1970, fifteen states, including this one, had legalized "therapeutic abortion," abortion permitted when the mother's physical or emotional health was deemed a significant risk to a healthy outcome. So I needed to be certified as a patient "at risk." My friend drove me to a private psychiatric facility where I met with a staff social worker. He coached me how to "present" my case to a psychiatrist whose written documentation would establish my tenuous emotional state, thus qualifying me for the procedure.

When I opened my eyes after the surgery, the OB/GYN was standing over me, demanding his fee. I propped myself up on the gurney in the recovery room, and signed over several hundred dollars' worth of traveler's checks to this small man.

We continue our walk through the forest. A large limb has fallen in front of us. I step over it, then realize that others will follow me on this path, if not today, in the days to come. As I bend to lift it, I am surprised by its weight. I wrestle with the fallen bough, and finally drop it down at the side of the path. It becomes a marker on the way. We continue, listening to the insects as they warm up their string section for the coming twilight concert.

June 1970 was not the right time for me to begin a family. I summoned up the courage to move ahead with determination and sought the assistance of trusted friends to help me. However, I intentionally kept my situation and my whereabouts from my parents. I did not confide in my beloved siblings or share my story with other dear friends. I did not turn to God or to Jewish sources. I chose silence. It was not a good time.

After the procedure, I boarded a plane for Seattle and immersed myself in the intensive Hebrew language program that provided a bridge to my subsequent graduate studies. I did not look back. Until now.

I now see that I was unwilling to accept the pervasive cultural message that love and pleasure lead, inexorably, to shame and degradation, any more than the fear of conception, or of contracting sexually transmitted diseases, should determine decisions about sexual activity. I was unwilling to be bullied or deterred. But I was not then able to name that determination with clarity. And I was not ready, then or subsequently, to speak or to write about my choice.

I have spent the years since then studying and teaching Jewish texts. Eleven years after my abortion, I began to study for the rabbinate. I remembered the pastor's first question, "Is the baby's father white?" I was appalled by the explicit racism of this query. Was there a difference between terminating a pregnancy of a biracial fetus or a white fetus? Would it be preferable to keep a mixed race individual from being born? The first question both defined and challenged my white privilege, suggesting that my choice of a non-white sexual partner would dictate a blighted future for me and my offspring. Conversely, a white baby would be acceptable to the world, either for me to "keep" or for me to give away. Even years later, the pastor's question sickened me.

The shame I carry is not about having made a series of choices that included terminating my unwelcome pregnancy years ago. My shame is about my silence about that choice. Both then and now, I am a person of privilege. My white skin, my education, and my class enabled me to seek and find safe and legal means to terminate my unintended pregnancy. My subsequent silence about my experience has been a fallen tree in my path, and I have, unconsciously, turned back from speaking about this essential injustice, this moral wrong, this stumbling block to human freedom that continues to define too many women's lives across the globe. The Passover *Haggadah* teaches, "we begin with shame and conclude with praise." But this journey is not simply from shame to praise. It is through shame to speech. My forty-year silence has been, for me, a wandering as circuitous as my ancestors' through the wilderness.

And then there was the pastor's second question: "Would you rather speak with a rabbi?" I would have preferred to speak with a rabbi. I was hungry for conversations about abortion and Jewish law and tradition, about the nature of the soul and the sanctity of the body. I was living in an America where many disapproved of abortion. And I knew that the voices of the progressive tradition in which I had been raised were often drowned out by strident so-called "pro-lifers," those who denied women's rights to control our own bodies and our own destinies. I wanted to speak with a rabbi who would take me seriously as a seeker and as a woman. I longed to speak with a rabbi who would not begin with racist assumptions about the sanctity of life and relationships. And I wanted to speak with a rabbi about God's place in this story.

I hoped that I could become that rabbi.

Our path has taken us to a clearing. We trudge up a short but steep rise, and are rewarded with a commanding view of the valley below. The aluminum roofs of the houses and barns below catch the late afternoon sun and glisten as if under water. The entire valley is bathed in gentle, golden light. We're far enough away that we hear no sounds of human or animal life. We're surrounded by the music of the afternoon breeze. The insects' symphony seems to have stayed behind us when we came out of the dense forest. We stand still in this exquisite moment, marveling in how far we can see and how much remains beyond our sight. I invited you to walk with me today because I want to continue to move through speech to praise.

These forty plus years have been, for me, years of blessing and celebration. I have been blessed to partner with sweet and generous souls and to raise children who have charted their own paths. I have been blessed to teach the tradition I love to those who hunger to learn, including some who will choose to teach those who follow them.

And I have learned how to begin to speak with God. We Jews are blessed with a tradition rich with God-talk, and I have studied with teachers who have helped me think deeply about how we image and speak with God. As a woman, as a feminist, as a progressive and questioning Jew, I continue to explore rich, evolving, and ever-changing conversations with the Holy One, the Source of all, the One of many names. As I reflect on this time in my life, I realize that God was with me on every step of this journey, however uncertain I may have been at the time. As I look back, I, like Jacob, see that God was in that place, and I did not know it (Gen 28:16).

My initial training as a volunteer chaplain at Planned Parenthood included observing, with their permission, every step of the patient's experience from intake through recovery. We were encouraged to visit the lab where the clinicians examined the POC, or "products of conception" to insure that the process was complete. I was profoundly moved by what I saw that day. I knew that for me, serving as a witness and guide for women choosing abortion is a holy opportunity, a calling.

In the daily morning service, as we prepare to recite the *Shema*, we repeat this petition to God: "Enlighten our eyes with your Torah and draw our minds near to You . . . that we will never be shamed." Joel Hoffman teaches: "'Never' is too weak to capture the force of the Hebrew . . . the proper meaning is 'never, ever!' but that expression sounds childish, and the original Hebrew does not." We shall never, ever be shamed.

I began to break my long silence by sharing my story with my daughters, now grown. I spoke with my siblings, who shared their own stories with me. Finally I spoke with my mother, now a widow. Each one listened with compassion and without judgment. Each expressed gratitude that now is a better time, a time of deeper understanding and greater openness, a time when silence can be broken without fear of rejection or reprisal.

If the twenty-two-year-old woman I was in 1970 came to me now, I would welcome her to sit with me. I would invite her to speak, and I would listen as my daughters and my siblings and my mother listened to me. I would listen to her questions, and invite her to hear, with me, the questions behind her questions. Deep listening invites discernment. And from discernment come new, more probing questions.

Over the course of my rabbinate, I have been blessed to speak with many women whose questions about transitions in their lives have led them to consider using ritual and ceremony to explore those experiences. Together, we talk about what each woman hopes to accomplish by acknowledging her transition from one state of being to another. We explore Jewish texts that reflect, echo, or illuminate her experience, and we consider utilizing ritual objects and performative words to deepen and enhance the ceremony.

Over the years, I collected prayers and rituals to mark the intentional conclusion of a pregnancy. But I did not create a ritual for myself. I see now that I was searching for a text that would, like other powerful texts from our tradition, help to illuminate my story, contextualize my experience, and perhaps enable me to see my experience as part of our collective, shared narrative.

Elie Wiesel teaches us that God loves stories. Our tradition is filled with stories crafted by rabbis, tales that answer questions raised by the biblical text, tellings that connect individuals, events, or places to enrich our reading and our understanding, even when the context of our lives seems to be profoundly different from that of our forebears. Texts, both ancient and modern, historic and newly imagined, can illuminate our paths, revealing hidden patterns, uncovering hints, clues, insights, wonders. Stories heal our brokenness, as sharing the experiences of and reflection upon our lives pushes back the heavy curtains of loneliness and isolation.

In the book of Numbers, five women, Mahlah, Noah, Hoglah, Milcah, and Tirzah are identified as the daughters of one man, Zelophehad. These sisters, who had no brothers, challenged Moses to consider them as their father's heirs, eligible to both inherit his land and to carry on his name. In the biblical world, women were considered the property of their father until they were acquired in marriage by a husband, so the daughters' request was both bold and courageous. Moses' positive response set a new legal precedent for men who died without male heirs.

These sisters are unique in the Torah for a number of reasons: they are the single group of five sisters mentioned by name, and two of their names appear only in this particular story. Tirzah, who may have been the youngest of the sisters, is mentioned again in the Song of Songs. Scholars debate whether Tirzah, and indeed each of the sisters' names, are place names transformed into names of individual women to make a point about the importance of equal inheritance. Is Tirzah, the youngest daughter, the same women mentioned in the Song of Songs? Her name is often translated as pleasure and beauty.

For the woman I was in 1970, for the women and men who come after me, I offer my version of Tirzah's story.

∞৩৩∞

I was twelve years old and had recently joined my sisters in counting our cycles by the moon. It was my custom to join one or more of my sisters in watering my father's sheep at the oasis not far from our compound. We loved skipping together and singing to the sheep as we accompanied them across the open spaces. Some days we were joined by BenAv, my companion and playmate from the days when we were very young. He and I often ran ahead of my sisters, racing one another to the top of the ridge, and then collapsing in laughter, trading stories and secrets.

One day, Hoglah and Milcah remained at home to help with the barley harvest. BenAv and I set out with the sheep for a long day in the sun. I noticed that he had suddenly grown tall, and that his voice had deepened. We took the sheep to graze, and then we set up our cloaks as a barrier from the midday sun. When we lay down in the shade to rest, our bodies touched, and I felt a strange and delicious fire sweep through me. BenAv looked into my eyes. "You are beautiful, Tirzah, fair and striking." We both knew the words of *Shir haShirim*, the courting song, the wedding song. The power of our connection amazed and slightly frightened us, but we continued to let our bodies speak to one another in this new language.

When I awoke, I saw that the sun had moved across the sky. I felt beautiful and strong and clear. This was not my time for love. I woke BenAv and we sat together, first in silence, and then with words. "Daughters of Jerusalem, swear to me by the gazelles, by the deer in the field, that you will not awaken love until it is ripe." We both knew that we were not yet ripe. We both knew that this was not our time to come together as a family.

We agreed that we would not be together again in this way. We returned home with the flocks.

In the days that followed, my sisters and I returned to the open spaces with the sheep; BenAv was busy with his family's herds. One day, Mahlah asked after BenAv. I told her that we had delighted in one another, and had decided that it was not time for us to be together. When the moon became round, my sisters began to bleed. I did not. Mahlah watched me when we rose in the morning and I checked my garments. She drew me close, and told me that it was time for us to visit the midwife. Shifra, named for the mother of midwives (Exod 1:15), cared for all women in their times of need. My sisters Mahlah and Hoglah were now her apprentices, learning the ancient craft of those who work as partners of the Holy One, helping women. A few months before, I had attended a neighbor's birth, and had watched in silence and wonder as a tiny, wrinkled baby had entered the world. My sisters stood at the neighbor's side. Together the women chanted "*B'sha'ah tova, b'sha'ah tova*": "this is the time, this is the good time."

Mahlah and I approached Shifra's tent. I carried a shofar, a ram's horn, I had carved the previous spring. Shifra looked at me with love and consternation as I offered my gift. "Five moons ago, we welcomed you into the circle of women who bleed with the moon. Why are you here today?" I met her kind eyes shyly. "I awakened love before it was ripe. This is not my time."

"Have you conferred with your sisters?" Shifra knew that since our mother died, the love between us had become a great source of strength.

"Yes." Mahlah added, "I speak for Noah, Hoglah, and Milcah."

Shifra turned to me. "With God's help, your moon cycle will be restored."

The midwife gave me a small vessel, and we returned to our tent. I followed Shifra's direction and drank the strange-smelling potion. My sisters held me as the liquid entered my body, and they cared for me and sang to me as the hours passed and my body expelled the unripe seed. On the second day, I joined my sisters at the evening meal. By the third day, I returned to the oasis with my sisters and the sheep.

When the moon was round again, I bled with my sisters. To celebrate my return to the sacred cycle of women, our family hosted a feast for the women of the village. My sisters crowned me with a garland of delicate desert flowers, and we feasted on a freshly-killed lamb from our flock. As the sun set and the stars rose, the women joined in ancient songs of thanks to the Holy One for my recovery. Their voices danced through the dark as they shared their stories of healing, singing to the Healer of all flesh. I watched their faces glow in the light of the fire and I learned how the women of my village care for one another from first blood until the time when women no longer count their days by the moon. I learned of seeds planted in love and in war, of other shoots, like mine, that were uprooted. Some women wept as they shared their stories. Other women uttered victory cries as they recalled their triumphs. As each woman concluded her story, her sisters and mine joined in a chant that gave wings to her words. One of the chants sounded like a lullaby; I remembered it from the birth I had attended. "*B'sha'ah tova, b'sha'ah tova.*" As the women's voices sparkled in the night, these words promised a future I could not yet see, a future when my "time" would be "right." Surrounded by the circle of my sisters' love, I fell asleep on a soft lambskin. Under the night sky, I dreamed of leading my sheep, a flock of ewes and new lambs, and watching them prance together across the hills.

∞ᘐᗡ∞

Every morning Jews begin our prayers with *Mah Tovu*, a poem constructed of five biblical verses, one from the book of Numbers and four from the book of Psalms. The final verse begins: "I offer my prayer to You, Holy One, *at this time of favor* . . . " The phrase, *eit ratzon*, echoes Tirzah's name. When is a time of favor? Joel Hoffman teaches: "the question is whether the speaker is praying for a time of favor or at a time of favor." Tirzah's tale is written about a time of favor.

I now live in a time of favor. And I continue, each day, to pray and to work towards a time of favor, a time when we all can love without shame, a time when we can choose when and how to begin our families, a time when every Jew who seeks spiritual guidance can find a compassionate ear and a listening heart.

Thank you for joining me today. You have heard me into speech, and have helped me find "a few words" in this, the right time, a time of favor. Perhaps, together we can open the way towards speech for each of our lost stories, continuing the process of revealing Torah. In telling, we take firm steps towards praise. Let us praise the Source of All, who enables each of us to find the right word in the right time.

13

My Life as a Talking Horse

Hybridity and Gender Equity as Jewish Values

WENDY ZIERLER

M Y LIFE STRADDLES TWO Jewish worlds.
 I spend my workdays as a professor of Jewish literature and feminist studies, helping to train rabbis, cantors, and educators for the Reform movement. I spend my evenings and weekends in modern Orthodox Riverdale, New York. On *Shabbat*, I alternate between various Orthodox *minyanim* and prayer groups—groups that are committed both to *halakhah* and to feminism, but where a traditional legal approach often forces a compromise with strict feminist principle. My weekday life actualizes my deepest feminist convictions, but places me at something of a remove in light of my commitment to Jewish law and observance. My *Shabbat* life puts me in the company of people steeped in Jewish law, learning, and practice, but relegates me, in one way or another, to the other side of a partition.

My work and the theory that undergirds it often compel a tearing down of binaries. I teach literature and feminism at a rabbinical school, which means that I am always bringing together seemingly disparate worlds: classical Jewish texts and modern literary sources, Judaism and feminist or queer theory. My teaching constitutes an extended argument for the place of seemingly secular, even heretical literary sources in the (sacred) canon of Jewish literary tradition.

Most of my writing has been dedicated to the ways in which modern Jewish women's writing can serve as a source of new, in some cases counter-traditional exegesis of tradition. I am convinced that the revival of the secular Hebrew language and the participation of women in this revival (against the background of so many years of women's Jewish literary and intellectual silence) is one of the great miracles of modern Jewish life.

Like the life I lead, the scholarly work I do doesn't neatly fit into the prefabricated categories of classical Jewish learning. It mixes approaches that are not often mixed, just as this essay combines the personal as well as the scholarly voice. I find myself, in this regard, a curious anomaly, a strange beast. Part-feminist / part-traditionalist; half-heretic / half-hieratic. I live inside and outside two worlds all at the very same time. So often, I find that it is my outsider stance that allows me to remain inside. I remain the thing because I am also its opposite. I cannot allow the categories to stand truly apart.

As a reader and writer of literary texts, I don't always draw a neat distinction between life and text, between personal life and story. Sometimes I even come upon a work of fiction that seems to speak for me very personally, which houses me in its very lines. Such is the case with one enigmatic, little-known story by American Jewish writer, Bernard Malamud, called "Talking Horse," a work of fiction that had led me on a search for my own "Talking Horse Tradition." This may seem like an arcane literary pursuit, bizarre, even laughable, hardly something said to constitute the foundation of Judaism or Jewish literature. And yet, tracing this tradition reveals a Jewish textual preoccupation with hybridity that helps me make sense of my own complicated Jewish self-definition. It also takes me back to my childhood, to the origins of my career, to some of my most basic and yet seemingly contradictory intellectual and ideological commitments as a scholar and a feminist. Permit me as I take you through this text and its inter- or pre-texts, on an analytical journey to the very center of my own mixed, hybrid self.

Bernard Malamud's "Talking Horse"

Malamud's "Talking Horse" (1977) is the story of a talking horse named Abramowitz, a creature who has trouble making sense of his mixed self and feels trapped in a role and identity dictated and enforced by a mute master, a circus trainer named Goldberg. Abramowitz wants to know how he came to be a talking horse; more than that, he longs for a way out of his current life. Like many short stories that begin with a large, boldface capital letter, "Talking Horse" begins with a boldface, upper case Q. for question, introducing the central identity problem that agitates the talking-horse protagonist:

> Q. Am I a man in a horse or a horse that talks like a man? Suppose they took an X-ray, what would they see?—a man's luminous skeleton, prostrate inside a horse, or just a horse with a

complicated voice box? . . . All I know is I've been here for years and still don't understand the nature of my fate, in short, if I'm Abramowitz, a horse, or a horse including Abramowitz. Why is anybody's guess. Understanding goes so far and no further, especially if Goldberg blocks the way. (p. 514)

Abramowitz has learned all the answers to scripted questions of his sideshow act with Goldberg, but none to his own, which include basic inquiries into origin, self, and purpose. Was he originally a man or a horse? Does his essence belong to one species or another? In being a talking horse—i.e., a human consciousness incarcerated inside the body of a horse, a creature of ideas and language as well as an animal of considerable size and speed—is he serving some kind of sentence? Will he ever be set free to discover the answers to his own questions?

Abramowitz's Jewish surname suggests that he is not just any talking horse, but in some way, a Hebrew or Jewish one. The G-sound of Goldberg's common Jewish name, underscored by the recurrent "geee, gooo, gaaa, gaaw"s of his unintelligible speech, point to a reading of the story wherein Abramowitz, evocative of the biblical Abraham, stands for the Jews, while Goldberg stands for an inarticulate God who permits no questions, subjects his people to endless inexplicable suffering, and reduces them to bestial submission.

Abramowitz is a modern, philosophically and scientifically inclined Jewish talking-horse, who hopes to resolve the mystery of his identity by means of an X-ray. He also dreams of the other lives he might live if only he could be liberated from the identity imposed upon him since time immemorial by God-Goldberg. On the one hand he fantasizes about being a horse, a purely physical creature of the land, "pulling a wagonload of yellow apples along a rural road" (p. 524). On the other hand, he dreams of being an "altogether free 'man' . . . who is maybe a doctor or lawyer helping poor people" (p. 525). God-Goldberg (in the form of a voice that speaks in Abramowitz's head) rejects both options. Regarding his dreams of being a majestically physical, graceful racehorse—the voice tells Abramowitz that he is too broken down, overweight, and sagging for that ever to come to pass—in short too much of a Diaspora Jew-horse. As for being a doctor or a lawyer, Goldberg's cliché-ridden voice admonishes Abramowitz not to "rock the boat," or "break up the act." Recalling the theme song from Mr. Ed, Goldberg reminds Abramowitz that "[a] horse is a horse even if he's a talking horse," and that "the law is the law, you can't change the order" (p. 523).

Still Abramowitz persists. And as readers we cannot help rooting for Abramowitz against God-Goldberg. We yearn along with him for Emancipation and Assimilation, for the breaking up of the brutalizing Jewish "act." If one can simply accomplish this—if one can free oneself from theologically determined, pre-modern forms of Jewishness and allow oneself, through questioning and political acts of self-liberation, to be reborn as a full-fledged modern—can one not discover a true, authentic, coherent self? Isn't that what we're meant to think?

Sarnia, Ontario, Canada. Population 75,000. Jewish population seventy-five. I'm sitting on the floor in my bedroom, sunlight coming through a half-open curtain, throwing a fat triangle of light on my oval-shaped, multicolor rag rug. It is a Saturday, *Shabbes* afternoon. I am bored, with nothing to do but contemplate the white-lit triangle on the floor on this long summer Sabbath day of rest decreed by God and my parents. Will it ever end, this vast, uncut lawn of a day, when we can't go the beach and can't watch the television and can't use crayons or paints? Margie West who lives three doors away and whose family isn't Jewish can do whatever she likes on Saturdays; what's worse: today and for the next three weeks they're away on a camping trip. Her bus-driver father, Bill Sr., has bought an old-school bus from his company, painted it blue, and turned it into a camper. And Margie is there on that bus, traveling across Canada. I can imagine no greater pleasure on earth than riding a blue bus to Winnipeg, because I have already seen, with my very own open eyes, the bed that her father has built for her, an engineering wonder, that pulls out from under one of the seats by night and that can be converted back into a seat by day. Since Marge is riding the blue bus, and since my father, who can't afford to keep the store closed on Saturday is out at the store, and since my mother makes the rest of us keep *Shabbes* even if my father's at work, and since my sisters and brother have all gone off to visit friends and my mother is napping, I am sitting in my room watching dust motes swirl in the light above the rag rug, a magical activity, perhaps for some, but not for me.

I lie down on my rug, world-weary, turn my head to my left and to my right, and to my amazement, right there, under my bed, is a shining dime. How it got there, I do not know. I do know that I am not allowed to touch money on *Shabbes*, but wouldn't it be fun to watch the dime roll along the carpet, throwing off bits of sun? Better yet, wouldn't it be nice to clasp that dime tight in my hand, and run down the street to the variety store, and buy a handful of Pixy-Stix straws with the sour and sweet powder that melts on your tongue, and run back before anyone knows where I've been? Only seconds later I am dashing down the street, the dime in hand. The door of the store gives off a guilty ring and bang as it swings open and then swings back shut. I place the dime on the counter. I grab five Pixy-Stix: red, purple, blue, yellow, and green. I run back, but tread carefully up the porch and into the house so as not be detected in my coming. I tip-toe upstairs, slip back into my room and fall onto my rag rug, panting. I tuck four of the straws into my bottom dresser drawer, under my pajamas, but open up the green one, slowly pouring the powder onto my tongue. Some of the green powder bounces off my tongue and dances with the dust motes in the air, and I think, how naughty and free I am having broken *Shabbes* this way, how utterly unlike anyone else in my family. But then again, my father works on *Shabbes,* and yet he is the one who makes *Kiddush* and *Hamotzi* at dinner and likes so much to go to *shul* when someone can cover for him at the store. Come to think of it, so do I. *Shabbes* is nice when it isn't so boring, and everyone is home, and I can walk to shul with Daddy, while he skips down the sidewalk and sings "Tea for Two." How is it, I wonder, that one thing can be two things all at the same time? Wouldn't it be easier if it were just one thing or another? And will I have to spend the whole long day trying to figure this out myself?

Talking She-Horses

Malamud's story is all about Abramowitz's long struggle to figure it out himself and break free; but as it turns out, freedom doesn't end up taking the tidy Enlightenment form that he or we might have expected. We get a clue that is going to be the case in that name Abramowitz, which refers not only to the biblical Abraham, founding father of the covenant with God, but also to the founder of modern Yiddish and Hebrew fiction, S. Y. Abramovitsch (1835–1917), otherwise known as Mendele Moycher Seforim. Abramowitz's novel, *Die Kliyatshe* (1873, published in English in 1955, under the title, *The Nag*) features a talking she-horse. In Abramovitsch's novel a young *maskil* named Yisrolik, a kind of false or misled visionary, is enlightened about failures of the Russian Enlightenment through his phantasmagorical conversations with a beaten-down she-horse. Haven't we seen this plot before?

Recall another important moment in the Jewish Talking Horse Tradition—the biblical story from Numbers 22 of Balaam the Gentile prophet, who is hired by the Moabite Balak to curse the Israelites. After securing permission from God, who adjures him only to speak that which God places in his mouth, Balaam rises early in the morning, saddles his she-ass, and sets out on the road. Three times on the way, Balaam's she-ass sees an angel of God standing before her brandishing a sword and therefore veers of course. Balaam beats the she-ass for doing so, at which point the she-ass miraculously speaks to protest this treatment. Eventually God opens Balaam's eyes so that he can see the angel himself, but only after the she-ass has spoken twice. Consider this in comparison to Abraham's felicitous sighting of the angel at the end of the *Akedah* story, which results in the sparing of Isaac's life. The she-ass is even more Abrahamic than Abraham, not to mention Balaam, for she sees the angel at the beginning of her journey, not just at its end.

On one level, this is a deadly serious story about two peoples at war, with one people endeavoring to curse the other. The cultural context here is one where people believe quite literally in the power of words to affect reality. In the midst of all this seriousness about words, however, comes comedy: a talking she-ass who upstages the prophet with her superior visionary powers. Not only does the Gentile prophet fail to see the angel of God on the road, he mercilessly beats his trusty she-ass almost to death. The Gentile prophet is thus shown to be an unfitting vessel for God's word. In contrast, the articulate and perspicacious she-ass gives noble voice to the downtrodden and abused, thus affirming the basic ethical values of the Torah. Shall we rename her Abramowitz too?

———

Fast forward a decade and a half. My family no longer lives in Sarnia. Shortly after my fifth birthday, my parents decide to give up the store and their small-town life and move to Toronto where we can live as fully observant Jews. My parents join an Orthodox synagogue so that for once, they do not have to be in the minority as Sabbath observers; my siblings and I are sent to Jewish schools and Orthodox summer camps. Most of my friends at school, a community school under Orthodox leadership, do not keep *Shabbat* as we do, which is okay with me as I have *Shabbat* friends in my *shul*. I secretly revel in our "greater Jewish excellence"—but here and there come moments of inchoate disgruntlement. Why is it that my brother can sing in a boys' choir and make a record and I cannot? Why is it that my conservative best friend can learn the *Haftarah* for her *bat mitzvah* and in our *shul*, girls do nothing at all? In the Canadian Jewish News, there is grumbling about Reform and now conservative Jews ordaining women rabbis. What, I wonder, should I think about that? There is no such being as a woman rabbi in Toronto in the 1970s and 1980s. There is no such thing as a woman teacher of Talmud or Bible or even Jewish History at my high school. No women principals. No women leading prayers. My brother goes off to New York to Yeshiva University, training to be an Orthodox rabbi, but what about me? Aren't I every bit as good a scholar?

Soon enough I too am an undergraduate at Yeshiva University, studying literature, art, and Jewish studies. As it happens, I take a course on the biblical book of Numbers and end up writing a term paper, which then gets published in a student journal, in which I offer a defense of the Gentile Balaam, over and against an exegetical tradition that seeks to malign him. In my reading of Numbers 22 and 23, Baalam is actually a decent guy, who refuses at first to do Balak's bidding (Num 22:13) and who ultimately blesses rather than curses the Israelites. What then does one do with those other biblical and post-biblical sources that heap every sort of lewd calumny on Balaam? My essay addresses these discrepancies by referring to two basic scholarly approaches. The first approach resolves the issue by relying on the Documentary Hypothesis and assigning the different biblical materials on Balaam to different biblical authors. The second, which deals primarily with the vilification of Balaam in post-biblical interpretation, situates these interpretations within the historical context of Roman and Christian persecutions of the Jews and views the writings on Balaam as instances of anti-Gentile polemic.

Little do I know, undergraduate neophyte that I am, that in writing up these findings I have wandered into forbidden territory. Unwittingly, I have cited two of the central methods of *Wissenschaft des Judentums*: 1) Higher Biblical Criticism, with its presupposition that the Bible is a composite document produced and redacted by humans rather than a singular document dictated to Moses by God; 2) the historical approach to classical Jewish texts, which suggests that in their interpretations of the Bible, the rabbis and the classical exegetes were influenced by their place and time. Just by mentioning these approaches, I have cast myself outside the Orthodox camp. In publishing this essay for my fellow Orthodox students, says one of my teachers, I have done the equivalent of placing an open electrical socket before a child.

Naïvely, I had thought that I was free to read and learn from everything that might enrich my understanding of Jewish sources. I had no idea that the quest for textual meaning could ever be anything other than laudable. And yet, the blessing of Torah that I had hoped to offer in my article has somehow been turned into a Balakite curse, a forbidden utterance.

Shortly after the publication of the essay, I find myself in the Yeshiva University library, commiserating in the stacks with my editor (who some years later would become my husband) and who earlier that week had been summoned to the office of one *Rosh Yeshiva* to be reprimanded for printing my piece. The same week, another *Rosh Yeshiva* had devoted thirty minutes of his Talmud class for the all-male students of Yeshiva College to debunking the various falsehoods and heresies of my article. One might think I was Benedict Spinoza, rather than a college junior, feeling her way through modern approaches to the study of Jewish text. I am dangerous enough that I need to be refuted, but not significant enough to be spoken to directly.

I am, if you will, but a talking she-ass, a figure who opens her mouth in speech incredibly and unexpectedly, significant not in her own right, but only insofar as she allows for others to clarify (in masculine voice) what is right and what is wrong in the eyes of God. Understanding goes so far and no further, especially if others, claiming to speak for God, block the way.

What Happens in the End?

What ever happens to Balaam's she-ass? How does her story end? Does she simply return, after her miraculous speech, to being a regular, ordinary donkey? Does Balaam ever hear her speak again? If so, do they turn it into a circus act, like Goldberg and Abramowitz, and go on the road?

The Bible does not provide an ending for the she-ass's story. Malamud's talking horse story, however, does offer an ending, and a surprising one at that. One day, after imploring his circus audience in an "impassioned speech on freedom for all" to "[h]elp me recover my original form," Abramowitz attacks Goldberg while he is watching a TV program on astronomy. Goldberg, fighting back, pulls at Abramowitz's ears, until, exposing an old wound, his head comes off on his hands. Out comes a man's pale skinned, dark-eyed, bespectacled head:

> As they tugged and struggled, Abramowitz, straining to the point of madness, slowly pulled himself out of the horse up to his navel. At that point Goldberg broke his frantic grip and, though the astronomy lesson was still going on in a blaze of light, disappeared. Abramowitz later made a few discreet inquiries, but no one could say where.
>
> Departing the circus grounds, he cantered across a grassy soft field into a dark wood, a free centaur. (p. 530)

What does one make of this ending, which also can be likened to a kind of circumcision of the (fore)head of the horse to reveal the other (truer?) Abramowitz hidden within? If the Abrahamic covenant of circumcision determines one's (masculine) Jewish identity, what kind of identity determination occurs here? If at the very beginning of the story, Abramowitz framed his quest for identity as an either/or question ("Am I a man in a horse or a horse that talks like a man?"), what does one make of this ending, where he discovers that he is neither man nor horse but both, not one thing, but two?

According to critic Robert Solataroff, the ending of this story teaches the very futility of the ideal of human freedom. After all, Abramowitz, the centaur, is a kind of monster, a being who can never really fit in or be at home in any single community.

Perhaps this is so. And yet, this reading does not acknowledge the possibility that being a centaur—that is, a hybrid—is a desideratum rather than a tragedy. As one of my students put it, centaur-hood seems to afford Abramowitz the best of both worlds. On the one hand, he has the intellectual capacities, literary sensitivities, even the manual dexterity of a human being. On the other hand, he has the physical strength, speed, agility, and grace of a horse. What if we were to read "Talking Horse," then, as a story of the postmodern Jew who enters a new kind of covenant, discovering that he is neither Jewish nor secular, neither body nor mind, but both? To be sure, his body is exceptional and the wood into which he is about to enter is dark and uncharted. But in departing from the circus grounds where he had been beaten and forced to perform a prescribed circus-act of identity, he is now able to canter freely across a grassy field. Is it not possible that his freedom inheres in not being forced to conform to one essential identity or another? Written against the postmodern social backdrop of late twentieth-century America and the fabulous success story of Jewish American life, Malamud's talking horse story conjures up a scenario wherein Greek and Hebraic elements—the lore of Abraham as well as the West—can conjoin, in a meaningful albeit enduringly challenging whole.

———

It's the end of the summer; the kids are back from camp, and the family, once again, has accompanied me for the weekend in the Hamptons where I am serving as scholar-in-residence at the same Reform congregation for the sixth year in a row. On Friday evening and on Saturday morning, my husband, three children and I walk across the grass from the house where we stay to the main synagogue building where we attend services. This is the only time we ever sit next to each other as a family in synagogue—I, my two daughters and son, and my husband (who has already prayed on his own back at the house). Together we sit, feeling a sense of at-homeness as well as dislocation in this gorgeous Reform prayer space, listening to the confident, seasoned speaking voice of the Senior Rabbi. Every year my eldest daughter, who is studying vocal performance, comments on the female Cantor's lovely voice. And every year I wonder whether my daughter herself might decide one day to become a cantor. Might she be able to find in such an uncharted wood—for an Orthodox woman, at least—her spiritual, familial home?

After services we attend the *Kiddush*, mingling and greeting, my son looking for that Yankees co-owner who promised to take him to a game after his *bar mitzvah*, my daughters repeatedly asking me what they're allowed to eat, as they know the food at Reform synagogues is not always kosher. My husband and I direct the kids to the wrapped items, the ones we can identify by brand, and to the fruits and vegetables. There is always something there, of course, that one of them would like to eat but that we cannot authorize. Alas, I say, grab yourself some more fruit. Soon enough we'll be eating lunch. They and I know, however, that it won't be that soon, as first I have to lead the Torah study session that often goes on for a while. If you're really hungry, I say, you can go back to the house and grab something there. I am impressed, however, that they all decide to stay. They're old enough now to sit through the session, even to chime in with their own comments. Their Orthodox day school education has made them adept readers of text.

After the Torah Study session, we cross the street to the Chabad House, where every year since we began coming here, we have been hosted for late *Shabbes* lunch, a remarkable Reform/Chabad collaboration. We cross the street as if into a different world, where the stories shared around the table are wonder tales about the deceased Lubavitcher *rebbe*, and the miraculous hand of God in helping the work of Chabad emissaries all over the world; where the women in the family jump up from the table to serve, while the men foster a joyous mood, by banging on the table and singing Hassidic melodies.

In years past, I have been asked about what I taught across the street, though I do not typically offer up much; our hosts are warm and gracious and I do not wish to offend. It has been a long time since I first learned that the questions I want to ask and the methods I want to use to answer them aren't always acceptable in the Orthodox, let alone the Hassidic community.

Despite all that I willingly withhold, when the Chabad rabbi asks me to tell him my feelings about the recent controversial decision of my Orthodox rabbi in Riverdale to ordain a woman and call her *rabbah*, I slowly but surely share my feelings about how women rabbis might contribute to the Orthodox community in so many important ways. Remarkably, he listens. Not just he, but his entire family, his wife, and twelve children. For what turns out to be five hours, we all sit and talk about modernity, women, and Judaism. The rabbi goes on at some length about how the Lubavitcher *rebbe* always supported women's scholarship and the capacities of women. As he speaks, I can't help thinking about the collection of Rabbi Wendy Zierler tags that I keep in a drawer in my bedroom, picked up along the way at various Reform rabbinical conventions or meetings, where it is simply assumed that if I teach at HUC-JIR, I must be a rabbi. There is something preposterous and pathetic about the collection of name tags stashed away like Pixy-Stix in my bottom dresser drawer, emblazoned with a title so expected, so run-of-the-mill, to the Jews on one side of this Hamptons highway, and so odd and impossible to those on the other. I do not dare mention in this company the name tags, nor the running "joke" between my husband and me that one day I might actually be ordained, becoming the first ever Orthodox Reform woman rabbi. That hybrid vision I keep to myself. Meanwhile, there is one excitable Chabad son at the table, who cannot take any of this any longer and who inveighs against feminism and its goal of making over a tradition that hasn't changed in 3000 years; mercifully, his own mother retorts on my behalf, "Yossele, what are you talking about? *Hassidus* itself was a major change!" And so it all comes back together instead of falling apart. This day, this afternoon, this conversation—all of it, my family and I together with it—are a centaur. Part one thing, part another. Certainly unconventional, and yet comfortably conjoined in this way, at least for the moment.

Q. Am I a woman in a horse or a horse that talks like a woman or both at the very same time? Understanding goes far and even further, especially if God opens the way. Shall we canter off to the dark forest of Jewish interpretation and see?

14

My Interfaith Friendships

Blessings and Challenges

BLU GREENBERG

WHAT WAS I DOING in the community room of a Christian church in Allston, Massachusetts, listening to opening hymns about the blood of Jesus flowing? It was 1957 and I was a young, Orthodox woman, newly married to a rabbi. I had never been in the home of a non-Jew, or for that matter, a Jew who did not keep kosher. I was in the church because my husband, Yitz, the new Brandeis Hillel Rabbi, had been invited to speak to a group of devout Christians about Judaism. The congregation was sweet and most welcoming, but the experience—albeit unintentionally—brought me back twenty years to when I was seven and was first told that I was a Christ-killer. I grew up in a loving, insulated Orthodox Jewish community in Seattle, Washington. My earliest recollections of interfaith relationships were negative ones. In addition to the charge that Jews had killed Jesus, I knew I could not ride my bike on Mary Jane's corner. And though no words were exchanged, at a tender age I grasped that the mud pie thrown into my open eyes had something to do with my being Jewish.

A year after the church visit, I invited my professor, Thomas Petti-grew, and his wife, Ann, to our home for *Shabbat* dinner. We became good friends. When it was our turn to visit them, Ann and I exchanged several calls to plan the Sunday brunch: cottage cheese, tuna, mayo, bread—all with kosher certification; green salad cut with a cold knife, everything prepared in glass bowls and served on paper plates. Ann was gracious and wanted to do everything right. She smiled with pride as she produced a loaf of bread from the kosher bakery, fifteen miles away. Perfect as the meal was, I still would not report it to my father. And yet, it was a powerful experience for me.

As I sat in that church basement, and even in the home of our friends, I felt a sensation that would return over and over in interfaith settings: the intense feeling of being a Jew in the larger world, carrying my portable faith with me. Though it is quite grandiose to think of myself as representing the Jewish people in these many encounters, I still had a profound sense of that responsibility. But even more, I felt stirrings of my Jewish soul, as I sat among non-Jews in friendship—or occasionally, enmity. I have come to appreciate interfaith dialogue as one of the dozen spiritual forces in my life—along with family, feminism, Israel, singing in *shul* on *Shabbat*—forces that generate a powerful, autonomous surge of emotion, accompanied by feelings of deep gratitude that I was elected to be a Jew.

I am indebted to my husband for bringing me into the world of dialogue, and even more for what he taught me about how to conduct it with integrity. In 1973, Yitz delivered a conference paper that was later cited in many Christian theological works. He wrote, "No statement, theological or otherwise, should be made that would not be credible in the presence of burning children." As time went on, I adapted that standard as a personal rule for dialogue: one engaged in dialogue should not speak words to the other that ignored their suffering. Neither should one say things *about* a dialogue partner that one did not or could not say directly to that partner. The temptation of the latter is often there, and I must admit have allowed myself some leeway around the *Shabbat* table with my family, but I have tried to say what I want to say directly, and not behind someone's back. Like Yitz, I have tried to speak the truth, not hiding behind platitudes. And certainly, I have tried to keep the reality—and the suffering—of the "Other" in my mind as I speak.

Post-Holocaust Encounters

In the early '60s the Jewish community was abuzz about the reconciliation work of the Catholic Church coming to grips with the role of Christianity in the Holocaust. *Nostra Aetate* was published in 1965 and included new directives for Jewish-Christian understanding, among them the mandate for Christian seminaries to engage rabbis to teach Judaism. This was a role priests had filled since time immemorial. The local Catholic women's college, Mount St. Vincent (CMSV) invited Yitz, by then a professor at Yeshiva University, to teach. I ended up teaching for him for ten years, loving those years at Mount St. Vincent, though there was hardly a Jew in sight.

One morning, on my way up to my office I heard a knocking at a back entrance that was always locked. I went down a set of stairs and opened it. A Catholic sister stepped in from the chilly winds and said, "My, that was an act of grace." I still smile when I think of how she offered thanks in christological language. What was my equivalent? I rarely sprinkled my words with *Baruch Hashem* or *Im Yirtzeh Hashem* the way more traditionally Orthodox Jews than I routinely did. Though I had inherited from my mother a deep consciousness of life's vulnerabilities, as a modern Orthodox Jew my everyday language was sophisticated, secular. I wondered if I ought to rethink it. I learned something about my Jewish self from the Catholic sisters every day, even if I did not actually change my speech.

Every afternoon at 12:30 in Room 104 Administration Hall, the nuns gathered for daily prayer. I had never witnessed women in group prayer before, other than the women in my *shuls* who were more observers or adornments than *daveners*. During my years at CMSV, I was beginning to engage Jewish feminism, and when Orthodox women prayer groups were founded, I was not shocked by them. I had witnessed the model elsewhere.

One spring, I was invited by the Sisters of Charity who lived on campus to give a series of lectures. They were an open-minded and forward-thinking group. Many Sisters taught college courses; most had given up wearing a habit a few years earlier. Midway through the first lecture in their living room on Pharasaic Judaism and Feminism, I realized the nuns had an agenda. I said, "If you want me to show how the Pharisees were chauvinists and Jesus was a feminist, I can't oblige because Jesus was also a Pharisee or at least came out of that tradition. Both have pluses and minuses re women's roles in their time." Though the sisters were feminists, they wanted so hard to defend Jesus. I recognized myself sitting there. I was beginning to hear feminist criticism of my heroes, the rabbis, and sometimes it hurt.

As I learned from the nuns, I learned from my students. I saw how open they were to learning about Judaism, including the parting of the ways and the painful history of Jewish-Christian relations of the last 2000 years. In my Jewish-Christian relations course, I felt myself crying on the inside as I spoke in dispassionate voice of inquisitions and exiles as well as of golden eras, and I appreciated how they listened compassionately. Yet, I also saw that no matter how hard they tried, no matter how much of the new scholarly/historical literature of rapprochement they had read, they could not get past blaming the Jews for deicide. A semester of reading David Flusser, Gregory Baum, Edward Flannery, Roy Eckhardt, et al. could not compete with the power of the church. "But it is written in the Gospels . . . " was the response from my students. I came to realize the potential negative power of a religious tradition—my own included—relying too heavily on authoritative interpretations of the "other" in ancient texts.

In 1967, Sister Rose Thering, a Racine Dominican, invited Jewish scholars, including Yitz, to give lectures about Judaism to priests and nuns. Sister Rose grew up in a religious farm family in Wisconsin amidst deeply rooted anti-Semitism. She first heard about living Jews when a Jewish pharmacist moved into town, and she remembered that even her father spoke the word "Jew" in a whisper, just as he spoke about Satan. In Rose's school and church, Jews were described as demonic and diabolical killers of Christ. Yet, the sources were nothing less than her beloved sacred Christian texts!

When Rose finished the novitiate, she took a job in a parochial school. It appalled her to see how much anti-Semitic material appeared in the standard textbooks. She was also growing in awareness of the Holocaust. She decided to write her doctoral thesis on the treatment of Jews in Catholic textbooks. When she presented her research findings to her superiors, her bishop told her to keep her information under wraps.

But he did not know Rose. Young as she was, she would not keep silent about what she saw as injustice and took her findings all the way to the Vatican. Her scholarly work played a significant role in the statement on anti-Semitism in *Nostra Aetate*, and on Catholic textbooks published after that important document. Rose also played a role in the movement to free Soviet Jewry and in establishing mandatory Holocaust education in public schools. She trained Christian teachers to teach Judaism and led thirty-three missions to Israel. She went head to head with Kurt Waldheim, with the nuns at Auschwitz, with anyone who spoke against Israel or Jews, and even with Jews who tried to hide their identity.

Rose related to Israel not only as the Holy Land but as the living, modern Jewish homeland. She understood. . . . In fact, whenever a Christian would use the term "Holy Land," she would recite her mantra, "Say Israel."

She loved our children, and they returned the feeling. One morning, she called for Yitz, and I answered the phone. He was in his study so I shouted to the kids downstairs to tell him Sister Rose was calling. Deborah, age eight, yelled up, "Our Sister Rose or Grandma's sister Rose?" It was fitting that the Jewish community of Metrowest, New Jersey, took care of her in her last years of illness, offering her residence, health care, comfort, and friendship.

One Friday night, Rose brought her boss, Msgr. John Oestreicher, with her for *Shabbat* dinner. I knew the Monsignor was a convert to Christianity, a *meshumad*, apostate, as we unlovingly called those who volitionally walked away from Judaism. Yet, here he was, doing good work on behalf of the Jewish people. I was thoroughly confused. At *Kiddush* on Friday night, I had an immature fantasy. He would hear the ancient words and traditional melody; it would take him back to his childhood; he would be overcome by nostalgia and would repent of conversion. But there he stood like any other Christian guest, respectful, without a flicker of emotion.

As a priest, he opposed the Nazis and had to flee during the war. In the '60s he drafted that part of *Nostra Aetate* that removed the deicide charge from Christian theology and liturgy. He literally fought anti-Semitism all his life. What was I complaining about? Yet, his mother and father died in Auschwitz and Theresienstadt. I tried to wrestle my ambivalence to the ground and mostly succeeded, but I could never stop wondering about his parents. Were they dismayed at his conversion or did not care? As they were taken to Auschwitz, were they grateful that he would survive?

The Holocaust work was incredibly rewarding. Whenever I think of Pope John XXIII, I feel great gratitude, mostly for what he did in terms of Israel, post-Holocaust theology, and relationships with the Jewish people, but also because he charted me along an important path in my life. Interfaith work in the early years primarily focused on how much we shared in common, how good brotherhood is, and how much the church needed to reform its teachings. It was meaningful work, and just to have known people of such moral vision as Sister Rose would alone make the whole interfaith journey worthwhile to me.

On a theological level, the Jewish-Christian encounter was gratifying because I could see how a religion could transform itself from centuries of teaching hate to genuine repentance, to friendship, to cooperation, to mutual respect. What Christianity had done in a short half century vis-à-vis Judaism has been nothing short of miraculous.

Women in Dialogue

Beginning in 1978 and lasting in various forms for a dozen years, Women of Faith in the '80s was an important home for me. Twenty women represented Jewish, Catholic, Protestant, and Muslim communities. Riffat Hassan, a Pakistani-American and early Muslim feminist who taught at the University of Louisville, was the first Muslim I got to know well. Outspoken and afraid of no one, she put everything right out on the table: Her religion (sexist and chauvinist, but misreading the true intention of the Qur'an on women); her marriage (failing); her family (still in Lehore); her daughter (getting Americanized); her writings (arousing admiration and anger). Riffat was a great friend of Israel and the Jewish people. Thirty years later, we are still friends.

One of our group was a very smart Christian leader whom I knew for a solid fifteen years before I realized that she was gay. At one particular meeting, this generally private woman wrestled aloud with her demons, her sense of being the end of the line of generations. She was then in her mid-fifties, single with no children, the only child of her mother who had recently died. If you were a religious woman, in those days, and did not marry, for whatever reason, becoming a mother was not an option.

A liberal Jewish woman in our group, and a dear friend of mine, tried to console our Christian colleague. "But you have led a very worthwhile and validated life. A woman should not feel as if her life is not meaningful just because she has no children. That is why," she continued, "whenever I speak to my children, I always make sure to say, '*if* you get married, *if* you have children'. I don't want to coerce or pressure them." I could not contain myself, even if it meant puncturing the empathy balloon that hung over us. "By God," I said, "that is no way for a Jewish mother to speak to her children! Whenever I speak to my children, I make sure to say '*when* you get married and have children . . .' If they don't get married, it will be their choice but I want them to know that these are our family's values that I hope they will choose as adults." A lively discussion followed. It was liberating to realize that women of a particular faith community did not have to present as one voice in interfaith settings.

Today, my own views have changed. I have seen how too many gay men and lesbians have been ostracized or marginalized by their religious communities and their families. And I have come to appreciate that sexual identity is not a matter of choice, but largely an inborn trait. Moreover, gay people can and do live rich family lives in covenantal relationships, often including children.

In 1982, I was invited by Hans Ucko, director of interfaith activities of the World Council of Churches (WCC) to join seven women of other faiths to prepare papers for the Decade for Women meeting scheduled for Nairobi, 1985. The Consultation, as we were called, was a colorful group: Christians from different parts of the world, a Hindu, a Muslim. In a million years, my path would not have crossed theirs, and I was grateful to feminism for providing this entry point.

One *Shabbat* morning, I found myself running like crazy through the streets of Geneva, searching for the meeting place of our group. I had not set an alarm clock and had overslept passed the starting time. Although I had been subsisting on sardines and *matzoh* in my room (there was no food that met my *kashrut* practice available to our group), as I ran, I laughed out loud at a recurring thought: what am I doing running through the streets of a strange city instead of being in *shul* this morning? Perhaps running and laughing out loud is why the Swiss quickly turned away from this American madwoman. And the more they turned away, the louder I laughed. I felt lucky and honored to be part of this eclectic and generous-spirited group.

From interfaith "trialogue," I gained insight into the commonality of our struggle as feminists. We all wanted to find equal dignity, rights and access in our faith communities. We all wanted to find resolution within, rather than jump ship as so many moderns had done. We shared a love for our respective traditions, understood that we were nurtured by them, and maintained that gratitude even as we chafed at limits and disabilities for women. The strategies to resolve our problems were different, but there was enough sameness to be instructive. I also came to understood more about Jewish law vis-à-vis women, as I learned about other traditions.

I have to admit that I was living in a bubble of happy interfaith experiences. Christians had made great progress during the previous twenty-five years in reaching out to other religions, especially Jews. The early Muslims I met were happy to be accepted as full members of the dialogue. Interfaith work was pleasant, non-confrontational, amicable, offered a larger view of the world and new friendships.

Little by little, however, during the '80s and following, many of the interfaith and feminist encounters and meetings moved on to politics, particularly of the Middle East. This was much more challenging territory for me.

Israeli-Palestinian Conflict

During the spring of 1967, as Arabs threatened to annihilate the Jewish state, we Jews involved in dialogue waited to hear support from our Christian partners. The silence was deafening; it felt to us like the bystander syndrome of the Holocaust all over again. After the exhilaration of Israel's victory in the Six Day War quieted down, we reassessed Jewish-Christian dialogue. We realized that we had to speak more openly about what Israel meant to us, not just niceties about commonalities. Otherwise, how could our dialogue partners know that support for Israel was our line drawn in the sand, that Israel was not an issue that was separable for us, from our very identity and survival as Jews?

Over the years, the topic became increasingly fraught. There were early signs, but I did not pick them up. One was a conversation in our Women of Faith in the '80s. At some point, Riffat remarked testily about the Occupied Territories, "Well, what the hell are the Israelis doing there anyway?" She had been a great supporter of Israel. Where was this derailed? At that point in my life, I did not grasp that the Palestinians still harbored fantasies of "getting it *all* back," *all* being the slice of land called Israel. Riffat, a kind and compassionate person, could not help but be drawn into their narrative. How I missed all this for still another ten years continues to baffle me. I should have made the connection then. It would have saved me much bewilderment and trained me to respond better in the coming years

A second bell went off during the International Consultation on Women in Interreligious Dialogue, in 1988, co-convened by Tarek Mitri of the World Council of Churches and Diana Eck of Harvard Divinity School. On the second day of the five day conference, I took a social walk on the beautiful grounds of Victoria University in Toronto with a kindly, elderly nun. At some point she turned the conversation to Israel. In her gentle nun's voice, she said, "Those soldiers over there, they are behaving like Nazis." I was thunderstruck, as if someone had punched all the air out of me. I was raging inside.

A personal principle I developed in dialogue was not to answer every last challenge or slight, or even mistruth as I saw it, but this I would not let go by. I wanted to say, "How dare you make that analogy?" but instead said, "How can you make that analogy? On the contrary, the Israeli army acts with great restraint under great provocation and threat. It has the most moral army anywhere in the world," (a refrain I would find myself reciting over and over in Jewish-Palestinian dialogue in the decades that followed). The nun was not convinced.

Later, I ran to a Protestant friend in the group, thinking she would be as affronted as I and chastise the nun for stepping way over dialogue boundaries. Instead she brushed off the remark. Other good Christian friends on the political left followed, as they perceived Israel to be no longer the underdog and victim of hostile neighbors' attacks but as the persecutor of Palestinians.

By 1989, on a visit to Israel just before the first *intifadah*, I realized we truly were sitting on a powder keg. I stepped out of a construction site and a young Arab worker fifteen feet away made an obscene and hateful gesture to me in broad daylight. I was shocked. And my Israeli sister-in-law's tone in speaking of Arabs was equivalent to the hatred I saw in the eyes of the young construction worker. I resolved to do something about it when I returned home.

Ten days later, I received a call from Reena Bernards, the mild-mannered, soft-spoken daughter of a rabbi and a woman active in Jewish communal affairs. Reena asked if I would help her organize a meeting between Palestinian and Jewish women. I jumped at the opportunity and said her call was serendipitous. First, we created a day for Jewish women at the home of a good friend and leader in the community. Then, Reena and I met with the woman organizing the Palestinian participants. We met at the offices of CLAL, a Jewish organization where my son JJ, executive director, always freed up space for our planning meetings.

I spent four years in active dialogue in this group, simply named "The Dialogue Project." It seemed heady and hopeful. Heady, in that I genuinely liked all of these women and believed we could be friends. The Palestinian women were educated, cultured, and very fine. They were family-oriented professionals, academics, and creative writers. Their husbands worked for the World Bank, and other important institutions. Hopeful, in that perhaps we women could model a solution of peaceful relations.

But it was also difficult, sometimes to the point of despair. At one retreat, each side (and we were honest enough to see the group constructed as two sides) selected core principles we wanted the other to accept. Number eight on our list was that the Palestinians stop the spiral of teaching hate, a shoe-in, I thought. Yet they would not agree: there would be no discontinuity in teaching hate to the younger generation until the day *after* a Palestinian state was declared. On the one hand, I admired their honesty. Even if I would have personally affirmed a teaching of hate and enmity, I would never have owned up to it in a dialogue setting. But here they were, standing firm and unified on their principle. On the other hand, this was terribly distressing to me.

During the second *intifada*, every time another suicide bomber carried out his evil plot I thought to myself, he was the product of that rejected principle. Once, the Palestinian women convinced many of the Jewish women to join them in a visit to the State Department to plead for a censure of Israel. Only our rules of veto stopped that foray. It was at that point that one of our leading Jewish members dropped out, discouraged. And it was also at that point that one of the Palestinian women, displeased that I had obstructed the State Department visit, tried to push me out of the group. But I would not leave. I had made an agreement with a Palestinian friend in the group not to give up until the end.

Our third year, we went together on a mission to Israel. The Jewish women accompanied the Palestinian women to Gaza, and to refugee camps. But they resisted a visit to *Yad Vashem*. After we visited Ramallah Hospital and spoke to the victims of Israeli retaliation, they relented and we paired for the visit. A Palestinian woman and I walked through the museum/exhibits together. Her only comment as we walked out into the sunshine was "You see, Blu, here is the proof that the Jews came here illegally."

Soon after the Rabin-Arafat handshake in 1993, the group ended. While the Jewish women and the world rejoiced at the symbolism on the White House lawn, the Arab women mourned, feeling they had not gotten a fair share. All of the Palestinian women wanted out.

Even though the group had disbanded, Reena Bernards still wanted to bring the experience to the wider Jewish community. She arranged for two Palestinian women and two Jewish women to speak to the Lion of Judah group, the top women contributors to the United Jewish Appeal. The meeting was held at the Ritz-Carlton hotel in Chicago. It was an inspiring program, and everyone spoke from the heart. We did not gloss over the difficulties but showed how even with the hurdles, we could present a model for peace and coexistence.

Afterwards, the five of us—reunited for an evening—met in the comfortable lobby of the Ritz-Carlton. Our tone was enthusiastic and a bit self-congratulatory, for indeed our presentation had been a success. Fifteen minutes into the conversation, I spotted a two-inch gold pendant draped against my Palestinian friend's beautifully cut, navy blue, wool, crêpe suit. She had not worn it during the lecture, but it was unmistakably there now. It was in the shape of Israel and the territories, the entire land. I interrupted the flow of conversation: "What is that pendant?" I asked, my stomach starting to knot. She replied calmly and with a smile, "It's greater Palestine." "Where is Israel in that map?" I asked. For two hours we argued. She did not remove or repudiate the pendant.

More disconcerting was the response of the other Palestinian woman, a moderate. She responded with a faint defense of the Greater Palestine pendant as "an educational tactic." Sleeping dogs awoke: should I now understand her comment at *Yad Vashem* not merely as insensitive but a statement that Jews simply had no right to be there? Why would someone who had worked so hard on coexistence, uphold someone who blatantly promoted an end to the Jewish state?

My Jewish friend who had dropped out was right. We had been fooled, and we were now a party to duping the Lion of Judah women. I wondered what I had been doing all this time. I had changed during these years, from believing that Jordan and Lebanon were enough, to understanding the longing and suffering of the Palestinians, to affirming their need for a state of their own. I argued with my right wing relatives in Israel, more now than a decade ago. But I felt that the de-legitimation of Israel's right to exist at all was intensified.

At a meeting of the Multi-religious Women's Network, established by Diana Eck, I introduced myself as an American Jewish Feminist Orthodox Zionist Jew. I added that somehow I felt like I was waving a red flag as a criminal for these multiple identities. Sometimes, even Jewish participants, even Israelis, were not prepared to fully back me on my stances. I wondered if the time had come for me to quit and let others step into my place at the interfaith table.

My questions intensified when I met with Reena in Washinton, DC. I looked forward to the visit as we had not seen each other in five years. She peddled her bike downtown and I gave her a big warm hug when she arrived. And then she told me that she was going to try to reconstitute the dialogue but that the Palestinian women did not want me in it. I was stung. And hurt. I had never been rejected from a dialogue before. I did not think that I behaved obnoxiously, yet I wondered whether it was not just my politics but my very presence as a Jew passionate about Israel that could not be tolerated. Could I have spoken more softly, made fewer challenges, responded to fewer insults, not defended every attack? They were suffering. This dialogue had been so hard, especially in comparison to Jewish-Christian and feminist interfaith dialogues.

With all this, did I want to stay in interfaith dialogue with Palestinian women? Yes, was my unequivocal answer, because like Jewish-Christian dialogue, and feminist dialogue, that, too had changed me. Changing oneself is about being alive, and learning, and I had learned a great deal. Dialogue is about learning to listen and listening to learn, and learn I did!

Looking Back

In interfaith dialogue, the rewards were enormous. At the most basic level, I met individuals whom I liked, sometimes loved, and gained from immeasurably. I met dozens of women and men who became powerful models for me, as well as lifelong friends.

As I reflect on almost half a century, I see that the two major historical events of our times, the Holocaust and Israel, have been the bookends of my dialogue work, with interfaith feminist activity bridging the two.

The feminist encounters were powerful: we shared a similar agenda, especially devout Catholics, traditional Muslims, and Orthodox Jews who faced similar challenges regarding religious authority, sacred texts, canon law, and starting points of greater inequity. From the early experiences of watching the sisters pray, to the many remarkable women of faith I came to know, my horizons were expanded, my worldview reshaped. From these women, I learned that self-pride ought to accompany a feminist journey. The work was not about a handout for women, but about an offering of justice to community and God.

What about political dialogue between Jews and Palestinians? I would certainly do some things differently; I need to know more, read more, prepare better. I now understand more fully that the narrative for each side is very different, even when we refer to the same set of "facts."

Dialogue has taught me things I wish I did not have to know. It made me realize how vulnerable Israel is, with so much hatred directed at her from around the world. The poison of anti-Semitism has spread not only to future generations but horizontally, to many corners of Western Europe, Asia, and Africa. It is my responsibility as a Jew to try to mitigate such hatred, whether through building friendships or confronting it or feeding back information. I know that the gain is very, very small for a lot of effort, but even that small gain is of value. I have seen how it is possible for love to replace hatred, and I have witnessed how the dialogic component is central to that process. And realizing what a tiny people we are, a tiny speck in the world, has made me both want to personally work harder and enlarge the universe of cohorts in the interfaith enterprise.

Has interfaith dialogue changed my sense of myself as a Jew? Yes, in all the ways described above, and still, in the Pettigrew dining room sense, just as inexplicable after all these years. I am a Jew in the world, elected to the joys and responsibilities and challenges that go with being Jewish. Sometimes, when I am out of the comfortable milieu with my own, I feel an awesome awareness of the covenant that my ancestors handed down to me, a covenant that I carry with me wherever I am, with great privilege.

Within my community—the Orthodox Jewish world—participation in dialogue is controversial. A decision of the eminent Rabbi Sololveitchik states that theological dialogue is to be avoided, although it is acceptable to meet to discuss issues of social justice. Why not theology? Over the years, some Orthodox Jews have felt that Orthodox Jewish presence might be taken as affirming the Trinity, which was still considered idol worship by some. Others worry that another's compelling narrative and beliefs might pull one away from one's Jewish faith.

I can testify to exactly the opposite outcome. Based on my experience, for one deeply rooted in the tradition, dialogue and interfaith friendships serve to enhance feelings of self and a sense of identity and strengthen knowledge of one's own religion.

Moreover, I believe that the cross faith encounters have made me a better human being, less insulated to the suffering of others and less inured to their pain. Simply put, I feel more connected to the world. When I read about the Tamils in danger, I remembered the sweet Tamil man I met in Glion years earlier who had fled from persecution and torture, and who worried about his extended family. I worried about them, too. Worry is a form of prayer. For me, that is the constant phenomenology of dialogue, a quickening of my Jewish soul, an expansion of my mind and an opening of my heart.

15

The Remembrance of These Things

War, Occupation, Parsley, Bitter Herb

Margaret Holub

> Why was the first Sanctuary destroyed? Because of three things that
> prevailed there: idolatry, immorality, and bloodshed . . .
>
> —BT Yoma 9b

When the United States invaded Iraq in 2003, after months of hellish foreplay, I felt dirty. Yes, I had marched and protested a bit, one of the worldwide millions. But I couldn't escape the nasty realization that this war was being prosecuted in some measure for my benefit, in order to keep me and my kind at the very top of the food chain for a while longer. Whatever the actual motivation for the war may have been, whether to keep oil cheap or to allow US businesses to set up shop wherever they wished or even (I write this with my fingers crossed) to prevent Iraq from developing weapons of mass destruction, it was clear to me that those in power in my government had my upper-middle-class white American interests at heart, even if I did not. Not only did I have little to gain by resisting, but, harder to admit, I had little to lose if my resistance failed. The war wasn't going to hurt me or anyone I knew, except in moral outrage (which, let's face it, feels good even while it feels bad . . .)

Maybe I would feel the pinch as the infrastructure around me got cut and crumbled—when the war began, for example, I was surrounded by an energetic local campaign to save school band and choir—but it ain't Baghdad here by any means.

For me as an American and a Jew, I had "boots on the ground" in two war zones at once. Soldiers were fighting on my behalf in Iraq, Afghanistan and in Palestine. And in Palestine, *al achat kamma v'chamma*, as in the lesser case, so much more so in the greater one, I am both a protester and a beneficiary of the failure of my protest. I can rail against Israel's draconian security measures while keeping a whole spare country in reserve for myself in case someday those anti-Semites in the woods here where I live really do amass some power to hurt. I can abhor Israel's messianic land grab and still drop in every couple of years to soak up the atmosphere of a society that runs on the Jewish calendar, language, and contiguity with the Torah.

So what of my more local pleasures: my modest six-room house, my compost bucket full of scraps that would be fought over in lots of places on our globe, my big problem of not having enough room in my closet for all my shoes, the slightly fancier, four-color cat food I buy at the grocery store because my three pets prefer it? Sometimes I allow myself to wonder, "Who makes all this stuff? And where? And how?" But the details send me into a panic. Just today, taking a break from the computer, I fixed a cup of fancy Chinese tea and read an article in the *New Yorker* about slaves—slaves!— picking oranges in Florida. And I was thinking guiltily, "I wonder if the organic ones are picked by those guys too?"

Elie Wiesel tells the tale, slightly fictionalized, I believe, about going back to his *shtetl* in Romania, years after surviving the Holocaust, and finding the neighbor who watched impassively from his window as the Jews of their village were herded into the central square and deported. Wiesel fantasizes shouting in the neighbor's face: "The dead Jews, the women gone mad, the mute children—I'm their messenger. And I tell you they haven't forgotten you. Someday they'll come marching, trampling you, spitting in your face. And at their shouts of contempt you'll pray God to deafen you . . ."

That fictional Romanian peasant had little to gain from the deportation of Wiesel and his family. Sure, he might have been just as happy to see the Jews go as stay, but for him the Nazis were just another occupier at the end of a long string of occupiers. He might have said, as a friend of mine does now and then: "I ain't got no dogs in that fight!" So my position is worse. I actually benefit from war and occupation prosecuted on my behalf. Or so I am promised by the US and Israeli governments, who couch their aggressions in concern for my safety and comfort. I'm not the bystander looking indifferently out the window. I'm the soldier in the square. Or at least I'm his employer. Or, to put my position in the language of the exodus from Egypt, the classical Jewish language used to speak about oppression, I am a pharaoh.

———

It happened that during the first couple of days of the war against Iraq, I was at a rabbis' conference, having the pleasure of praying morning and night in the company of a very smart and committed *minyan* (quorum for prayer). It's unusual for me to have access to a *minyan* at all on a weekday morning, much less one full of women wearing *tefillin*. The Reconstructionist prayerbook, which we were using, is carefully designed to be both mystical and modern, open to multiple genders, short on anthropomorphisms, full of beautiful interpretation of what otherwise might seem klutzily literal. I could hardly have asked for better praying equipment, or a better setting in which to try to deploy it.

Squirming as I was in my self-awareness as a pharaoh, I predictably found the *geulah* prayer difficult, even degenderized and demilitarized to read, "Blessed are you, ETERNAL ONE, the champion of Israel." I was also challenged by the various petitions in the *Amidah* to save and heal, eradicate and destroy, redeem and rebuild on our behalf. But more than being uncomfortable with what was on the page, I found myself hungry for something I couldn't find anywhere in the book. It was during that first morning, moping and daydreaming as much as I was praying, that I first found myself wishing that there were prayers for pharaohs to say.

———

Prayers, texts, and rituals tell us who we are and where we stand in the cosmos. So when I pray something like "Praised are You O Lord, King of the Universe . . ." that tells me who, at least according to the prayerbook I'm using, rules the world. And when I go on to say, for example, "Who makes peace and creates everything," that fills in the picture somewhat further.

I find this genuinely helpful. I try on, in this instance, the thought that I am not myself the King of the universe, and that the world in which I dwell is in fact ruled. I may not even exactly believe it—these are not, after all, my own words. I am reading them out of a book. But for the duration of the prayer I allow myself to live in the world the prayer portrays. For at least that moment, I live in a universe in which my power is limited, a world in which there are rules and a ruler. This information provides a context for my own plans and schemes, and my understanding of my own agency.

As I was praying at my convention, while the bombs rained down on Baghdad and beyond, I felt like I was grasping at the words of my *siddur*, trying to figure out my place in this bloody new arrangement of things. "Is there something in here to situate me properly?" I kept asking—"something to give me a better perspective from which to consider this moment in which I am living today?"

Indeed the service is full of prayers for peace, though each one has to be surgically modified to ask for peace not only for the Jewish people but also for the rest of the universe. And even so there is that discomfort if we feel that the State of Israel is actually preventing peace, so that just asking for everyone else's *shalom* in addition to ours doesn't fully rectify the problem. I wasn't exactly sure what peace would look like right then, but I knew I wanted it. I like very much Rabbi Brian Walt's insistence that we say "*na'aseh shalom*," "let us make peace," rather than putting it all on the shoulders of some saving God. But if this is the full solution, then why was I there wrapped in my *tallit* addressing God at all?

More comforting to me in that tight and frustrating place were those statements, and they are legion, that simply say that God is Master, Source, Heart, Spring, Rock, and Center. I have found comfort and clarity in many difficult moments over the years by remembering that God, and not I, is King and Queen of the universe; that this world, with all its complexities, is God's beautiful world; that human beings, with all our horrors, are created, like the rest of the world, in the divine image. Somehow, from some perspective, from some distant vantage point, even this situation we're in at this very minute must somehow be good, be *tov*. This is what is, with all its mix of cruelty and beauty. I have a lot more exploring to do at this edge. I think that there is something importantly true here, even if I can only hold it in my heart for a split second.

But what is the moral recommendation here? Perhaps I would do best to remove myself to some perch from which I can look at what is without hysteria and simply observe, listen, and find a way to be present with a whole heart. That certainly appeals to the helpless and anguished part of me. I am, after all, not the King. In this respect I think of my Buddhist friends in their pursuit of equanimity. Equanimity would be a good beginning, or at least it would feel better than horror and depression. But even though horror and depression are my problem, they are not the world's problem. By making my own feelings my central concern, I am really making myself the victim once again. I am the victim of the emotional trauma of being a pharaoh. That's not really the problem I want to fix.

———

Jewish tradition has given us one great, holy tool for dealing with moments when we are perpetrators of harm against others. And that is *teshuvah*, repentance. Maimonides teaches that to make a full confession one must: articulate one's sin in detail to both your victim and to God; feel and express great remorse; restore the wrong done in every material way possible; and then, when the opportunity next arises to commit that sin, choose not to do so.

The liturgy of *teshuvah* is most extensively developed for the *yamim noraim*, the Days of Awe. It is then that we make ourselves abject before God and our community, recalling, confessing and expunging our sins in hopes of entering the Holy of Holies pure and radiant on Yom Kippur afternoon. In preparation for that moment, we recite the *avodah* service; we recount in great detail the steps taken by the *Kohen Gadol*, the High Priest, on Yom Kippur, his purifications and changes of dress, the sacrifices and dashings of blood as he entered the Holy of Holies and atoned for himself, his family and his people.

> Fortunate is the eye that saw all this—for the ear to hear of it distresses my soul. . . . But our ancestors' iniquities destroyed the Temple, and our sins delayed the final redemption. However the remembrance of these things can be our forgiveness and the affliction of ourselves can be our atonement.

This might be the saddest moment of the entire Jewish year, when we open our hearts to the naked recognition of what was lost by our people's sins. We feel the collectivity of our wrongdoings and their malignant effect on the course of history. In an intact world the mystery and the elegance of the Temple would have continued forever. But our cruel and oppressive behavior—and we have only to read any of the latter prophets to see that cruelty catalogued in explicit detail—broke the ancient order, destroyed what was meant to be perpetual, threw it off its axis and left us heartbroken.

Praying that prayer, reciting the tragic end of the *avodah* service, places us in a reality of shame and regret, wishing so desperately that we could roll back the clock and be just a bit less exploitative, treat the widow a little better, not degrade the sacred offerings in quite such a vulgar way. Oh, if only we had shown a bit more respect for the deeper truths, for the enduring institutions, for human decency! If we had just managed to hold back, to control our appetites, to exercise discernment, then perhaps our heart and the heart of our people, would not have been shattered.

That's a prayer I could have used reciting when the war began. That's a prayer I could recite every day of my life, every day that I dwell in the upper 10 percent of the world's wealth, every day that I meditate on which kind of new car I should buy or how I would like to redesign the guest bathroom.

For the sin of craving what I don't need.

For the sin of throwing out half of what I craved yesterday.

For the sin of owning things built by slaves, with toxic materials, shipped heedlessly around the world.

For the sin of instigating war to keep these things at my fingertips so that I barely need to expend energy to reach for them.

For all the sins we never imagined a generation or two ago would be available to us, for all the new sins of affluence and power, for all the sins we were praying for all these centuries to have the opportunity to commit—*s'lach lanu; m'chal lanu; kapper lanu*. Forgive us, release us, clear us of accountability.

These sins of pharaoh-hood are very hard to extricate oneself from. Moral integrity requires that we try to get at least a bit untangled, but we never really escape. This is why being a pharaoh is a spiritual predicament and not merely a moral failing—because the path of atonement is so damnably complex and partial and frustrating. If one could cease being an oppressor by simple, decisive action, then it would probably be immoral to waste any time in prayer. As it is, even with the best intention in the world we can make only tiny moves out of the sticky web of voraciousness and exploitation upon which our positions in life depend. And then just about every step has some kind of counterpunch, so that you take one step and then begin to realize that your very step created further problems, like kicking in quicksand. One only has to think for a moment about the moral politics of recycling—"greenwashing," outsourcing trash, generating extra power to turn a small fraction of our recyclables into something resalable, then marketing these new/recycled products to the same small privileged class that threw them out in the first place, while pitching most of our nicely recycled trash right into the landfill—to feel how not-simple solutions really are.

I flail, along with my conscientious classmates: we do recycle. We shop at the farmers' market. We support progressive causes in Israel. We participate in dialogues. We vote left. We march. And even as we earnestly and energetically do these *mitzvot*, we know in our souls that they don't begin to touch how deeply we profit from our place in the food chain. They don't come near to Maimonides' final step in the path of *teshuvah*: we know that, presented with the next opportunity to commit acts of war, occupation and enslavement, we will do so again and again.

It is the very vexing nature of the problem that makes us need to pray. We need to pray because we are stuck, because atonement is not simple, because the pathway is not obvious. If I take Maimonides' four steps as a road map for atonement, as I regularly try to do in my small private world, then, just to start with, how do I articulate my sin in detail? How many shoes, for example, make their owner a sinner? What is the sin in paying your taxes knowing that over a third will be used to support the current military? What is the sin in wondering if it is truly the whole amount that is sinful—if we wouldn't actually do well to spend something on the military, just not as much as we do, just not in the way we do? What is the sin in not having a better idea about how to run the world, even if you are appalled by the way it is presently being run? What is the sin in being confused and despairing?

I can be like Rabbi Nachman and go outside into the field and pour out my heart to God like a child to my parent, let all this shame and confusion pour out of my brain and into the cosmos, hope that it is received and responded to. I can and I do. But I can only do that for my individual and private self. I have no language, no equipment for being part of a community of perpetrators of war and occupation turning our hearts towards God in *teshuvah*.

I think back to that day when US soldiers bombed Baghdad, to opening my prayerbook and knowing I needed words that weren't there: words that would command me daily, constantly, with my people, to consider the impact of my choices and actions on the rest of the world, my own choices and actions and those of the Jewish people. Those words would say to me every day, "You live in a position of privilege. And privilege has costs and responsibilities associated with it. The wisdom of our people asks the following of you as *teshuvah*, as turning towards God from the complex and compromised place in which you live today. And it asks this not only of you privately but as a Jew, as a member of a nation that partakes of a collective covenant with the divine." These words would give me the challenge and the opportunity to live into this consciousness for at least as long as it takes me to recite them. And maybe to close the *siddur* and act with clarity and integrity.

The prayerbook cannot tell me what I need to do today, from my desk in Albion, California, not with that level of specificity. This I need to figure out with my own local community, inquiring together as to how this mandate might be fulfilled in our particular time and place. And it is the place for my individual conscience to call me to my own personal response.

I don't look to the prayerbook to give me daily marching orders. But I do look to it to situate me in the world, to tell me, "This is where you stand" in this beautiful, God-filled world, this world full of crisis and inequity, sorrow and cruelty—this world in which it matters where you stand and which direction you walk. I look to the greater wisdom of our people, its guiding and shaping power, to speak not just to me but to us, to keep us and sustain us and guide us through this moment.

I wrote the first draft of this essay in 2003, as the US-led war in Iraq was just beginning. It is now 2012, and this year most of the American troops have been withdrawn from the shambles that is now Iraq. On the personal front, for all the reasons of nine more years of life, I have gotten somewhat better at holding that larger perspective that sees all, and not just the favorable, as being God's holy world. This includes my own self; I am a little better at seeing myself as not only a pharaoh, not only an occupier, but also a simple being trying to live in a large and complex world. Rereading my own words above, I feel some compassion for how ashamed and outraged I was to be placed by class, citizenship, and religion into such a morally untenable position in history. This year a new text has arisen for me, shining a light on the same quandary and helping me to see it differently. It comes from the *seder*, where the drama of Pharaoh and slaves is spelled out most clearly and explored most deeply.

For many years now I have loved the second half of the *seder*, the *afiko-men*/Elijah half, in which the Angel of Death is vanquished and the world is redeemed. At our table we always finish the *seder* with a round of Yellow Submarine: "And our friends are all aboard—many more of them live next door . . . " It's a vision of the world we all wish for, and I love to dwell there for a couple of hours, a little loopy with Manischewitz, singing freedom songs with my dearest people. I don't love the first half of the *seder* nearly as much. I find it strange and disjointed and somehow troubling.

This year it occurred to me for the first time that there are really two quite different tales of redemption celebrated in the *seder*. There is my beloved post-dinner messianic narrative, in which history as we know it ends and all is completely and finally resolved for good. But first we enact a whole other version, in which parsley is dipped in saltwater, horseradish in apples and wine, in which we say "*dayeinu*" knowing full well that no part of that redemption was truly "enough," not even the whole story, much less any one part of it standing apart from the rest.

This first telling I now think of as the narrative of ambivalence, or call it "the *seder* of proximate reality." This is how redemption happens in our messy present world: even at best, one year you're the parsley and someone else is the tears. The next year you are weeping while someone else thrives. One year we eat the bitter herb and the next year we are force-feeding it to someone else. And so it really is: history cycles. We find ourselves at different points "in every generation." Some years we need desperately to see ourselves as though we were redeemed from *Mitzrayim*, from the "narrow place" of enslavement. At other times—and now is probably such a point for many of us—we need to see ourselves as people who make some part of the world a *Mitzrayim* for others.

I still long for language, text, and liturgy that chastens us when we are eating the parsley of someone else's growth and aspiration without compunction. And we may be witnessing the development of some of this language, arising from a challenging corner of the Jewish community today. These days I am beginning to participate in the call for boycott, divestment, and sanctions to end the occupation of Palestine. I am doing so with other Jews—rabbis, in fact. In order to speak this call into our own Jewish world, we need to look at the words and gestures of our tradition from this place of struggling with our dominance and privilege. Here I am a Jew, with other Jews, looking at our role in the world as pharaohs, as occupiers and oppressors. As we do this work, however hesitantly and awkwardly, new words and gestures are emerging—words of prayer as well as words of action.

Here, as always, the most important hope is for *yetziat mitzrayim*, for an end to oppression—not for a more perfect prayerbook or Passover *seder*. But we can watch—and be—Jews struggling with our capacity to oppress and enslave, even while we hope for a world in which this cycle of parsley and saltwater is forever abolished.

I am not the king or the queen of the universe, and no amount of repentance will free me from my small but morally difficult place in this moment of history. War, occupation, torture, despoliation of the earth and more are done on my behalf day after day—for my safety, my well-being, and my pleasure. The moment will shift. My Jewish ancestors lived in very different circumstances, and generations after me will as well. I am not free to abdicate from my place in the movement of history, and I can only change it in the most minute ways. Because I am not free to escape the predicament of history, I cannot fully repent either. At best I, and all of us, can be honest about who we are on the *seder* table: parsley or saltwater, bitter herb or sweet mortar.

However the remembrance of these things can be our forgiveness.

And so I continue to pray.

IV

Be Still and Know
(Psalm 46:10)

16

Shattering and Rebirth

My Midlife Gap Year

DAYLE A. FRIEDMAN

I AM FIFTY-FIVE YEARS OLD, and I am in the midst. As my eldest child prepares to leave home, I swing between feelings of delicious pride and bouts of unabashed moroseness. My father is on hospice care, precariously balanced at the edge of life. My dream job recently ended, so I must re-imagine a career trajectory I had thought was settled. I am basically healthy, yet in the past year I have contended with a knee injury that required frustratingly slow rehab, a sudden hospitalization, and a cancer scare. As my first-born takes off, her twin siblings hurtle relentlessly into full-blown adolescent drama. My husband and I endeavor to maintain humor; the kids make sure we stay humble.

This is a time of flux, loss, and confusion that will lead me, I pray, to transformation. Like so many of my Baby Boomer peers, I am in transition to my Third Chapter, as sociologist Sarah Lightfoot-Lawrence calls the twenty-five years beyond fifty. I am far from winding down. With any luck, I might yet have a long swath of productive years ahead. Having spent the last thirty years of my career accompanying others in the awesome terrain of growing older, I am somehow astonished to find myself at the trailhead of aging's path. How will I *grow up* as I grow older?

In this reflection, I shall attempt to make sense of this moment in life's journey. I am in the midst of a new beginning, but I am not starting from scratch. This restart emerges out of both the beauty and the shards of what has come before. It is a birth out of brokenness.

I find solace in a teaching of Rabbi Isaac Luria, the sixteenth-century master of Kabbalah. According to Luria, the world we live in, the life we have, was born out of a cosmic shattering (*shever*). God had intended to fill the world with the divine light, but the world could not endure this effulgence. God contracted Godself in order to make room for the world, but, in a devastating cosmic accident, the vessels intended to hold God's light shattered.

The light that was abundant and omnipresent was suddenly hidden and dispersed—encased in shards (*klipot*) of the vessels that had been meant to contain it. So now, the divine is limited and concealed in a world of darkness. In the wake of the cataclysm, we human beings are alive—there is space for us in the world—but we are in darkness. It is up to us to locate and liberate the sparks of light hidden within the shards that surround us. This Third Chapter transition is, for me, a new beginning emerging out of shattering. I am trying to figure out how to find—and lift up—the sparks that can light the way forward, so that I can repair myself and the world around me.

Career: Hitting a Brick Wall

I am sitting in my office, surrounded by piles of files, open boxes stacked books, and overflowing trash. This space, long a tranquil haven, decorated with art and mementoes that always made me smile, is now chaotic and sad. The walls are bare, except for the needlepoint made for me by a long-ago nursing home congregant, bearing the words, "Aging is not for sissies." I have spent days on end plowing through the detritus of eight years of beloved work and crushing frustration. Almost all of the mountains of papers, representing programs, classes and lectures, plans, flyers, grant proposals, and correspondence, end up in the recycling bin. I am leaving, and my program is ending. No one will need these records.

It took me a long time to accept the fact that the project I dreamed up, founded, and directed was not going to endure. In retrospect, it seems that I was making my way through Kübler-Ross' stages of grieving (denial, anger, bargaining, depression, acceptance). When it looked like the program was unsustainable, I refused to accept it. I loved this work. I had the opportunity to share my passion with beloved students, colleagues, and trainees, and to constantly develop new skills. I was not going to let it thing die. I drove myself to exhaustion trying to muscle through obstacles, and indeed somehow managed to temporarily stave off the inevitable. I felt angry, resentful, and lonely as I struggled to keep it going.

And then one day, as I sat in *shul*, it came to me in a flash: this is not going to work out. And it is nobody's fault. Just like that. Not exactly a *bat kol*, a divine voice, but a moment of revelation, to be sure. The truth I had tried so hard to evade was in my face, and it felt liberating to let go of the draining work of evading reality.

I felt like Sisyphus putting down his boulder. I was relieved to be freed from carrying an impossible burden. But as I was appreciating a new lightness of being, I was also peering into an abyss. I had failed to build a sustainable effort. Even with successes, we did not manage to manifest the funding needed to secure the project for the future. I could feel gratified by what we had done, I could offer rational analysis about objective causes for this turn of events, but none of that changed the fact that I had not accomplished what I had hoped to.

The sense of failure cut deeply. And I had no idea what I wanted to do now that my dream was no more. On hearing my account, one particularly wise colleague said, "You have suffered a loss, but you've had no funeral to mark it. This is a death. You are grieving." And I was—for my shattered expectations, for my wounded pride, for my sense of being on a trajectory.

I felt alone, but truly, I had plenty of company. Many peers were thrown off-course as businesses and non-profits scrambled in the wake of the Great Recession. Organizations collapsed, restructured, merged, and downsized, and none of this was good for workers in midlife. Many people found themselves out of work and wondering how they would move forward in a world where experienced individuals were viewed as overqualified or undesirable. Even if their job loss was obviously the fault of a plummeting economy and not their own performance, they felt disheartened and shaken. Many of us wondered what we might have done differently. And now what?

Welcome to Middle Age: Illness and Death

Around the time I turned forty, a dear friend dropped dead while hiking with his wife. He was forty-six. When I shared my outrage and shock, my friend Margaret said, "Welcome to middle age." I did not appreciate her comment and thought to myself, what a cynical, jaded thing to say. This is just an aberrant, untimely tragedy, not a harbinger of things to come. I knew that illness and death were inevitable features of aging. I gradually came to understand that Margaret was right: we cannot escape midlife unscathed by vulnerability and loss.

My family and I were recently brought into intimate encounter with mortality as we accompanied two dear ones to their deaths.

It is Friday night. My sister-in-law, Doris, has asked me to spell her so she can have a couple of hours to dance, to breathe, to recharge. I sit with Steven, her fifty-nine-year-old husband. This healer, who brilliantly married conventional and alternative medicine to treat intractable illnesses, has brain cancer. Steven is lying in his bed. His once-elegant frame is now emaciated. His formerly precise speech is now slurred, labored, almost impossible to decipher. We chat (what do you talk about with someone who is clearly dying, but doesn't want to discuss it?). Steven: it's tiring for me to talk. Me: we don't have to talk. Steven: could you please massage my feet? We sit for a long time. I rub his feet, and silently pray for him. Steven: thank you for the blessing. Me: which one? The touch or the one I said silently? He says: both.

We are at the gravesite. The impossibly crisp fall day contrasts entirely with our abject desolation. We take turns shoveling dirt. My eleven-year-old daughter, Anat, hides behind David, my husband, as if not seeing could make Uncle Steven's death not be real. Avram, her twin, sobs convulsively as he buries his head in Bubbie Miriam's lap. Anya, my sixteen-year-old first-born, collapses in my arms, her tears searing me with pain. My children's grief is wrenching. Steven's death is unspeakable. I am a comforter by trade, but I cannot make any of this better.

We are back in the cemetery. The ground is snow-covered, but it is raining, and the path to the grave is wet and muddy. David is stoic; Doris is stunned. Anat wants to get away, anywhere but here. Anya is awash in tears. Avram is wracked with sobs, but this time, he cannot put his head in Bubbie's lap, because we have come to bury her, just three months after Steven. We all knew my amazing mother-in-law would die eventually, but she seemed to have nine lives. She had survived the Ghetto, the camps, the death march, the slow-creep loss of her beloved to a wasting illness, the cancer that took half her stomach, but even she could not survive forever. How will we live without her? No one will tell us about Warsaw, the lost home, grandparents, aunts, uncles, cousins. There will never again be someone who will delightedly invite me to share a chochmeh from the children in a daily phone call. Or call me up after I mentioned an issue I was facing and say, "You know, I was thinking . . . " and offer advice in the form of a perfectly apt Yiddish or Polish proverb introduced with the words "My mother used to say . . . " It feels like the heart has been wrested from our family's body.

I am aware that I am immensely blessed. I have a brilliant, kind, and infinitely patient partner. I have loving, creative, and never boring children. I am sustained by webs of friendship and community. I have a rich connection to text, tradition, and practice that nourish me greatly. I feel I have made a contribution through my work.

Still, these family losses are shattering, more troubling than my professional disappointments. I am crestfallen that all of my years of accompanying elders through illness and dying cannot make Steven's agonizing death any less traumatic. I am shocked that, as much as I thought I understood the complexities of end-of-life decision-making, the reality is just plain messy. I am unprepared for the immensity of the hole left by Miriam, the raw pain I feel every time I lift the phone to call her.

Tikkun: The New Path

The Benedictine priest, Richard Rohr, suggests that it is beyond midlife when our life's true purpose can be realized. In the first half of our lives, he says, we are consumed with the construction of the "container"—the outer structures of our life—work, home, and family. The second half is where we have the opportunity to become who we truly are meant to be, to construct the essential "content" of life, what Carl Jung calls a spiritual outlook. The shift from the "first half" way of being to the "second half" happens through failings and fallings. Rohr writes, "The supposed achievements of the first half of life have to fall apart and show themselves to be wanting in some way, or we will not move further. Why would we?" Rohr suggests that we arrive at our life's fulfillment only through shatterings, or, as he calls them, fallings and failings. When certainty disintegrates, we are, in the words of Elizabeth Lesser, *broken open*, and in this way, we become available for real learning and growth.

Rohr says of the second half of life, "the way up is the way down" or "the way down is the way up." In Jewish tradition, this insight is expressed quite similarly: very often, progress comes by way of *yeridah l'tzorech aliyah*, a descent for the sake of ascent. We grow into the fullness of our human potential, but only through spiraling down through disappointments and limits. If there is a *tikkun*/repair/redemption ahead for me in this Third Chapter, it seems that it will come only as I confront the shards of vulnerability here on the downside of my descent.

Seeking Sparks amidst the Shadows

My job is over; my family is reduced by loss, at the same time that the demands of parenting and daughtering are intensified. How do I move forward? I want to know: how can I grow from this pain? How can I harvest all I've experienced? I am determined to learn something from all of this.

I start by literally cleaning up my act. In order to set up my home office, I must wade through the boxes and boxes of disorganized detritus I had put aside, but never organized. With help, I go through each piece of paper. I don't need to hold on to most of the physical items, but I do get to savor both sweetness and disappointments of earlier jobs.

More profoundly, I begin to clean up my own act. A business coach suggests that I invite family, friends, and colleagues to reflect on my strengths and weaknesses in an unvarnished "360 review." This is not easy! I am touched to learn about gifts and qualities others respect, but what really gets my attention are their reflections on a couple of glaring flaws.

It hurts to confront this feedback; I see how I fall short of my own ideals. I feel the urge to defend or deny, to withdraw into the shell of my *klipot*. But I am also pulled toward the sparks—I don't want to shut down, I want to grow. Slowly, I begin to notice these shadow traits as they manifest in the moment, and to work at developing alternative ways of responding.

I probably miss more opportunities than I seize, but I am becoming at least a bit more awake. Each time I succeed in acting in a new way is a spark of possibility, of healing. I hope that my husband and kids, those most immediately in the path of my shadow traits, will benefit at least a bit from any sparks of patience and compassion that get liberated in this process.

Looking Ahead

What will I do with the rest of my life? I am coming to realize that I cannot now, nor will I ever (except in hindsight) be able to answer this question completely. Instead, I am trying to discern the next part of my path. It's like the Quakers teach: God may not be able to show us exactly where we'll end up. But we can ask God to light the next step. With help from guides (a beloved spiritual director, mentors, and friends), and with the precious luxury of time, I set off to find my way.

Many observers of this emerging life stage I am entering have noted the need for experimentation in making this transition. Mary Catherine Bateson suggests that time is needed as one searches for the next step in beginning what she calls Second Adulthood. Marc Freedman, in his book, *The Big Shift*, argues the need for a "gap year" for adults.

I am on my own gap year. This is an interlude in my life when I don't need a full-time job. I am building a practice and laying foundations for future projects. I have created a website to share the spiritual resources I'm developing for later life. I enjoy the creative side to this pursuit, and the way it allows me to interact with all sorts of people I know and don't know yet.

I am also working at recalibrating the balance of work and the rest of life, or perhaps rethinking what work is most central for me. I have had the time to become a regular at my kids' sports games and to focus on my own physical well-being. I have done things I never believed I would. I have learned to bake *Challah*, walked a half-marathon, and become a passionate baseball fan. I travel frequently to visit my Dad as he travels the rollercoaster ride toward dying. I work at being a better partner, friend, and sister.

I have gotten greater clarity about my guiding values and aims. I realize that I long for a less frantic pace and taut texture for my life. Through a magnificent rabbinic fellowship offered by the Institute for Jewish Spirituality, I study meditation and practice yoga, both of which challenge my impatience and perfectionism. I am not "good" at these pursuits, yet they nourish and ground me in ways I would never have expected. I work to wrestle email into a less consuming and tyrannical force in my day. I study piano and find myself writing melodies, which I set to texts from the tradition. I am surprised and delighted when I have opportunities to sing and teach them in religious services and presentations.

I am both reaping lessons from the experience I've amassed to date and learning from scratch. There are divine sparks to be discovered in both modes of being. I am endeavoring to glean wisdom from my studies and decades of work, and to share it in a new book. My friend Julie, with whom I sit weekly and write, reminds me, "We are the seniors (as in high school)." We have learned stuff that can have value for others. It is both scary and exhilarating to put it down in black and white.

And yet, I am a learner. As I set out to deepen my meditation studies, and to grow my skill as a spiritual guide, I decide to start with the basics. In reflecting on my past, I come to recognize a pattern: I have never started anything in my adult life at *Aleph* (A). I started *Ulpan* (Hebrew immersion program) in *Kittah Bet* ("B" class), I began rabbinical school in the second year, I became a certified chaplain without the typical path of going through four units of clinical pastoral education, and I became a spiritual director with only informal peer training. I was always in a hurry, and mortally afraid of being bored. But I was also always skidding into the next thing, without building a foundation upon which I could securely rest. I always felt just a bit, or even more, an imposter, since I didn't go the length of the road. Now, I will savor my learning, step-by-step, and in a community of peers. I am committed to cultivating more patience and humility. I will start at *Aleph*.

Shever v'tikkun—Brokenness and New Beginnings

I am in the midst of this new stage, and, I hope, of my lifespan. I hope for a long road ahead. I know that I will face many more shatterings and new beginnings as I grow older. I pray that, as I descend through the inevitable losses and changes ahead, I will find the strength to remain open, grow deeper and wiser, and manage to find the sparks to bring blessing to my precious family and friends and to all of those I touch.

> May we grow fruitful as we age
> Ripe and abundant and sage
> Keep our hearts open, to all we face
> Present to goodness, even a trace.
> Renew us, let our spirits soar.
> Sustain us, Our Rock, for more.
> (Ps 92:16–17)

17

Letting Go and Drawing Close

Laura Geller

WHEN MY SON WAS eighteen months old, it was time for me to wean him. He was ready. I was ambivalent. I remember a conversation I had with a much older woman. She said: "You are going to have to wean your child many times in your life. You might as well learn to do it now."

So how does a young Jewish mother learn how to wean her child? If the mother is a rabbi, she goes to a concordance, (remember this was 1984, before the internet!) looks up the Hebrew word for weaning . . . and checks every reference. So that's just what I did. And to my delight, I rediscovered a verse that was very familiar because we read it every Rosh Hashanah: "And on the day Isaac was weaned, Abraham made a great feast" (Gen 21:8). Then I remembered that in the *hafatarah* for Rosh Hashanah morning, Hannah weans her son Samuel. I had read these texts for many years . . . but I never paid attention until the story connected to me.

I was clearly not the first Jewish mother who needed to learn how to begin to let a child grow up . . . to feel the need for some kind of ritual to mark this important passage. The texts didn't tell me the details of the ritual . . . who knows how Abraham and Sarah celebrated? And why Abraham made the feast, not Sarah? All we know is that there was a great feast. Who knows how Hannah and Elchana celebrated? All we know is that it involved prayer and a sacrifice, *korban*, an offering of thanksgiving.

So I created a ritual. My ritual brought women friends together; we began with *havdallah*, the ceremony that epitomizes separation. We studied texts about weaning, and each woman shared a story about letting go as we embroidered small triangles of fabric that were later sewn together into a *kippah*. My son wore his proudly until he outgrew it and realized that it was sort of funny looking! The ritual concluded with my giving my son his first *Kiddush* cup because now he could drink on his own.

Joshua is thirty now, about to get married. He and his lovely bride are considering using that *Kiddush* cup as the first cup in their wedding ceremony. His getting married requires a different kind of weaning, letting go. His sister who lives across the country has a *kippah* created at her weaning and her own *Kiddush* cup as well. My children have grown up. I am growing older. I am still learning about letting go.

In a class that was part of the Institute for Jewish Spirituality's alumni retreat, our teacher, Rabbi Shelia Weinberg, taught about the Hebrew word *koof—resh—vet*—"to sacrifice." It is a metronym, a word that means two almost opposite things. It means "to draw close" and at the same time "to let go." I realized at that moment that from the weaning ceremony forward I have been struggling with what it means to offer a *korban*, to let go and to draw close.

When I was forty, my marriage to my children's father ended in a very devastating way. It felt as though I was trapped in a never-ending earthquake; there seemed to be no place to stand. How could I, a nice Jewish girl from Boston, and a rabbi yet, be so humiliated? How could I let go of the image I had of my life . . . that I had married the right man, that he loved me, that we had the perfect family? It was as though the pillars of my Temple had been undermined, that the Temple itself was destroyed. I remember how helpful was the advice from Rachel Adler, who urged me to read Lamentations, the book we read to remember the destruction of the Temple. And she was right; putting my personal pain within the context of the Jewish story was actually comforting, and ultimately even redemptive.

But redemption didn't come immediately. I spent the next many years of my life alternatively burying the pain I felt and experiencing it burst forth at moments that completely surprised me. The very first time I tried to meditate, at my first retreat with the Institute of Jewish Spirituality ten years after the divorce, I dissolved into tears. Just quieting down for a few minutes enabled the pain that was just below the surface to spill out. I had obviously never really let go. All the rage, the sadness, the pain over time not spent with my children because both my ex and I believed that joint custody was best for them, exploded into uncontrollable tears. My teacher, Rabbi Jonathan Omer-Man, counseled me to work on forgiveness—toward my ex and his girlfriend—and compassion for myself and the world. His counsel: "You can't draw close to who you want to be until you can find a way to let this go."

Through the Institute for Jewish Spirituality I learned new spiritual practices, particularly meditation and spiritual direction. Though I still struggle with a regular practice of meditation, I have discovered what my teachers often talk about: it leads to the opening of the heart. The slowing down, the attention to breath, the quieting of the chatter that goes on in my head, the temporary abandonment of my never ending "to do" lists, somehow shifts the center of attention from me and my drama to a sense of connection to something much bigger than I am. It also has mysteriously led me to understand that it isn't helpful to cling to a story of being a victim. Meditation has helped me let go of that story. It has also helped me notice how often what is difficult in my relationship with congregants and even friends is my confusion between what is, and the story I am making up about what is.

My mediation teacher Sylvia Boorstein teaches that the only correct answer to the question "How are you?" is "I couldn't be better," because if I could be better I would be better. And that everyone is on the same airplane, experiencing the same turbulence. This knowledge makes me a little less judgmental and a little more compassionate. I remember the moment when I felt this teaching opened my heart. I was leading prayer during a *bar mitzvah*, holding the Torah we had just taken out of the ark. The parents and grandparents of the *bar mitzvah* were lined up on the *bimah*, ready to pass the Torah from generation to generation. I looked out over the congregation, full of strangers who never come to synagogue, only there because of their connection to this family. Suddenly, instead of my usual judgment of them, I felt love. They had all come to be with this family, to honor a sense of tradition, to connect to something bigger than themselves. I felt my heart melt in my chest so powerfully that it was almost frightening.

Congregants tell me they experience me differently now: softer, more compassionate, more accessible, more honest. Much of that is the result of meditation and spiritual direction. I meet monthly with my spiritual director, a Protestant minister about my age who once pastored a church about the same size as my synagogue, so she understands the work. Spiritual direction helps me ask the question: how do I understand God in my life right now and what is the invitation that comes out of whatever particular challenge I am wrestling with at the moment? I have been meeting with her for over ten years now and I am learning to pay attention to what I need to let go of and to what I want to draw close.

A third spiritual practice that I have come to more recently is the study of *mussar*. Initially through the work of Alan Morinis, I have been able to study *mussar* with a group of congregants and, with them, focus on cultivating *middot* (character traits) like humility, acceptance, forgiveness, and gratitude. The work involves focusing on a *middah*, studying traditional texts that raise questions about how it manifests in our lives, and then noticing the choices we make around that *middah*. Over time, with journaling and reflection, I begin to notice some difference in the way I interact with other people and the way I view myself.

All these practices have opened my heart. They have enabled me to finally be with a man who loves me, supports me and really knows me. Through this work I am probably a better mother, definitely a better friend and I am finally becoming the rabbi that I was meant to be.

I'm sixty-two now. *Pirkei Avot*, in describing the stages of a life, says; "At sixty for *zikna*." *Zikna* is hard to translate. It means "meditation," or "maturity," or "old age." Some commentaries read the word as an acronym for *zeh sh'kana chochmah*: "the one who has acquired wisdom." I feel that I have acquired wisdom—though the challenges and the blessings in my personal life, through the opportunities and the difficulties of my professional life, including those that resulted from my being one of the first women to be ordained a rabbi.

What is the wisdom I need now as I enter into this new stage of my life? What will I have to let go of? What will I have to sacrifice? Who am I when I am no longer Senior Rabbi at Temple Emanuel of Beverly Hills, no longer considered an influential rabbi? I already feel the creeping invisibility that comes with growing older, no longer chosen for the committees and boards on which I once served. I recognize that I was asked to serve on many boards because for years there just weren't that many Jewish professional women around, and feminism had succeeded in getting people to understand that every organization board, committee, and program needed at least one! But still, I am struck by how often I react negatively whenever I hear that "ensuring the Jewish future" means only one thing: reaching out to unaffiliated Jews in their twenties and thirties. I hear myself saying: "What about me and my cohort of aging baby boomers? We're not dead yet and we still have a lot to contribute!"

Not long ago I sat in a room with a group of rabbis, many of whom were once powerful leaders of their communities. Younger colleagues introduced themselves as rabbis of their synagogues; the retired ones just spoke their names. What will it feel like when I am "just" Laura Geller? To what do I want to draw close? What do I need to let go of? How do I figure it out?

Several years ago, as my mind wandered while meditating, I surprised myself by noticing that one thing I really wanted to do before I died was to become fluent in Hebrew. It surprised me for two reasons. One was to find that I was actually beginning to think about dying. The other was that mastering Hebrew was at the top of my bucket list. After all, my Hebrew was adequate. Maybe it was about feeling authentic, or maybe just curiosity. So I went back to college . . . the intensive Hebrew language immersion program at Middlebury College offered by Brandeis, characterized by the pledge only to read, write, and speak the language of the immersion for seven weeks. It was just me and about forty other students, with the oldest being half my age! I lived in a dorm with other students, sharing a bathroom where I felt very confident leaving my cholesterol medicine on the counter because no one else would need those pills for about thirty years. Meditation does lead to surprising insight!

Meditation, spiritual direction, *mussar* work . . . it all helps me reflect with more clarity on my metronym; what does it mean "*l'hakriv*." To these practices, I add what I learned when I first confronted the challenge of weaning: the power of connecting the Torah of my life to the Torah of tradition. So I again turn to a story I have known for years, but now feels more urgent and compelling, the story we read in Genesis 12.

"And YHVH said to Abram, 'Go forth from your land (*lech l'cha*) and from your birthplace and from your father's house, to the land that I will show you. And I will make you into a great nation, and I will bless you, and I will make your name great, and [you will] be a blessing'" (Gen 12:1–2).

It is only recently that I really heard the truth of feminist scholar Savina Teubal's insight that Avram and Sarai are not a young couple at the beginning of their lives, but rather mature adults beginning "a quest into the unknown at a later stage of life." Savina used that story as the text for what she called a "croning ceremony" on her sixtieth birthday. I had the privilege of being there. For me the most powerful moment was when Savina donned a *kittle*, the white garment in which she wanted to be buried. That gesture connected this stage with the truth that undergirds it: there is less time ahead than behind; how can one find meaning and purpose in the time that is left? It was for this ceremony that Debbie Friedman and Drora Setel wrote the now well-known song: "*Lechi Lach*" (the imperative feminine of *lech l'cha*, meaning: go, really go). The words are: "*Lechi Lach*, to a land that I shall show you; *Lech lecha*, to a place you do not know. *Lechi lach*, on your journey I will bless you; and you shall be a blessing, *lechi lach*."

As I listen to the call of this biblical story I notice that this journey begins for Abram and Sarai with the directive to go from their land, their birthplace, their parents' house. In Savina Teubal's words: "to disregard unwanted pressures left by parents or culture or tribe." What work do I still need to do, through meditation, spiritual direction, *mussar*, prayer, or even therapy, to finally let go of unnecessary baggage? To be a blessing?

This biblical story challenges me in so many ways to ask what the invitation is at this moment in my life that will help me let go and draw close.

First, letting go: their names are changed from Avram and Sarai to Abraham and Sarah; to each name God adds a *hey*, the last letter of God's own name. My name will one day be changed as well: from Senior Rabbi to Laura; from synagogue leader to a Jew in the pews; from a mother to a mother-in-law; someday even (God willing) from mother to grandmother, and inevitably, sometime in the not-too-distant future, from daughter to orphan. And here too is drawing close: I trust that my *mussar* work on gratitude, acceptance, forgiveness, and especially humility will help me discover surprising blessings and even the presence of God in my new names.

Second, drawing close: Abraham and Sarah made a new covenant at this stage of their life. It is time for me to make a new covenant as well. That covenant begins with Eric Erikson's acknowledgment of the need "to gather the experiences of a long and eventful life into a meaningful pattern . . . time for remembering and weaving together many disparate elements and for integrating these incongruities into a comprehensible whole." Reb Zalman Schacter describes this life review as an "exercise for Sages in training." The important point of this looking back is to be able to forgive myself (and those I love) for not being perfect, to be able to see myself clearly and accept who I am with gratitude. And then I can make a new covenant—with promises to God, to myself and to those I love who will live after me.

The biblical story describes how Abraham and Sarah offered a sacrifice, a *korban*, a letting go and a drawing close. Me too: letting go of old dramas, letting go of my fear of invisibility, letting go of my jealousies, letting go of my need to be in the center of everything. And a drawing close: to a spiritual practice that honestly confronts the challenges of forgiveness, humility, acceptance and gratitude. And I want to draw closer to exploring opportunities to learn from and share my learning with both younger and older people; to give back to others and to continue to work toward repair of the world; to take more deep breaths, and to trust that God will bless me on this journey. If I draw close to all this, then I can be a blessing. *Lechi Lach.*

18

Leaving Egypt Again

Aging with Awareness

SHEILA PELTZ WEINBERG

It is well known that the mystery of the going out from Egypt (*yetziat mitzrayim*) was that awareness (*da'at*) was in exile and in a diminished state. No one knew how to serve God with joy and an expansive mind, with the fullest consciousness.

—*ME'OR EYNAYIM*

You shall speak of the going out of Egypt all the days of your life.

—THE PASSOVER *HAGGADAH*

WHEN I TELL MY husband that I got the senior discount on the train, he always asks, "Did they card you?" Well, the fact is: I have not been carded. The people giving senior discounts have absolutely no trouble seeing that I am of "age." No matter how the boomer generation shifts the definition of middle age, or how many times we say, "Sixty is the new forty," I am beyond middle age.

Age is both real and not real. What is really old? When I was nineteen and not married, I thought I was really old because my sister was married at eighteen. When I was thirty-one, the divorced mother of two young children, and came up with the idea of becoming a rabbi, I thought I was really old to start rabbinical school and a new profession. By the time I started rabbinical school, I realized I would be really old, forty, when I graduated. I also understood that I would probably be forty anyway. So what the heck!

Now I have five grandchildren and a daughter going to her twentieth college reunion. My friends are getting hearing aids and we are all losing words. We are exhausted more easily. Deeply exhausted. We are retired or talking about retiring. More and more people my age are dying and no one is saying that they are dying young.

In Jewish tradition, Ecclesiastes is seen as the book for the autumn of our lives; it is read in synagogue when the leaves fall and a wintry chill stirs in the air. I am interested, however, in exploring the relationship between the story of Passover, the Springtime epic, as guidance for this time in my life. I am moved by the Hasidic notion that the Exodus is the story of the liberation of awareness (*da'at*). Indeed, the Passover *Haggadah* instructs us to retell the story "in order for you to remember the day of the going forth from Egypt all the days of your life . . ."

What would aging be like if I saw it as a time of liberation, of deepening awareness, of strengthening my soul and my connection to the sacred unity that underlies all life? How might I see the Exodus story as a liberation of awareness? How might I apply this awakened awareness to the obstacles and shadows that cloud my consciousness as I age and face the inevitability of constricted places?

Mindfulness and Torah

When I moved to Massachusetts to become the first full-time rabbi of the Jewish Community of Amherst, I discovered it was located only forty-five minutes from an American-Buddhist meditation center. Insight Meditation Society (IMS) was leading the way in bringing Buddhist mindfulness teachings into many fields of contemporary life, from medicine and psychotherapy to education and art. I decided to try it. I was attracted to the idea of sitting in silence and letting go of the wordiness of my rabbinic life.

My first ten-day silent retreat was unbearably difficult. I was bombarded by my own endless stream of words, complaints, demands, and desires. It was also life changing. Sitting for ten days with my own mind and hearing the wisdom of teachers who had spent years looking at their minds, made me realize that I was not my thoughts! In fact, I was not even sure I knew if there was an "I" there at all. Instead there were experiences of connection to a clear quality of awareness that witnessed the arising and passing, moment to moment, of thoughts, moods, emotions, physical sensations, full-blown mind states, and detailed narratives. Awareness (*da'at*) was emerging from exile in these moments and offering this mind the possibility of a true liberation.

Even on that first retreat, some twenty-two years ago, the language of *Yetziat Mitzrayim*, the going forth from the narrow (*tzar*) place of *mitzrayim*, the land of constricted consciousness, spoke to my immediate experience. I realized that it was possible to train the mind and heart to remember this going forth all the days of my life, as a daily, immediate, life-affirming, and sustaining practice. This practice enables me to teach Torah through the lens of mindfulness and to teach mindfulness through the language of Torah.

One of the early mindfulness teachings I encountered is the Buddhist "five hindrances." It made sense when the teachers categorized a series of mind states in this way. I know these five intimately, both in meditation and in ordinary life. I see them so often, on and off the meditation cushion, that their existence is undeniable. What I do not always remember is that these five "friends" are an essential part of both practice and of life. These five energies keep awareness (*da'at*) in exile, in a contracted and limited state. Yet, the worst thing to do is to repress them, fight them, hate them, pretend they are not there. Cultivating the capacity to meet each one again and again with wisdom and love actually ends up expanding and freeing that very awareness. In other words, without the descent into Egypt, the narrow place, liberation does not occur.

Aging as Constriction

Getting old can be viewed as constriction on many levels. We get shorter; our joints don't have the elasticity they once had, we forget more easily and it is harder to learn anything new. Our potential narrows. There are fewer new opportunities, experiences, and friends. Our senses weaken in what they can receive from the world and what we do receive is often jarring. Sexual energy often abates. We are more aware of the shrinking distance between this breath and our last. So, I am asking myself: Is there a way to bring liberation into this period of my life? Is there a way to use the teachings of mindfulness and indeed the "five hindrances" themselves to free awareness so that I might see clearly and bring myself into a wise relationship with God, spirit, the holy, self, others and the world?

I want to explore this question in several dimensions. I will look at each of the hindrances in turn. I will note where they appear in the story of the Exodus and how they show up in my practice and my life as I age. In each case I am asking: Is there guidance here for working with these energies at this moment in the life cycle? Is there wisdom that might reduce suffering, increase joy and connection, and open the flow of the divine light of creation that calls us forth into freedom?

Sloth and Torpor

I teach meditation in a variety of retreat settings. When I stop giving instructions, and the room is quiet, especially if it is at night or after a meal—the sounds of rhythmic snoring are often heard. There will be a fair amount of head bobbing, drooping, and swooping. People are tired, yes, but the energy of sloth and torpor, not being able to mobilize the attention to stay awake and focus on the object of attention, is very common. Even in long retreats, after plenty of time for rest and sleep, that grey, murky, muddy mush sometimes sloshes over the mind. I admitted to a meditation teacher once that I was asleep through most of the sits. She said, "You are probably wearing yourself out by persecuting yourself for falling asleep. Just stand up. Open your eyes. Don't get into a conflict with your own sleepiness."

Early in the Exodus story, Moses speaks about the possibility of liberation to the children of Israel but "they do not hear because of shortness of breath from hard labor" (Exod 6:9). The slaves are suffering from sloth and torpor. They are worn out. They are not used to hearing anything other than the calls of their taskmasters and the groans of their own weary muscles. This very inability to hear anything beyond the very personal and immediate constricted quality of their state keeps them enslaved, impervious to the possibility of an expansion of their awareness and their lives.

I get tired more easily at this age. I notice this especially after travel and after babysitting my little grandchildren. There is a deep fatigue that lodges in the bones. It is a purplish color. Very heavy. I don't often have the energy to go out at night. It is harder to inspire myself with enthusiasm. Older people doze a lot. Like toddlers, we tend to nap. Sometimes we are just plain tired from not sleeping well during the night or from medication or pain. I do notice that when I struggle with being tired, I exhaust myself even further. When I bring a loving, accepting, non-judging awareness to the experience of being spent and tuckered, desisting from the commentary and the fright, the energy will revive. I can rest and renew myself. I can bring peace and ease to this moment and realize with joy that there are still moments of energy and excitement that spontaneously arise. When I name this truth, instead of struggle, awareness and liberation arise. The divine quality of awareness, represented in the Exodus story by Moses and augmented by the voice of Aaron, continues as the story unfolds.

At Passover, the act of baking the *matzah* (unleavened bread) represents the antidote for sloth and torpor. This simple bread wakes me up, arouses my interest, and forces me to count each moment. Because Jewish law stipulates that *matzah* is baked for no more than eighteen minutes, I must watch attentively so that the dough does not rise. *Matzah* is crisp, flat, and basic. It keeps my puffy sense of self in check, spares me delusions of grandeur, reminds me of my purpose, and helps me to pay attention and to keep focused.

Aversion

As animals, human beings are hard wired to resist the unpleasant. This survival strategy makes us run from the predator. We are able to flee from danger—fire, flood, or the enemy at our heels. This instinct is designed for extreme stress. However, we use it for the multiplicity of common human stressors in ways that are not skillful and that obscure the intrinsic luminosity of our own minds and hearts. Aversion comes in many flavors. Its main point is to get rid of unpleasant thoughts, moods, and feelings. It can manifest as blame, shame, anger, hatred, fear, worry, judgment, or any other constricting and conflict-inducing energy.

I am sitting in meditation and I start to get unpleasant sensations in a spot in the middle of my back. I am upset. I don't like this and I don't want it. I know that I am not supposed to move around until the bell rings. I move a little anyway but the pain does not get better. I am now really mad. I am also worried. "What if this gets worse and worse and I am in need of major therapy or even surgery and I don't have any time to schedule that in my busy life?" The aversion is a constriction. It constricts the pain in the back, which is already a constriction.

My mind is getting smaller and smaller. I am also feeling judgment toward myself as a poor meditator who should be in a state of calm and ease, even "bliss," by now. Now I am getting annoyed at the whole enterprise. Maybe this retreat was a bad idea. Maybe I should have gone to a spa where I would have had a massage and an aromatherapy sauna. Maybe these are the wrong teachers or the wrong practice or the wrong group of people. My mind is racing and creating diversion from the possibility of bringing calm, alert, and non-judging awareness to this moment. This is aversion.

When we meet the Israelites in flight from Egypt they are in a similar predicament. The Egyptians are pursuing them. For real. Their response is one of fear, a core aversive reaction, but then it moves quite quickly into blame, hatred, and hyperbolic delusion and ultimately doubt of the entire enterprise. They say to Moses: "Because there were no graves in Egypt, have you taken us away to die in the wilderness? What have you done to us taking us out of Egypt? Is this not the very thing we told you in Egypt saying, 'Let us be, and we will serve the Egyptians for it is better to serve the Egyptians than to die in the wilderness'" (Exod 14:11).

Doubt

When things do not go according to plan, or there is an experience of frustration, unpleasantness, or threat, there is a strong tendency for the mind to construct an elaborate narrative that negates our intention. "You thought you wanted to get free. Nonsense." "You were on a spiritual path? Get over it!" "You want to reduce your own suffering and the suffering of others? How naïve can you be?"

As I age there truly are many unpleasant things. There are things that I do not like, did not invite, and would prefer were not here. In this list: aches and pains; the fact that I don't know what a lot of the younger people seem to be doing or talking about, never mind the technology; the way I look; the fact that there is no one ahead of me in line and peers are dying; the fact that I did not accomplish anything near what I thought I would or get the recognition I believe I deserve; my invisibility to younger people; the stuff I have accumulated and can't figure out what to do with; my own mind; my digestion; not having enough money; certain relationships. I could go on.

Everyone has their own growing list. For the popular writer Nora Ephron, it was all encompassed in her aversion to her own neck. She wrote a whole, hysterical book about it. And it is very funny. This aversion to reality can lead to severe doubt, which is a kind of depression—another form of contracted awareness. Nothing makes sense any more. There is no purpose. Why were we ever born?

When I practice mindfulness, I name the moment as unpleasant. That's it. I cultivate again and again the pure awareness of Moses who tells the Israelites, "Have no fear! Stand by, and witness the deliverance, which YHVH will work for you today; for the Egyptians whom you see today you will never see again. YHVH will battle for you; hold your peace" (Exod 14:13–14).

Rabbi Alan Lew, of blessed memory, developed an entire practice based on this text. Yes, of course there is fear of decline, dementia, disability, and depression. I cannot banish fear, anger, judgment, or any other aversive reaction. But I can witness to it in this moment as a thought, or as a bodily sensation. I ask myself: "What is true in this moment?" No identity. No permanence. Nothing solid. Every mind state is passing through. When it is named, it dissolves. It does not need to congeal into a state of doubt.

I want to believe this can be a way of dealing with aging. I don't really know. I want to trust that God's deliverance (*yeshuat YHVH*—the saving power of the Universe as blessing and benevolence) will be available in this very day. I want to believe that it can be accessed when I soften the clutching of certainty and rest in the arms of Life that is so much vaster than any aversion or any doubt. I want to believe that I will have practiced letting go of small discontents and resentments so skillfully that I will be able to handle the bigger ones.

As Rabbi Abraham Joshua Heschel writes, "The aged thinks of himself as belonging to the past. But it is precisely the openness to the present that he must strive for." The "openness to the present" is what dissolves the hindrances. The "openness to the present" is what brings awareness (*da'at*) out of exile. The openness to the present is the path of practice and the path of the Exodus. I remind myself again and again, it is here, in this moment only, that I am safe, that I am at peace, that I am part of all that vibrates through eternity.

The healing of aversion is symbolized in the Passover *seder* by the sweet *charoset*. When I chew the bitter herb it is mixed with a delicious paste of apples, nuts, and honey. In working with my own mind in meditation as well as in life, thoughts and words of gratitude, blessing, prayer, and chant often soften the edges of the painful moments, the dark moods, the bitterness. I find ways to sweeten the mind so that doubts, and the other habitual aversions, have less room to proliferate. This reminds me not to get caught in the futile battle of fighting the bitter with the bitter.

What balances doubt? At the *seder* perhaps it is the four cups of wine and the warmth of gathering with dear friends. We let the mind relax and with it we soften and open the heart. Critical doubt surely serves me in my life, but sometimes doubt is resistance, reluctance, or my own willfulness masquerading as intellect. That is when a heart releasing agent, like wine or friendship, is the reassurance, the medicine I need.

Desire or Lust

Our animal nature is also hard wired to desire the pleasant. This too is in service of our survival, assuring that we propagate the species and consume nutritious food. There is nothing the matter with liking what is pleasant, in moderation, but a hoarding mentality quickly takes over when something is pleasant and the contracted energies of greed, lust, and clinging may quickly follow suit. No sooner do I taste a delicious cookie than I am wondering if and when I can have a second one. Our culture is based on cultivating a desire for more. The economy is predicated on increasing greed and stimulating lust—cultivating dissatisfaction.

In meditation it is easy to see desire arise. I often ask students to do walking meditation. The invitation is to walk back and forth in a small area, bringing attention into this moment of sensation as their feet meet the ground. Some folks see this as an invitation to do fancy footwork. They get bored. They walk backwards. They go to the bathroom. They get a cup of tea. They are looking for a more interesting place to walk back and forth. For twenty minutes!

I understand this. I am waiting for a train. I take my smart phone out of my bag just to check. Then a few minutes later I check again. I want experience, excitement, something interesting. I am sitting in meditation and the mind is going off into planning the same shopping trip for the seventeenth time. The airport is a tough place. The stores really do not have anything I need but they stir the wanting mind. What might give a little comfort? What might add a monetary zing to an otherwise dreary plod through endless corridors teeming with strangers?

The Israelites are great models acting out the hindrance of lust. Who can fault them? They were slaves with no experience exercising independent judgment. Their sense of self-esteem and intrinsic worth has been systematically negated by the system. So it is not surprising that they lust and kvetch and are easily deluded. Right after crossing the sea (Exod 15:23), they are complaining to Moses: "What shall we drink?" It is not just that they are asking for a drink; they are complaining. Yes, the waters were bitter but how bitter were they really if all Moses had to do was throw a tree into the waters and they become sweet? The people don't like the taste. Okay. But after their thirst is slaked, they imagine how wonderful things are back in Egypt, recalling it in a totally idealized way (Exod 16:3). When the manna arrives they want to save it until the next day, against Moses' instructions, and of course it rots.

Desire for "what is not" makes it so hard to accept manna, "that which is," the great teacher of trust, patience, gratitude, and limits (Exod 16:20). Then again they thirst for water and their desire turns into doubt and blaming Moses. "And the people thirsted there for water; and the people murmured against Moses, and said, 'Why have you brought us up out of Egypt, to kill us and our children and our cattle with thirst?'" In the account in Numbers, we find fantasy merges with desire and doubt: "We remember the fish, which we ate in Egypt free of charge; the cucumbers and the melons and the leeks, and the garlic; but now our bodies are dried up; there is nothing at all save the manna to look at" (Num 11:5–6). Unable to rest in this moment, in the presence of what is being presented, the Israelites need to wander for forty years in the wilderness.

Awareness is trapped or concealed in the wanting to do and have more, wanting what is not present or possible, wanting what ultimately will not satisfy. This persists and may intensify as we age.

When I turned sixty I really wanted to do something dramatic. I did. I went trekking in Nepal. It was exciting but also exhausting. I was invited to speak in New Zealand this summer. I said, "Yes." I am not sure that came from a true desire or simply to satisfy the FOMO factor—Fear Of Missing Out. I think my son Ezra coined that term. It can afflict a person of any age. The question is how much depth and satisfaction is found in acting from that intention? Am I cultivating wisdom and a sense of freedom? Or am I trapped by my own delusions and desires?

Excessive wanting obscures awareness, much like the other hindrances. One could say, it obscures the connection to God's presence. It keeps me dissatisfied and held hostage to my sense of being separate, other, and alone. It obscures joy and connection and reduces my ability to enjoy life as it is, which is not my creation, but a fleeting and precious gift.

In the Passover *seder*, the bitter herb, *maror* is often understood as the suffering the slaves endured in bondage. But I would like to see it as a symbol of the energy that balances lust and desire. It reminds me that the end of the sweet is the bitter. I know this when I pursue "too much of a good thing." *Maror* teaches me how greed, lust, and clinging can transform the most pleasant experience into the constriction of suffering. It teaches me the impermanence of pleasure, as well as pain. This profound understanding creates freedom in my mind.

Restlessness

When I am restless, I have too much undirected energy. I cannot set a clear intention. I have *shpilkes*. This is not right and that is not right either. I have a lot of worry about the future. How is this going to turn out? Planning mind is fueled by the restless mind. I rehearse the same thing again and again. How many times do I need to review the menu for dinner? Restlessness is impatience, and a lack of faith. My father was always the first to leave a gathering. He would sit in the car while my mother made her endless goodbyes.

The electronic media surely fire our restlessness because we now always have something to scan, to check, to surf. Restlessness resists being here. It assumes that there is resolution, somewhere better to get to and an elusive perfection awaiting us. I work with restlessness just like with the other hindrances. As I embrace the energy, while I might feel temporarily uncomfortable, the vibrant and fluid force moves through the mind and a clear and wide awareness, like a cloudless sky, reveals itself.

The classic story of restlessness in the Exodus narrative is the story of the golden calf. "And when the people saw that Moses delayed to come down from the mount, the people gathered themselves together unto Aaron, and said unto him: 'Up, make us a god who shall go before us; for as for this Moses . . . we know not what became of him'" (Exod 32:1). Despite the immediacy of the deliverance, the experience at Sinai, Moses' dedicated leadership and his steadfast relation with God, the people lose interest, lose faith, and get restless. They need something more immediate to keep them engaged. They have a limited capacity for abstraction. They need an activity, a symbol and a concrete object to engage their deficient attention span.

How does restlessness manifest as I age? I am noticing less patience with people and activities that are purely obligatory. I am aware that there is less time to repeat the same old mistakes. This is a positive restlessness. It is a window into a new sense of my own confidence as a person. I get restless and impatient with things I used to feel I needed to do. Slowly I come to realize that I don't have to do them. I don't even have to make excuses. There is restlessness in trying to please others that can fall away as one ages. It leaves a freedom that is fresh and spontaneous.

As a congregational rabbi I felt great pressure to be someone who was always interested in others. Always. The truth is I was not always interested. I also had to demonstrate how "spiritual," "deep," "serious and seriously Jewish" I am. Especially as someone in the early wave of female rabbis, I felt so compelled to get it right. Shoring up a persona of "spiritual" has a grave downside, like any persona—intellectual, manager, healer, etc. So much energy is invested in the persona, the false God, that the true God, the true life force, one's unique passion, is concealed, and at worst, even buried alive.

Now I am wondering what it is like to let it go. This means letting go of the longing to be seen as anything in particular. I believe that in the realm of having, doing, and knowing (including having a persona or a fixed identity of any kind) there is never enough. In the realm of being, however, there is always enough. How I long to settle, in these last years, however many they may be, into the calm abiding of being enough and allowing relationships, work, pleasure, and creativity to emerge form that wellspring.

At the Passover *seder* we are invited to lay back on super comfortable chairs or to just "lounge around." Reclining as free people counters restlessness. We place the body in a position of repose, in a place of faith and trust. This posture opens a door to relaxing the fretting brow and the urge to pace the floor. When I am relaxed in my body, my mind is relaxed as well. I have a chance to ponder relationships, causes and consequences. I have the opportunity to live purposefully at whatever stage of life.

Opening to Wisdom

The *seder* symbols may be the medicine that help us address the hindrances so that our awareness is truly liberated. *Matzah*, flat bread baked in haste, may be the antidote to sloth and torpor. The intentional preparation of *matzah* forces us to pay close attention so that the dough does not rise; this attention reminds us of our purpose. *Charoset*, sweet and delicious, is the healer of aversion. The bitter *maror* balances lust and desire. Reclining as free people counters restlessness. The four cups of wine counter the wobbling mind, filled with doubt.

Ultimately, the *seder* reminds us to liberate ourselves from our own, sometimes unreasonable expectations of ourselves, our own constricted places. As the Hasidic commentator taught, each of us is, after all, the greatest taskmaster of our own lives. Whatever the circumstances of our particular stories as we age, we are served best by the practice of compassion and kindness, an intentional practice of opening our hearts toward the truth of each moment. This is the approach that yields wisdom. *Limnot yamienu ken hoda v'navi levav chochma* / "Teach us to treasure each day so we may open our hearts to wisdom" (Ps 90:12). As Heschel says, "Wisdom is the substance upon which the inner security of the old will forever depend. But the attainment of wisdom is the work of a lifetime."

19

A Heart So Broken It Melts Like Water

BARBARA EVE BREITMAN

Summer 1996

I AM FORTY-SIX YEARS OLD. I'm riding in an ambulance across a beach teeming with vacationers. They have formed a crowd and peer into the windows at me. My forty-six year old robust, athletic, generous husband lies next to me, unconscious. He collapsed after we got lost on a strenuous hike thrashing through thick brambles and tall, thorny bushes. I am thinking, "What am I doing in here? I'm supposed to be out there with you, looking at some stranger in this ambulance." An hour later, he is declared dead.

Shock is hard to capture in words because memory fragments. I instinctively touched Chaim's body. He was still warm. "They must have made a mistake. Wouldn't he be cold?" I remembered he had a joint in his pocket and I was afraid the police would arrest us for drug possession. I fumbled around and removed it. "This is ridiculous. I'm fishing a joint out of your pocket. If you were alive you would be laughing." I could hear the doctor and nurses murmuring in the hall. "What do we do with her?" What do they do with me? I realized, "Oh, we are at a rinky-dink hospital on Block Island. They probably haven't had to deal with more than bee stings and broken legs in years." Actually, I probably thought that later. A nurse came in. She was the only one who ventured near me. "The chief of police will be here soon. He will take you with him." "I need a Jew to stay with him. I can't leave him alone. Is there a Jew on this island? I mean a rabbi? Anyone who knows anything about Judaism?" She left. More murmuring in the hall.

Time passed. An eternity. A second. Now I am sobbing. I put my head on his chest. I cry out his name. I stroke his face. This isn't happening. A stunned Jewish looking man walks into the room. In my memory, his face looks like a terrified animal being thrown to the lions. He tells me he leads services on the island but he doesn't know much. He asks me what I want him to do. "Chant '*El Maleh Rachamim*'?" "I don't know how." "Okay. Will you please stay with him when I leave? I'm sorry."

The chief of police arrives. He takes my hand. He looks into my eyes with his eyes. Suddenly I feel grounded. This *is* really happening. Chaim is lying dead on that gurney. "You are going to come with me. I will take you to where you are staying. Do you know where you are staying?" "I can't remember. We've been here only two days." I describe something and he knows what I'm talking about. "I am going to rent a plane. You and your husband's body will fly off the island to Providence. Is there anyone there who can meet you?" My husband's BODY? *Chaim, where did you go? How can you have left me with only your body?* "What? Say that again." "Don't worry. I'm going to stay with you." The officer's name is Bill McComb. Months later I think, McComb. Like *Makom*. He was an angel. No, he was the only person who knew how to be with me. I always meant to send him a Christmas card. I never did.

This was the second shock to happen within a year. I could only do what had to be done.

Summer 1995

A first cousin of mine, who had suffered from schizophrenia since her early twenties, was murdered. She left two traumatized daughters, ages six and twelve, with no parent to care for them. The girls had spent years in and out of foster care, in California and Oregon. They were terrified by their mother's "break downs," their lives repeatedly disrupted as they moved from home to home, school to school. Despite the agony of her psychosis, my cousin loved her children dearly and tried against all odds to provide for them like a Jewish mother. She volunteered to clean the dance studio to get them free ballet lessons. Suddenly, she was gone forever.

In the midst of this nightmare, I had a sense of clarity unlike anything I had ever experienced before: I felt like I had been put on the earth for this moment: to take her children in and make a stable and permanent home for them. While my husband had daughters from a previous marriage, I had not had my own children. I wanted them but could not have them. Though it was unfathomable that the blessing of children had come to me through the brutality of my cousin's murder, my heart was wide open, full of love and I was ready to become the girls' adoptive mother. My husband was more conflicted, but willing.

The girls had been in foster care during the months before my cousin died. Chaim and I flew to Oregon and when the Child Welfare social worker met with us, she asked if the state could place the children with us, in Pennsylvania. I wanted to take them. Chaim didn't. He was afraid my cousin would never willingly relinquish her children and would camp out on our lawn or in our living room. I knew his fears were justified, but I was completely distraught. I asked him to promise that if the children were at risk of being separated from each other or abused, if the state proceeded to terminate my cousin's parental rights, which they were threatening, and the girls became available for adoption, we would welcome them into our home. He promised. The local Jewish community in Oregon rallied to the crisis, found a single Jewish woman ready to become a permanent foster parent, open to adoption. The children were due to transfer to her on July 1. I was agonized that I would lose them forever. On June 28, my cousin was murdered.

Chaim said he felt like Jonah. He had refused to go where God was sending him. He could no longer avoid the call.

Fall & Winter 1996 . . . Spring 1997

My sense of order and meaning shattered when my young husband dropped dead on the beach. Though I never lost clarity about caring for the children, the universe lost coherence. "There is no meaning except what we build painstakingly, one toothpick at a time," I said to a colleague. As I struggled daily with the challenges of single mothering and working to provide for my family (with enormous help from beloved friends and community), I searched for wisdom that could restore coherence. Although I had long been a student of Judaism, I could not initially find what I needed there. In my search, I discovered a book entitled *The Gifts of Suffering* by feminist, Jungian, Buddhist psychologist Polly Young-Eisendrath. Seeing it on my night table, my daughters were puzzled by the title. "*The Gifts of Suffering*? What kind of crazy book is that?" In the second edition, the publisher changed its name to *The Resilient Spirit*.

The Buddhist idea of the impermanence of the self struck me as compelling and true: trying to hang onto things as they were, resisting the inevitable losses and traumas that life brings, denying the truth of impermanence, increases suffering. I learned that the Buddhist concept of reincarnation could be seen refracted through the lens of depth psychology, as a process we undergo within a single life span. Each of us dies and is reborn many times in the course of *one* embodied lifetime. As illness, death, and loss strip away what is most familiar and precious, we must die to an old identity, to give birth to a new self.

As I struggled to encompass these difficult truths, an experience sealed them into my heart. I was invited to *Shabbat* dinner at the home of people I barely knew before my husband's death. Lighting the *Shabbat* candles, they sang "As we bless the Source of Life, so we are blessed . . .", a song recently included as an alternative *Barechu* in Reconstructionist and Jewish Renewal prayer books, but not used as a blessing for candle-lighting. I was stunned. I had been present when that song was written. Many years earlier, as one of the women leading *Shacharit* services at *B'not Esh*, a Jewish feminist community, I had led the group in a guided meditation and sent them out into a spring morning to "receive Torah." Faith Rogow composed that song. Suddenly I realized: that was another lifetime! The child whose hand I held, who was now my daughter, had not been born then; I had not met the man who later became my husband and whose death I now grieved. My *life* was not over, a terror that woke me in the middle of the night. Our life together was over. *That* life died with him. But I had lived other lifetimes. I knew how to give birth to myself. I had done it before. Birth was excruciatingly painful. But I knew how to do it. I would do it again. Mysteriously, Faith's song returned as *torah*.

Turning and Returning: Wheels of *Teshuvah*

In Judaism, the idea that we die and are reborn many times in the course of a single lifetime shimmers through the concept of *teshuvah*. Commonly translated as "repentance," *teshuvah* means "return" and refers to the process of turning and returning to God over and again. According to rabbinic tradition, *teshuvah* is among the primordial things that existed before creation; *teshuvah* is imagined as woven into the warp and woof of creation, into its very structure. Without *teshuvah*, the world could not cohere; there would be no inherent meaning in the universe nor would it be possible for human beings to create meaning by repairing our lives. In Judaism, repentance and forgiveness are interwoven with any images we have about cycles of death and rebirth.

The Sefat Emet, a nineteenth-century Chasidic *rebbe*, teaches that the letters of *teshuvah*, *tav—shin—vav—vet—hey*, are the very ones that make up the phrase *tohu va vohu*, "chaos and void," with the addition of the letter *shin*, alluding to the "darkness over the surface of the deep," the *khoshehk* there at the beginning, before God speaks the universe into being. Creation begins in formlessness and darkness. Light is created afterward. In the process of *teshuvah* it is as if we create and re-create ourselves, beginning in darkness and turning toward light. In the Chasidic imagination, the *tohu va vohu* and *khoshekh* remain always at the heart of creation. Over and again, we can be plunged into those dark waters. As we search our souls, face the chaos within, cry out for help, ask for forgiveness, we remake ourselves, dying to an old way of being and giving birth to a new one. The Slonimer Rebbe, Shalom Noach Berezovsky, writes in *Netivot Shalom I, Nitivei Teshuvah*: "How can *teshuvah* help? The answer is the Blessed Holy One created the unique medium of *teshuvah* through which one becomes reborn. Not only does a person correct wrongdoing through *teshuvah*, s/he actually becomes a new person. For this reason the sages say that even the complete *tzaddikim* cannot stand in the place where those who have done *teshuvah* stand. . . . One who has done *teshuvah* is a new creation . . . *like a convert, like a newborn* (BT *Yevamot* 22a)." The Slonimer Rebbe goes on to quote the author of *Pri Ha-aretz*, Rabbi Menachem Mendel of Vitebsk, who writes concerning this: "Through *teshuvah* one is elevated to a dimension prior to the creation of the world."

The traditional Bedtime *Shema*, intended for daily reflection, to take an accounting of soul at the end of each day, mentions *gilgulim*, literally "wheels," referring to the transmigration of souls. This little known Jewish mystical belief in reincarnation has been removed from most liberal *siddurim*. Here is one version of this prayer:

> Master of the Universe, I hereby forgive anyone who angered or antagonized me or who sinned against me—whether against my body, my property, my honor or against anything of mine, whether he did so accidentally, willfully, carelessly, or purposely; whether through speech, deed, thought or notion; whether in this transmigration or another transmigration. . . . Whatever sins I have done before You, may You blot out in Your abundant mercies, but not through suffering or harmful illness. May the expressions of my mouth and the thoughts of my heart find favor before You, my Rock and my Redeemer . . . (*The Complete Artscroll Siddur: Nusach Sefarad*)

I don't believe sin causes illness and suffering, nor do I imagine being able to achieve the transparency of soul this practice requires. Yet, the prayer remains a touchstone. A year after my husband died, I was deeply troubled that I had not loved him enough. A dear friend said, "From a spiritual perspective, we come here to learn how to love. He died before you knew fully how to love." Her words gave me relief as I struggled with things I could not change. They enabled me to be honest about my failures, but to encompass them with hope. I still have not learned how to love as completely as this prayer asks me to do. But these words give me a direction toward which to incline my heart.

Perhaps what unfolded in my family might have been different if my grand-parents had understood why the rabbis believed in "the immense supernal power of *teshuvah*." *Teshuvah* can stop karma from passing from one *gilgul* to the next, one generation to the next. This may be why Jewish tradition teaches that even the complete *tzaddik,* the most righteous, cannot stand in the place of one who has done *teshuvah*. A person who does *teshuvah* transforms what otherwise unfolds as fate.

My cousin was five years older than me. Her mother, the eldest of four children, had been baby-sitting at age eight for her two younger brothers, aged five and three, when the little one was run over by a trolley car. Her immigrant parents blamed the little girl for his death. My mother was born months after this tragedy, the baby whose birth was a sign of redemption to her parents. My aunt's soul was forever tormented, still recounting these memories as she prepared, at age ninety, to attend the trial of her daughter's murderer.

My cousin and I grew up with this narrative, only daughters of two sisters with radically different legacies. My cousin was haunted by her mother's endless, troubled repetition of the story. Perhaps it had driven my cousin mad. My mother told the story bewildered by events that occurred when she was still in her mother's womb. She benefitted, but struggled, with the unearned grace of being the blessed and beloved child, while her sister was unjustly assigned the mark of Cain as a small girl, by parents who couldn't bear the weight of their own guilt. I knew that when my mother and aunt were elderly, I would be the one to step in and help my cousin, whatever that meant.

As shocking as her murder was, my sense of living in a meaningful universe did not shatter with my cousin's death. The intensity of her children's need and my desire to provide healing, hope, and possibility to their lives, gave my life even more meaning than before. The words of my ninety-four-year-old aunt echoed in my mind, "She was ready to leave this world and all her suffering. She knew you would take care of her girls." I will never know if this is true. I think it was not. My cousin wanted to live and raise her daughters.

What I learned during the two years of shattering is one of the great mysteries of life: loss and grief can be catalysts of spiritual growth. We all try to minimize loss, avoid pain and suffering. It is only human. Certainly pain does not necessarily lead to spiritual growth. It can lead to bitterness, despair, and isolation. But grief *can* be "a birth process from ego to spirit," as Miriam Greenspan describes it. At moments when I thought my life was over, when grief dropped me to my knees, that awareness had the power of revelation.

Still reeling from my husband's death, I decided to participate in a Clinical Pastoral Education (CPE) program for which I had registered months earlier. Though I was concerned about whether I could serve as a hospital chaplain, I found myself able to meet people in the midst of illness with what felt like deepened compassion. As we shared experiences in our multi-faith CPE group, a Catholic laywoman told me I should know about "spiritual direction," a contemplative practice of companioning people on the spiritual path. She pointed me to the Shalem Institute for Spiritual Formation, an ecumenical Christian program, which I eventually attended. For almost a decade and a half, I have worked with other colleagues to bring a contemplative practice of regular, disciplined spiritual companionship into the liberal Jewish community, drawing on wisdom from the Jewish tradition that I needed but could not find during the years of crisis recounted here.

A spiritual director who works with survivors of trauma says, "It can take something as powerful as trauma to release the ego's tyrannical hold on consciousness." Loss shatters our illusions of control. We realize that we have no control over what matters most. We feel the great discrepancy between the enormity of our personal pain and the implacability of an unresponsive universe. The ego is unseated from its place at the center. When life unfolds as we would like, the ego can be lulled into the delusion that suffering happens only to others. Though we know we are as mortal as the next person, we are often shocked when suddenly, the "other," the stranger, is us. As I rode in the ambulance on the beach seventeen years ago, at the moment of greatest loss, what was my mind telling me? "This shouldn't be happening to you." That is how the ego sounds when it is shoved off its throne and cracks. Shattering lets the light in.

Tzubrochenkeit: Brokenness

In 1998, I began meeting with my dear friend, Elliot, for healing and learning. We had been in graduate school together in our early twenties, studying Jewish mysticism. He finished his doctorate and become a professor. I dropped out after two and a half years, eventually made my way to graduate school in social work and became a psychotherapist. It had been a difficult decision to leave the doctoral program in the department of religion in 1975. Like many daughters of Jews striving to be "American," I never had a formal Jewish education. If I had been a boy, my parents would have sent me to Sunday school to study for *bar mitzvah*. They did not consider such an education of equal necessity for a girl. Though my passion was to study *Kabbalah* and *Chasidut*, I lacked the foundation needed to walk the labyrinth of Jewish mysticism, a path that required extensive prior learning.

Elliot is a scholar who yearned to bring to life the texts he teaches in academic settings. He wanted them to be used for the healing he knows they contain. I wanted to touch my suffering with the wisdom of the tradition. I shared my experiences on the path of grief and he taught me about the tradition of *tzubrochenkeit*, brokenness.

Judaism, especially the mystical tradition, speaks of the transformation that can happen through suffering and *teshuvah*, using metaphors of smashed tablets, shattered vessels, and broken hearts. A well-known *midrash* says that the Ark of the Covenant carried through the desert contained both the broken tablets that Moses smashed when he came down from Mt. Sinai to discover the Golden Calf *and* the whole tablets he carved the second time he ascended the mountain, after the people had done *teshuvah* for their sin. Both the broken tablets and the whole tablets had an honored place in the holy Ark. Both our wholeness and our brokenness are sacred. I asked, do I really think of my brokenness as wholeness? Reb Menachem Mendel of Kotzk taught, "Nothing is more whole than a broken heart."

A famous story about the *Baal Shem Tov*, recounted in Buber's *Tales of the Hasidim*, helped me understand.

> Once the Baal Shem Tov commanded Rabbi Zev Kitzes to learn the secret meanings behind the blasts of the ram's horn, because Rabbi Zev was to be his caller on Rosh HaShanah. So Rabbi Zev learned the secret meanings and wrote them down on a slip of paper to look at during the service, and laid the slip of paper in his bosom. When the time came for the blowing of the ram's horn, he began to search everywhere for the slip of paper, but it was gone; and he did not know on what meanings to concentrate . . . Broken-hearted, he wept bitter tears, and called the blasts of the ram's horn from his heart . . .
>
> Afterward the Baal Shem Tov said to him: "Lo, in the habitation of the King are to be found many rooms and apartments, and there are different keys for every lock; but the master key of all is the ax, with which it is possible to open all the locks on all the gates. So it is with the ram's horn: the secret meanings are the keys; every gate has another meaning, but the master key is the broken heart. When a man truthfully breaks his heart before

> God, he can enter into all the gates of the apartments of the King
> above Kings, the Holy One, Blessed be He." (*Or Yesharim*)

The Kabbalistic interpretation differs from what the tale stirred in me.
I thought of when my world had lost coherence, when I searched for wisdom unable to find it. I had wandered through many rooms, trying different
keys, opening some doors. But it was not until I broke my heart open to God
and wept bitter tears that I began a process of transformation. This felt true.
Something happens when our hearts break open. When we reach the limits
of our understanding and our effort, of our ability to make meaning in ways
we have known, of our capacity to shape things to happen as we wish they
would, the ego gives way to the heart and we glimpse a greater horizon, a
more encompassing truth.

The Baal Shem Tov's first successor, the Maggid of Mezhirech, gives
voice to the most radical mystical transformation that can come from the
breaking of the heart:

> "God is close to the broken hearted" (Ps 34:19) . . . But only a
> heart broken into several pieces so that his heart melts within
> him like water. Thus it is written, "to the broken hearted," (*nish-
> berei lev*) in the plural . . . For in the case of an earthenware
> vessel, its breaking is its repairing. (cf. BT *Shabbat* 16a) That
> is, man, who is an earthenware vessel made of shards of soil, is
> purified by his breaking—that is, the breaking of his heart; but it
> must be broken so that it is no longer fit for its original use. (For
> the text see Rivkah Schatz Uffenheimer, *Hasidism as Mysticism*.)

As long as we believe we are separate and self-contained, whole and
intact as an earthenware vessel appears, we cannot draw close to God. When
our suffering opens us to the suffering of others, when we recognize our
shared vulnerability, compassion crumbles the illusion of separation, our
hearts melt like water. We can no longer live as we had before.

Now . . . For the Moment . . .

It is seventeen years later. My older daughter just graduated with a masters
in social work and she is passionate about helping homeless families. She
works at a program that houses families in churches and synagogues until
they can get into more permanent housing. She eats with them, babysits for
the children, takes mothers to the emergency room, moves them from place
to place, feels at home with the homeless and spends hours doing case man-
agement so they can access the services they desperately need and deserve.

At age thirty, she has abundant energy and zeal not only to help individual families, but to work to change policies and improve the programs and laws that serve and dis-serve people who do not have homes. She knows her own life experience fuels the passion for her work and she struggles, as a new professional, to discern how much of her personal story to share with the families. My younger daughter graduated a year ago from college with a degree in photography. This summer she is directing the photography program at an arts camp where she went as a child and discovered her love of picture making. I remarried and teach Jewish spiritual direction with my husband, Avruhm, and other colleagues at a Jewish retreat center. I've helped to bring the practice of spiritual direction to more than one rabbinical school. This is another lifetime. This one is more comfortable and "how life is supposed to be." But I learned too deeply and well that the wheels, the *gilgulim*, never stop turning.

I dedicate this article to Phyllis and Arthur, who rented a plane and flew from Philadelphia to Providence to meet me.

20

With the Song of Songs in Our Hearts

Tamara Cohn Eskenazi

WHAT SENSE CAN WE make of a biblical book that begins with a female who says: "Oh that he would kiss me with the kisses of his mouth!"? Check again. Yes. This is indeed in the Bible, and yes, she is saying this to the one she loves. And it gets worse—or better (depending on your point of view)—when she exclaims, "Let us hurry" as she urges him to take her into his chamber. The woman's boldness and eagerness continue when she asks him, a few verses further, to tell where he takes his lunch break. She wants to be sure to find him quickly and not waste her time or their time, looking for him in the wrong places. "Tell me you whom my soul loves, where do you pasture your sheep . . ." (Song 1:7).

Welcome to the Song of Songs, *Shir HaShirim*, the amazing, short poetic book in the Bible.

Ariel and Chana Bloch begin their introduction to Song of Songs as follows: "The Song of Songs is a poem about the sexual awakening of a young woman and her lover." The Blochs' beautiful translation of the poem and their helpful commentary guide readers through the intricacies of the Song, offering an excellent contemporary tool for modern and even postmodern readers.

But is the sexual awakening of a young girl worthy of preserving as Scripture, as sacred tradition of a people? The rabbinic sages obviously didn't think so. They chose to read the Song allegorically, as a love song between God and Israel. But apparently not everyone saw it that way. And a debate ensued. One rabbi claimed the Song should not be declared holy because they sing this Song in the local tavern. The tradition, however, credits Rabbi

176

Akiva, one of the most illustrious rabbis of his generation, with pronouncing that "The Song of Songs is the Holy of Holies!" Akiva was famous for his mystical interpretation of Scripture. Even the small signs above the letters in the Bible were endowed, he claimed, with power to transport us to the sublime upper regions and closer to God. But to call this book The Holy of Holies? What could this mean?

When the Temple still stood, the Holy of Holies was the inner sanctum, the most sacred place in the sanctuary. It was accessible only to the High Priest. The tradition from Akiva's time held that even the High Priest could enter the Holy of Holies only once a year, on the Day of Atonement, Yom Kippur, and even he was deemed to be in such danger that the acolytes tied a rope to his ankle in order to be able to drag him out should the power in the Holy of Holies kill him.

Why was he at risk? Why would anyone be at risk in the presence of the holy? The Holy of Holies was the most intense manifestation of human-divine connection. We tend to think of the holy as ennobling and even comforting, a healing power. But in the ancient world, including the Bible, holiness was akin to how we think of nuclear energy or radiation. Here, ironically, Hollywood can be helpful. The famous film *Raiders of the Lost Ark* depicts the dreadful consequences to those who, unauthorized, dared to open the holy ark that had been stolen from the Temple in Jerusalem millennia earlier. As they open the doors, they smolder and melt down before our eyes.

We probably should consider a less horrific image. Think of nuclear energy and other sources of radiation: the right amount of radiation can heal. The wrong amount can kill. Right tools, right skills, and right steps, then, would be essential for survival and thriving.

Is that what Rabbi Akiva meant? In his days the Temple was no more, destroyed by the Romans several decades earlier. How then is the Song a Holy of Holies? At the very least we can suppose that the Song, for Akiva, was the most intense nexus of divine presence, available now that the Temple was gone. Is it perhaps the only place where access to God's presence is to be found in its purest form? And if so, is love, rather than elaborate rituals or even ethical teachings, the surest path to God?

What about the Blochs, and their "young girl" who first awakens to her sexuality?

Growing up in Israel, as I did, meant that I was introduced to various sections of the Song in folk music and folk dances. Like my friends, I knew passages such as "*Dodi li ve'ani lo*"—"My beloved is mine and I am his," or "*libabhtini akhoti kalah*,"—"you ravished my heart, my sister, bride" (Song 2:16 and 4:9). But none of us knew that these songs came from the Bible. Yet, we came to internalize these phrases and many others from the Song.

Unbeknownst to me, the embodiment of these lyrics during my formative years made them a prism, a lens through which my adult, scholarly self, decades later, related to the Song in its biblical context.

However, whatever awakening I had when I fell in love in America did not come through the language and the imagery of the Song. My own awakening as a transplanted Israeli who discovered life, and life in English, in Brooklyn, required a different language. There was no Bible in my world when I first fell in love with Howie Cohn. There was, fortunately, great literature: Henry James, Colette, and poets like T. S. Eliot and Blake. When Howie, my husband and first love, suddenly died, leaving me and our two young children bereft of all we took for granted, literature was a source of solace. By then I had read world literature. Lao Tzu was a revelation, as was Buber.

It was Buber who brought David Eskenazi and me together after each of us lost our spouse. As two recently widowed adults with children, we explored the reality of *I and Thou*. I had the language now. But David was the one who lived it, from the first time we met to the day he died twenty-five years later.

At first there was the magic of rediscovery. Both of us came from a marriage in which we deeply loved our spouse and expected the relation-ship to last forever. Both of us were unprepared for the deep devastation, the havoc, that losing our loved ones unleashed. And neither of us expected to fall in love again. But there it was, unbidden and for that reason all the more potent. I had not yet become a scholar. I had not studied or even read the biblical version of Song of Songs. The love lyrics that accompanied our falling in love came from popular songs of the early '70s, and from the world of classical music that bypassed word language. We were mystified by the power of new love and fortunately heeded its call. Our kids were swept along as we all reconstituted ourselves into what years later came to be called a "blended family."

It would be a lie to say that the early years of this marriage were easy. In Denver in the early 1970s, there was no language for a family like ours, and no support. This is why our family of seven faced several difficult years, although all the children grew to become beautiful, caring adults who retain a strong sense of family and commitment to one another and the world at large. We were very lucky.

It was with David, the Director of the Denver Jewish Community Center, that I discovered the Judaism that was unavailable to me in secular Israel or in Jewish Brooklyn where Judaism was what you did once a year on the High Holy Days, where buying the new hat and dress for services constituted the most intense preparations. And it was with David's support that I went back to college and discovered not only the world of literature but also the Bible. Of course you know the Bible when you grow up in Israel. But now in my thirties, as a returning college student, I studied it with new eyes, amazed by wisdom that I had sought in the sacred writings of other cultures. The company I now kept included Moses, Jeremiah, Job, and yes, Song of Songs.

Falling in love with David, after I had already been awakened in my first marriage, taught me—taught both of us—the capacity to awaken again. Discovering one's self in relation is not, we learned, a one-time only experience.

The Song of Songs is about discovering the self, the other, and the world. In this book we follow young lovers who court and cavort in the springtime of their life. She tells us, "I am black and beautiful" (1:5), confident of her beauty and her power. Her lover agrees, describing her with the most delicious metaphors, alive with abundance and energy: "Your eyes are doves" (4:1); "Your hair is like a flock of sheep gliding down mount Gilead" (4:1); "Your breasts are like two fawns, twins of a gazelle" (4:5); "Your neck is like the tower of David" (4:4).

Here is how the woman describes the man she loves and how she understands the effect of his love on her. Most translations render the following words of the woman this way:

> My beloved speaks and says to me: "Arise, my love, my fair one, and come away." (Song 2:10; NJPS)

The more accurate translation goes this way:

> My beloved answered (*anah*) and said: "Arise, my friend, my beautiful one and go forth!" (*Qumi lach raiti yafati u-lechi lach*).

There are several noteworthy messages enmeshed in the Hebrew that are lost in the usual translations. First, the woman understands the invitation or coaxing as a response ("answered") to a question, yet no question has been uttered. The lover's words, then, are a response to something not yet articulated. More importantly, the language is not only of romance but also of friendship. These lovers have many different ways of being with one another, friendship among them. Finally, and most importantly, this is not merely an invitation to come away but to go forth. The last words are identical to those God issues to Abraham when God says, albeit cast in the Song, in a feminine form since they are addressed to a woman: "Go forth (*lech lecha*) from your native land and from your father's house to the land that I will show you" (Gen 12:1; NJPS).

Now in the Song, the lover exhorts the woman: *Lechi lach*, "Go forth!"

Why should she venture forth? We then hear the man's description of the world outside the woman's domain: The buds appear, ready to bloom, and the chirping of birds is heard everywhere:

> for now the winter is past,
> the rain is over and gone.
> The flowers appear [are seen] on the earth;
> the time of singing has come,
> and the voice of the turtledove
> is heard in our land.
> The fig tree puts forth its figs,
> and the vines are in blossom;
> they give forth fragrance. (Song 2:11–13a)

At first one might think, as most interpreters assert, that this is an invitation for the lovers to roam the beautiful countryside and enjoy the beauty of nature. But more is at work and more is at stake.

The man repeats the call:

> "Arise, my friend, my beautiful one and go forth!" (Song 2:13b)

And now we learn why:

> O my dove, in the clefts of the rock,
> in the covert of the cliff,
> let me see your face,
> let me hear your voice;
> for your voice is sweet,
> and your face is lovely. (Song 2:14)

This is not merely an invitation to see and enjoy nature. It is a call to the woman to blossom, to be heard, to be seen. One lover tells the other: "It is not enough to see the buds beginning to bloom and hear the birds singing. It is time to see you and hear your voice. It is your time to blossom, like nature in springtime."

The Song depicts love as a dialogue between two equals who awaken one another to their possibilities. Truth be told, I only understood these words because David lived them. And I only began to teach the Song this way after he was gone, and language was what remained. Our marriage was a perpetual invitation for me to bloom by a man who daily gave witness to words like "My friend," and "Arise . . . and go forth," even though he never read those lines in the Song. In relationship with David I discovered what it means to be coaxed by love into becoming. The Tamara that David first met had not finished school. Until then I dabbled in courses in some fine universities, but due to circumstances beyond my control, including child-care obligations and frequent moves, I never lived long enough in one place to sustain an academic education. Only with David's encouragement did I enroll and complete in rapid succession, BA, MA, and PhD.

And it was with David as inspiration, and with the sorrow of losing our first love and discovering each other as backdrop, that I wrote my first academic paper, "Song of Songs as an Answer to the Book of Job" (1981).

The paper delineated some important connecting themes between Job and the Song, including distinctive linguistic features. In modern Jewish editions of the Hebrew Bible (in contrast to non-Jewish Bibles), the Song directly follows the book of Job. I tried to show how the questions that remain unanswered in Job find responses in the Song of Songs. That answer is the renewed immersion in life and in love.

In the aftermath of David's sudden death after twenty-five years together, Song of Songs became a lifeline. It is only now, having read a recent article about an extraordinary ninety-two-year-old widow, that I can see how and why the Song worked its magic. Norma Zack began writing love poems when her husband of sixty-three years died. In his essay about Norma, the journalist David Suissa writes: "The hole in her heart was still there. She missed him more every day. As simple as it sounds, she needed to find something else to love. She didn't just miss her husband, she missed the very act of loving him. That act of loving kept her alive." Yes. Love is how we move forward.

Norma fell in love with words and produced beautiful poems in which she explores loss and the path to an ongoing love of life. "Will I be content to hear the day's sounds and songs / And know that he does not? / How can I stop dreams for him / When I have lived within his dreams?"

I fell in love with Bill Whedbee, a biblical scholar like myself but with a deeper knowledge of the Bible because he studied it from an early age.

> The voice of my beloved!
> Look, he comes,
> Leaping upon the mountains,
> Bounding over the hills.
> My beloved is like a gazelle
> Or a young stag. (Song 2:8–9)

Bill was a runner, bounding over the hills. His voice reached me across the chasm that was opened by loss after David's sudden death. It was a voice that answered questions I didn't know I had. And it allowed me to continue to go forth "Arise, my friend . . . and go forth . . ." (Song 2:10).

Towards the conclusion of Song of Songs, the woman says:

> . . . Under the apple tree I awakened you
> There your mother labored with you
> there she who labored, gave birth to you. (8:5)

Our relationship, the woman seems to say, is tantamount to a new birth, as momentous as your first. Our relationship is a return to the primal moment, now as a reborn man or woman.

The woman repeatedly calls her beloved "the one whom my *nefesh* loves." *Nefesh* is typically, aptly even if not sufficiently, translated as "soul." It refers in the Bible to a person's entire being, not to a disembodied spirit lodged in a person. All of us are a living *nefesh*. This fullness of two mature lovers as they meet one another and give birth to one another's wholeness seemed to be our destiny, Bill's and mine.

The coupling of adults in their early sixties can be, and was for us, the re-creation of Eden, a return to a garden after a life already filled with exquisite joy and deep sorrow, but now reclaimed in the face of loss. As Phyllis Trible observes, the Song is the Garden of Eden reclaimed. The title of her chapter on the Song, "Love's Lyrics Redeemed," captures this redemptive power of the Song that is enacted in the protective world of a garden. Although death has not been vanquished, it has met its match "For love is as strong as death . . . Its sparks are sparks of fire, the flame of Yah" (Song 8:6). Yah, we know, is a reference to Israel's God, YHWH (as in *Hallelu-yah*, usually translated as "Praise the Lord"). This love, the poet declares, is divinely fueled.

Trible points out the many echoes, allusions, and reversals of the Garden of Eden narrative that transpire in the Song. Once again we have a man and a woman; once again, animals gently surround them. The tension created in Genesis 3, however, disappears in the Song. "No serpent bruises the heel of female or male; no animals are indicted unfit companions for humankind. To the contrary, the beasts of the field and the birds of the air (cf. Gen 2:19) now become synonyms for human joy. Their names metaphors for love" (156). If the senses in Genesis 3 led to temptation and fall, they are instruments of revelation in the Song: "Fully present in the Song of Songs from the beginning, these senses saturate the poetry to serve only love. . . . The embraces of lovers confirm the delights of touch (1:2; 2:3–6; 4:10, 11 . . .). The glance of eyes ravishes the heart (4:9; 6:13)" (154). Of particular interest is the word "desire," *teshukah*, which appears only three times in the entire Hebrew Bible. In Gen 3:16 desire places a woman under a man's control. But the situation is reversed in the Song when the woman declares "I am my lover's and his desire [his *teshukah*] is for me" (Song 7:10). In Genesis, Trible writes, "her desire became his dominion. But in the Song . . . desire becomes her delight," restoring mutuality (159–60).

The garden in the Song became a world for me and Bill to explore together. Here was a place in which to recover from loss and rediscover life's abundance. Here were words that blossomed into lush flowers broadcasting their scent, gentle animals like deer and doves everywhere; undulating fields of grain and bright red pomegranates, the air dense with spices such as cinnamon and nard.

The awakening of a young girl to her sexuality could not compare with the awakening of older lovers who discover each other anew and who bring with them a much deeper and wider landscape to be discovered.

"Who is your lover?" "What does he look like?" the female chorus in the Song ask the woman (Song 5:9). "My lover is fresh and ruddy . . ." she says (5:10).

> His head is finest gold, His locks are curled
> And black as a raven.
> His eyes are like doves
> By watercourses,
> Bathed in milk,
> Set by a brimming pool.
> His cheeks are like beds of spices,
> Banks of perfume
> His lips are like lilies;
> They drip flowing myrrh. (Song 5:11–13)

Oh, I recognized him even though his hair was now grey, and yes, his eyes are doves, always communicating. Bill was perpetually young even at sixty. Others described us together as "aged adolescents." In fact, neither of us had the ordinary teenage life we read about or see in movies. I grew up in war-torn Israel. Bill, a stone's throw from Disneyland yet largely oblivious to its charm. Both of us were serious youngsters, buried in books. His text, from early age, was the Bible. Both of us discovered our first romance with our first spouse.

Now, at sixty, freed from the constraints of a family under one roof, romance could be rediscovered. There were beaches and orange groves to roam, even vineyards to frame our new adventure. Above all, there was our common language.

Each of us had discovered independently Adrienne Rich's book, *The Dream of a Common Language*. It held a dream neither of us expected to see fulfilled. And now, at sixty, a common language was springing from within us. The language was us.

Bill, a seasoned biblical scholar and an award-winning professor, had taught a course on "Love in the Western Tradition." He could regale and court me in my own language, the one deeply embedded in my *nefesh*. And he had never before spoken these words of love aloud, the Hebrew did not as yet have an audience.

Ani ledodi v'dodi li. "I am my beloved's and my beloved is mine!" Yes, we could say, did say this in Hebrew and in action. Mutuality, reciprocity, equality. We were like the lovers in the Song, twins of a gazelle, matched in heart and mind, able at long last to speak our being in the languages and texts that formed us. The text that shaped our very life now flowed from us and guided our dance, infused us with new and hitherto unfathomed depth of intimacy. Each word resonating in many chambers of the heart, chambers that, like the rings of a tree, only multiplied and expanded with time.

Adrienne Rich describes such moments in *The Dream of a Common Language.* "Since we're not young, weeks have to do time / for years of missing each other." Like the poet, I too wondered, "Did I ever walk the morning streets at twenty / My limbs streaming with a purer joy?"

As our wedding approached, Bill wrote the following to Rabbi Sue Levi Elwell who was to officiate at our wedding:

> Certain key lines have often sprung up in my relationship with Tamara, often poetic lines that enliven and embody our love for one another. "Love is as strong as death," the famous quotation from Song of Songs . . . has embedded itself in our union. Both of us had known death intimately. Yet love proved as strong as death—not stronger than death, not negating fully the terror of death or its sense of separation, loss and wounding. Love has helped to keep us alive for life and to the possibility of renewed life—not as a panacea, but as a hard-won insight gained from living life fully even when staring death in the face.

―――――――

"Love is as strong as death." (Song 8:6). You only really know that when a loved one dies.

The *Shabbat* before he died, when his body was wrecked with the ravages of pancreatic cancer, Bill, perhaps hallucinating from medication, but more likely reaching deep into his being, said, "Let us be naked. It is the garden, the Garden of Eden." That garden was his last habitation.

The books we owned did little to ease his life in those painful months of slow defeat. But the texts that he inhabited stood by him and within him, to the end. I do not need to wish each *Yizkor* that he "may rest in the Garden of Eden." I know that the Garden of Eden was his final stop, even when breath was still in him.

Is the sexual awakening of a young girl holy? Of course it is. But let us not delude ourselves by thinking that an awakening to love is a once in a lifetime experience.

We wake up every morning. If we are like Abraham Joshua Heschel, our sense of wonder remains acute. The discovery of another person, the becoming in relation to another person—a friend, a book, a child—are there.

"You are what you eat," we say. You are also what you read. Bill was a walking biblical text. First, he read and studied the Hebrew Bible as a young and zealous Christian. Then he studied it as a biblical scholar at Yale, where he became (in his words) "a post Christian pagan with a Jewish heart." Eventually, his Jewish heart enlarged its domain when he converted to Judaism shortly before our marriage.

Spring has come again many times now since the winter that took Bill away from me. The ground above his casket is green, nurtured by the body below. Years later, my soul, my *nefesh*, keeps speaking with Bill. He continues to be the voice I hear when I close my eyes or look at the world around me. The beds of spices remain as the stubble on his face that still rubs my cheeks when I place my face against the freshly mowed grass on his grave.

Now what?

The seasons return. It is spring again as I write. The voice of the turtle dove is heard in our land, and now is my turn to sing these words to loved ones—family, friends, students: "Arise up my friend, my beautiful one, and go forth. It is time to hear your voice and it is time for you to blossom." (Song 2:10).

Biographies of Contributors

Rabbi Rachel Adler, PhD, teaches courses in Modern Jewish Thought and Judaism and Gender to the next generation of rabbis and Jewish educators at Hebrew Union College-Jewish Institute of Religion in Los Angeles. Her essay, "The Jew Who Wasn't There" (1971) is often cited as the beginning of Jewish feminist thought, and her bold reading of Jewish theology, *Engendering Judaism* (1999) won a National Jewish Book Award.

Barbara Eve Breitman, LCSW, DMin, a psychotherapist in private practice, works at the interface of psychotherapy, pastoral care, spirituality and Judaism. She was instrumental in developing the Reconstructionist Rabbinical College's (RRC) program in spiritual direction, and at RRC she serves as Assistant Professor of Pastoral Counseling and Director of Training of the Jewish Spiritual Direction Program. A founding faculty member of *Lev Shomea*, a program of *Elat Chayyim*/Isabella Freedman Jewish Retreat Center, she co-edited *Jewish Spiritual Direction: An Innovative Guide From Traditional and Contemporary Sources* (2006).

Rabbi Amy Eilberg, MSW, directs interfaith dialogue programs in the Twin Cities, including at the Jay Phillips Center for Interfaith Learning and serves on the adjunct faculty of United Theological Seminary of the Twin Cities. One of the founders of the Jewish Healing movement, Eilberg co-founded the Bay Area Jewish Healing Center. The first woman ordained as a Conservative rabbi by The Jewish Theological Seminary of America(1985). She is the author of the forthcoming book, *From Enemy to Friend: Pursuing Peace in our Lives and in our Work* (Orbis Books, 2014).

Rabbi Sue Levi Elwell, PhD, works with synagogue leaders to keep congregations healthy and vibrant through the Union for Reform Judaism. The founding director of the Los Angeles Jewish Feminist Center and the first rabbinic director of *Ma'yan: The Jewish Women's Program of the JCC of Manhattan,* Elwell served as editor of *Lesbian Rabbis: The First Generation*

(2001), *The Open Door: A Passover Haggadah* (2002), and as poetry editor of the award winning *The Torah: A Women's Commentary* (2008).

Rabbi Tamara Cohn Eskenazi, PhD, is Professor of Bible at Hebrew Union College-Jewish Institute of Religion (HUC-JIR) in Los Angeles, the first woman appointed to the Rabbinical Faculty at HUC-JIR. She is the Editor of *The Torah: A Women's Commentary* (2008), which won the National Jewish Book of the Year Award. Her publications include *In an Age of Prose: A Literary Approach to Ezra-Nehemiah* (1988), *Telling the Queen Michal Story* (1991) and the *JPS Bible Commentary on Ruth* (2011; winner of the 2012 National Jewish Book Award in Women's Studies). She was ordained in 2013 (HUC, L.A.) Eskenazi also recently received a National Endowment for the Humanities Fellowship (2012–2013).

Ellen Frankel, PhD, has had a rich career as a writer and editor, and has most recently written the libretto for *Slaying the Dragon*, an opera based upon a true story. After heading the Jewish Publication Society for eighteen years, she now serves as its first Editor-in-Chief Emerita. Her publications include *The Five Books of Miriam* (1997), which was published in Hebrew as *Midrash Miryam*, (2007), *The Jewish Spirit: A Celebration in Stories and Art* (1997), and three books for young people. Frankel also contributed to the ten-volume commentary series, *My People's Prayerbook* (Jewish Lights).

Rabbi Dayle A. Friedman, MSW, offers spiritual guidance, training, and consultation through *Growing Older*, a private practice in Philadelphia. She founded and directed *Hiddur: The Center for Aging and Judaism* of the Reconstructionist Rabbinical College where she served on the faculty. The founding director of chaplaincy services at Philadelphia Geriatric Center, Friedman is the author of *Jewish Visions for Aging: A Professional Guide for Fostering Wholeness* (Jewish Lights, 2008); editor, *Jewish Pastoral Care: A Practical Handbook from Traditional and Contemporary Sources* (Jewish Lights, 2nd edition, 2010) and the forthcoming *Provisions for the Journey: Jewish Wisdom for Growing Older*.

Rabbi Laura Geller, Senior Rabbi of Temple Emanuel of Beverly Hills since 1994, was the third woman to be ordained by Hebrew Union College and the first woman to be selected to lead a major metropolitan synagogue. She was twice named one of Newsweek's 50 Most Influential Rabbis in America and was featured in the PBS documentary "Jewish Americans." A frequent contributor to the *Huffington Post*, she is author of numerous articles in books and journals. She is a Fellow of the Corporation of Brown University.

Blu Greenberg, a pioneering feminist in the traditional Jewish community, is founding President of the Jewish Orthodox Feminist Alliance. Dialogue work has been another long term passion of hers. She's participated in numerous interfaith and inter-denominational enterprises and was co-founder of the Dialogue Group (Jewish-Palestinian women) and founding member of the Jewish Women's Dialogue. Her books include *On Women and Judaism: A View from Tradition* (1981), *How to Run a Traditional Jewish Household* (1983), and *Black Bread: Poems After the Holocaust* (1994).

Rabbi Julie Greenberg works with individuals, couples, and families in her *Counseling with Soul* practice. A licensed Marriage and Family Therapist, she serves as spiritual leader of Congregation *Leyv Ha-Ir~Heart of the City*: Philadelphia's Center City Reconstructionist Congregation. She is the author of a forthcoming book, *Just Parenting: Building the World one Family at a Time* (2013). Greenberg and her family were featured in the cover story of *Lilith Magazine* (Summer 2010).

Rabbi Margaret Holub serves as the spiritual leader of the Mendocino Coast Jewish Community and spent a recent sabbatical in South Africa interviewing Afrikaner church leaders about their experiences of apartheid. The author of "A Cosmology of Mourning" in *Lifecycles, Vol. 1, Jewish Women on Life Passages & Personal Milestones* (1994) and "The Good, the Bad, and the Possible: Some Thoughts on Jewish Women Making Community" in *Lifecycles, Vol. 2, Jewish Women on Biblical Themes and Contemporary Life* (1997), she currently serves as co-chair of the Rabbinical Council of Jewish Voice for Peace.

Rabbi Nancy Fuchs Kreimer, PhD, is the force behind a range of initiatives and programs that bring together interfaith thinkers, writers, and activists, with particular emphasis on building bridges of understanding and respect between Muslims and Jews. She is the founding director of the Department of Multifaith Studies and Initiatives at the Reconstructionist Rabbinical College. She blogs at www.multifaithworld.org, and her articles periodically appear online on the religion page of the *Huffington Post*. She is the author of *Parenting as a Spiritual Journey* (1998).

Rabbi Vivian Mayer brings together her gifts as a teacher and interpreter of traditional text skills with her pastoral skills in her work with rabbinic students as the director of the Preparatory Year and the *Bet Midrash* at the Reconstructionist Rabbinical College. She served as rabbi of Congregation *B'nai Israel* in Danbury, Connecticut for ten years, where she also served as a chaplain for Jewish women at the Federal Correctional Institution in Danbury.

Rabbi Vanessa Ochs, PhD, is a prolific writer and teacher whose books span three decades of Jewish feminist thought. Professor in the Department of Religious Studies of the University of Virginia, her books include *Inventing Jewish Ritual* (2007), *Sarah Laughed* (2004), *The Jewish Dream Book* with Elizabeth Ochs (2003), *Safe and Sound: Protecting Your Child In Unpredictable World* (1995), and *Words on Fire: One Woman's Journey into the Sacred* (1990; revised 1999). She served as Consulting Editor for two issues of *Nashim* dedicated to the theme of Jewish Women's Spirituality (2005: 9 & 10).

Rabbi Hara Person is a visionary editor, a writer of both poetry and prose, and an individual who shepherds ideas into books. She works as Publisher and Press Director for the Central Conference of American Rabbis. The Managing Editor for the award winning *The Torah: A Jewish Woman's Commentary* (2008), her publications include *That You May Live Long: Caring for Aging Parents, Caring for Ourselves* (2003), and *Stories of Heaven and Earth: Bible Heroes in Contemporary Children's Literature* (2005).

Judith Plaskow, PhD, is widely recognized as the first Jewish feminist theologian. Her first book, *Standing Again at Sinai: Judaism from a Feminist Perspective* (1991), challenged and changed the way Jews think about gender, revelation, community, and God. The co-founder and for ten years co-editor of *The Journal of Feminist Studies in Religion*, she is the author of *The Coming of Lilith: Essays on Feminism, Judaism, and Sexual Ethics, 1972–2003* (2005). Plaskow retired as Professor of Religious Studies at Manhattan College in 2012.

Rabbi Ruth H. Sohn has spent a career as a teacher of Jewish texts. She currently directs the Rabbinic Mentoring Program, Hebrew Union College-Jewish Institute of Religion, Los Angeles, and serves on the faculty of *Morei Derech* Spiritual Direction Training Program of the *Yedidya* Center. Her essays and poetry have appeared in many publications. She is the author of *Crossing Cairo: A Jewish Woman's Encounter with Egypt* (2013).

Ellen M. Umansky, PhD, is the Carl and Dorothy Bennett Professor of Judaic Studies, Fairfield University. She is the author of *From Christian Science to Jewish Science: Spiritual Healing and American Jews* (2005), *Four Centuries of Jewish Women's Spirituality* (1992; rev. ed. 2009), and two books on Lily Montagu. She is working on a book-length work of constructive feminist theology.

Rabbi Sheila Peltz Weinberg pioneered in developing the practice of Jewish meditation. A co-founder of the Institute for Jewish Spirituality, she directs the Jewish Mindfulness Meditation Teacher Training. She is the author of *Surprisingly Happy: An Atypical Religious Memoir* (2009). She served for thirteen years as rabbi of the Jewish Community of Amherst (Reconstructionist), after years of service in Hillel and Jewish communal service agencies.

Wendy Zierler, PhD, brings her talents as a reader and interpreter of traditional and modern texts to her work as Professor of Modern Jewish Literature and Feminist Studies, Hebrew Union College-Jewish Institute of Religion, New York. She is the co-editor and translator of *Selected Works of Hava Shapiro* (2008) and *And Rachel Stole the Idols: The Emergence of Modern Hebrew Women's Writing* (2004). She served as Consulting Editor for two issues of *Nashim* dedicated to the theme of Gender and Books (2008: 15 & 16).

Authors' Endnotes

Chapter 2
On Raising a Son
One Mother's Search for Wisdom
Hara E. Person

I am indebted to the work of Bruno Bettelheim, *The Uses of Enchantment: The Meaning and Importance of Fairy Tales* (New York: Vintage, 2010); Joseph Campbell, *The Hero with a Thousand Faces* (Princeton: Bollingen, 1968); and Jane Yolen, *Touch Magic: Fantasy, Faerie, & Folklore in the Literature of Childhood* (Little Rock: August House, 2000).

In particular, in Campbell, 325–26; 97, and 365; and in Bettelheim, 76 and 127–28.

Chapter 3
Between Sisters
Ellen Umansky

The quotation from Lori Hope Lefkovitz comes from *In Scripture: The First Stories of Jewish Sexual Identities* (Lanham, MD: Rowman & Littlefield, 2010), 84; and Elisabeth Schüssler Fiorenza's statement can be found in *In Memory of Her: A Feminist Theological Reconstruction of Christian Origins* (New York: Crossroad, 1983), 29.

Chapter 4
The Face under the *Huppah*
Relating to My Closest Stranger
Nancy Fuchs Kreimer

Rilke's words are from Stephen Mitchell's translation of *Letters to a Young Poet* (New York: Random House, 1984), and Freud's from *Civilization and Its Discontents*, first published in 1930. The Marilynne Robinson quotation is from her novel *Gilead* (New York: Picador, 2004), 66. I learned about *tzelem elohim* from Tikva Frymer-Kensky, "The Image: Religious Anthropology in Judaism and Christianity," in *Christianity in Jewish Terms*, eds. Frymer-Kensky, Novak, et al. (Boulder, CO: Westview, 2000), 321–36; and from Ya'ir Lorberbaum, *Image of God, Halakhah and Aggadah* (Hebrew) (Tel Aviv: Schocken, 2004).

David Grossman writes about the *luz* bone in *Writing in the Dark* (New York: Farrar, Strauss & Giroux, 2008), 76. His character's quotation is in *Be My Knife* (New York: Picador, 1998), 6.

My teacher, Ira F. Stone (*A Responsible Life: The Spiritual Path of Mussar* [New York: Aviv, 2007]), has taught me much of what I know about Levinas and *Mussar*. Neuroscience sources include Timothy D. Wilson, *Strangers to Ourselves: The Adaptive Unconscious* (Cambridge: Harvard University Press, 2002); and Marco Iacaboni, *Mirroring People: The New Science of How We Connect with Others* (New York: Farrar, Straus & Giroux, 2008). For more about neurogenesis, see http://www.sfn.org/index.cfm?pagename=brainbriefings_adult_neurogenesis.

Chapter 5
Loving Our Mothers
Vivian Mayer

The quotation from Lori Lefkovitz is from *In Scripture: The First Stories of Jewish Sexual Identities* (New York: Rowman & Littlefield, 2010).

Chapter 8
El Na Refa Na La
Please, God, Heal My Daughter!
Amy Eilberg

I adapted the translation of *Adon Olam* from *Kol Haneshama Shabbat Vehagim*, 2nd ed. (Wyncote, PA: Reconstructionist, 1995), 458.

Chapter 9
Facing Pain, Facing My Fears
Ruth H. Sohn

The translation from the Zohar is by Daniel C. Matt and can be found in *The Zohar*, vol. 4, Pritzker ed. (Stanford: Stanford University Press, 2007), 343.

Chapter 10
My Mother as a Ruined City
Insights from the Book of Lamentations
Rachel Adler

Tod Linafelt's writing on Lamentations can be found in *Surviving Lamentations: Catastrophe, Lament, and Protest in the Afterlife of a Biblical Book* (Chicago: University of Chicago Press, 2000).

Elaine Scarry's work is *The Body in Pain: The Making and Unmaking of the World* (Oxford: Oxford University Press, 1985). My quotation from Kathleen M. O'Conner comes from *Lamentations and the Tears of the World* (Maryknoll, NY: Orbis, 2002), 3–4.

For more about ancient Near Eastern mourning, see Nili Fox, "Clapping Hands as a Gesture of Anguish and Anger in Mesopotamia and in Israel," *JANES* 23 (1995) 49–60.

Chapter 11
Wrestling with God and Evil
Judith Plaskow

The following classics: Albert Camus, *The Plague*, trans. Stuart Gilbert (New York: Modern Library, 1948), 117–18; Fyodor Dostoyevsky, *The Brothers Karamazov*, trans. Constance Garnett (New York: Modern Library, n.d.), 254; Thorton Wilder, *The Bridge of San Luis Rey* (New York: Washington Square, 1970).

My quotation from my own essay, "The Coming of Lilith: Toward a Feminist Theology," can be found in *The Coming of Lilith: Essays on Feminism, Judaism, and Sexual Ethics, 1972–2003*, ed. Judith Plaskow with Donna Berman (Boston: Beacon, 2005), 31–32. The essay was originally published as "Epilogue: The Coming of Lilith," in *Religion and Sexism: Images of Woman in the Jewish and Christian Traditions*, ed. Rosemary Radford Ruether (New York: Simon & Schuster, 1974), 341–43. Mary Daly's quotation comes from *Beyond God the Father: Toward a Philosophy of Women's Liberation* (Boston: Beacon, 1973), 33. The story about the airplane ride is from Nelle Morton, "The Goddess as Metaphoric Image," in *The Journey Is Home* (Boston: Beacon, 1985), 157–58.

Chapter 12
In the Right Time
Reflections on an Abortion
Sue Levi Elwell

Andrew Ramer's masterful *Queering the Text: Biblical, Medieval and Modern Jewish Stories* (Maple Shade, NJ: Lethe, 2010) inspired Tirzah's story. For Etty Hillesum's musing, see *An Interrupted Life: The Diaries of Etty Hillesum 1941-43* (New York: Washington Square, 1981), 55.

In 1973, the Supreme Court passed Roe v. Wade, establishing the right to legal abortion in all fifty states. For further reading about Jane and abortion support in the years before Roe v. Wade: http://www.uic.edu/orgs/cwluherstory/CWLUFeature/TribTheater.html and *The Story of Jane: The Legendary Underground Feminist Abortion Service* by Laura Kaplan (Chicago: University of Chicago Press, 1997). Daniel Schiff's *Abortion in Judaism* (Cambridge: Cambridge University Press, 2002) is a comprehensive compendium and analysis on the topic. Ritualwell.org is the best source for contemporary rituals and prayers on abortion.

Machlah, Noah, Hoglah, Milcah, and Tirzah are introduced in Numbers 27:1-11. Their story continues in Numbers 36 and Joshua 17.

Every day, observant Jews review the Talmudic rules of textual exposition, set by Rabbi Yishmael in the first century BCE. One of those rules is that similar words that appear in different contexts are meant to clarify one another. This principle applies to the name Tirzah, first introduced in Numbers 27:11 and then again in the Song of Songs 6:4.

Joel Hoffman's commentaries appear in *My People's Prayerbook: Modern Commentaries, Vol 4: Seder K'riat HaTorah/The Torah Service* (Woodstock, VT: Jewish Lights, 2000), 72, 70.

Chapter 13
My Life as a Talking Horse
Hybridity and Gender Equity as Jewish Values
Wendy Zierler

In this essay, I refer often to Bernard Malamud's short story, "Talking Horse," which can be found in his collection, *The Complete Stories* (New York: Farrar, Strauss & Giroux, 1977). All page number citations from this story are marked in parentheses in the body of the essay.

For more on Balaam, see "Balaam: The Prophet of the Nations," in Judith Baskin, *Pharaoh's Counselors: Job, Jethro and Balaam in Rabbinic and Patristic Tradition*, Brown Judaic Studies 47 (Chico, CA: Scholars, 1983), 75-114.

For a view that my naïve efforts to introduce modern criticism into traditional text study are part of an impossible enterprise, see James L. Kugel, "Apologetics and Biblical Criticism Light," in *How to Read the Bible: A Guide to Scripture Then and Now*, reprint ed. (New York: Free Press, 2008). For an alternative view, see Benjamin Sommer, "Two Introductions to Scripture: James Kugel and the Possibility of Biblical Theology," *Jewish Quarterly Review* 100/1 (2010) 153–82.

The citation by Robert Solotaroff comes from his book *Bernard Malamud: A Study of the Short Fiction* (Boston: Twayne, 1989), 131–32. For another representation of the idea of the Jew as centaur, see Moacyr Scliar, *The Centaur in the Garden*, trans. Margaret A. Neves (New York: Ballantine, 1984).

Chapter 15
The Remembrance of These Things
War, Occupation, Parsley, Bitter Herb
Margaret Holub

The Elie Wiesel reference is from his novella *The Town beyond the Wall*, trans. Stephen Becker (New York: Schocken, 1982), 162. Rabbi Nachman of Bratzlav is a Hasidic rabbi known for his teachings about prayer, including the recommendation that one go out to a field and pour out one's heart (*Lekutei Moharan*).

Chapter 16
Shattering and Rebirth
My Midlife Gap Year
Dayle A. Friedman

For a brief, clear exposition of the teaching of Rabbi Luria regarding the shattering at the start of creation, see Karen Armstrong's *A History of God: The 4,000 Year Quest of Judaism, Christianity, and Islam* (New York: Knopf, 1993), 269–70.

The idea of the "third chapter" comes from Sarah Lightfoot-Lawrence, *The Third Chapter: Passion, Risk, and Adventure in the 25 Years after 50* (New York: Sarah Crighton, 2009). Richard Rohr's teaching can be found in *Falling Upwards: A Spirituality for the Two Halves of Life* (San Francisco: Jossey-Bass, 2011). His work is indebted to Carl Jung's *Modern Man in Search of A Soul* (New York: Harcourt Harvest, 1955). I have also found helpful in thinking about midlife the work of: Mary Catherine Bateson, *Composing a Further Life: The Age of Active Wisdom* (New York: Knopf, 2010); Marc Freedman, *The Big Shift: Navigating the New Stage Beyond Midlife* (New

York: PublicAffairs, 2011); Elizabeth Lesser, *Broken Open: How Difficult Times Can Help Us Grow* (New York: Villard, 2004); and Carlo Strenger and Arie Ruttenberg, "The Existential Necessity of Midlife Change," *Harvard Business Review* 86/2 (2008) 82–90.

Chapter 17
Letting Go and Drawing Close
Laura Geller

Alan Morinis' teaching on *mussar* can be found in his book *Everyday Holiness: The Jewish Spiritual Path of Mussar* (Boston: Trumpeter, 2008).

The insights of Savina Teubal are recorded in "Have You Seen Sarah?" in *A Heart of Wisdom: Making the Jewish Journey from Midlife through the Elder Years*, ed. Susan Berrin (Woodstock, VT: Jewish Lights, 1997), 183. See also "*Simchat Hochmah*," in Ellen M. Umansky and Dianne Ashton, eds., *Four Centuries of Jewish Women's Spirituality* (Boston: Beacon, 1992).

Reb Zalman Schachter describes his ideas about life review in Zalman Schachter-Shalomi and Ronald S. Miller, *From Age-ing to Sage-ing: A Profound New Vision of Growing Older* (New York: Warner, 1995). Like many others, including me, Reb Zalman is indebted to Eric Erickson, *Identity and the Life Cycle* (New York: Norton, 1980).

Chapter 18
Leaving Egypt Again
Aging with Awareness
Sheila Peltz Weinberg

My opening quotation is from *Me'or Eynayim*, a Hasidic text translated by Arthur Green in Menahem Nahum of Chernobyl, *Upright Practices, The Light of the Eyes*, Classics of Western Spirituality (New York: Paulist, 1982). Rabbi Alan Lew describes his practice in *A Jewish Meditation Practice for Real Life*. My closing quotation comes from Rabbi Abraham Joshua Heschel's essay "To Grow in Wisdom," which was initially delivered at the 1961 White House Conference on Aging and can be found in Heschel, *The Insecurity of Freedom: Essays on Human Existence* (New York: Farrar, Straus & Giroux, 1965). My teacher, Sylvia Boorstein, has written many books. You can learn more about them online at www.SylviaBoorstein.com.

Chapter 19
A Heart So Broken It Melts Like Water
Barbara Eve Breitman

These sources have contributed to my thinking: Polly Young-Eisendrath, *The Resilient Spirit: Transforming Suffering into Insight and Renewal* (Reading, MA: Perseus, 1996); Miriam Greenspan, *Healing through the Dark Emotions: The Wisdom of Grief, Fear and Despair* (Boston: Shambala, 2003); Estelle Frankel, *Sacred Therapy: Jewish Spiritual Teachings on Emotional Healing and Inner Wholeness* (Boston: Shambala, 2003); Howard A. Addison and Barbara E. Breitman, eds. *Jewish Spiritual Direction* (Woodstock, VT: Jewish Lights, 2006).

To learn more about Hasidic teachings, I recommend Howard Schwartz, Carol Loebel-Fried, Elliot Ginsburg, *Tree of Souls: The Mythology of Judaism* (New York: Oxford University Press, 2004); Rami M. Shapiro, *Hasidic Tales: Annotated and Explained* (Woodstock, VT: Skylight Paths, 2004). The Torah commentary of the Sefat Emet has been translated by Arthur Green. The teaching of the Slonimer Rebbe comes from *Netivot Shalom I, Nitivei Teshuvah*. The version of the bedtime *Shema* comes from the *Complete Artscroll Siddur, Nusach Sefard*. Martin Buber recounts the story about the Baal Shem Tov and the key of the broken heart in his *Tales of the Hasidim*, 2 vols. (New York: Schocken, 1947; reprinted, 1991), 64. The Maggid of Mezritch teaching is in Rivkah Schatz Uffenheimer, *Hasidism as Mysticism: Quietistic Elements in Eighteenth Century Hasidic Thought* (Princeton: Princeton University Press, 1993). Faith Rogow's "As We Bless" can be found in *Ivdu Et Hashem B'Simcha: A Siddur* compiled and published by Rabbi David Zaslow, 3rd ed. (Ashland, OR: Zaslow, 2003), 66.

Chapter 20
With the Song of Songs in Our Hearts
Tamara Cohn Eskenazi

The quotation from Ariel and Chana Bloch's translation and commentary is from *The Song of Songs* (New York: Random House, 1995), 3. David Suissa's essay about Norma Zack is "Norma's Love," *The Jewish Journal*, February 22, 2012. Phyllis Trible's observations are from "Love Lyrics Redeemed," in *God and Rhetoric of Sexuality*, Overtures to Biblical Theology (Philadelphia: Fortress, 1978), 144–65. Adrienne Rich's poem can be found in *The Dream of a Common Language: Poems 1974–1977* (New York: Norton, 1978), 26.

Glossary

Unless otherwise noted, the words in this glossary are Hebrew.

Adon Olam—Lit: Lord of the World. A hymn that is part of the daily and Sabbath liturgy.

Adonai—often translated as "Lord." The word read aloud in place of the four Hebrew letters *Yud—Hey—Vav—Hey* (YHVH) that are, according to traditional Jewish belief, not to be pronounced.

Amidah—Lit: standing. A central prayer in daily and Sabbath liturgy.

Bar Mitzvah—Lit: son of the commandments. The ritualized celebration of a Jewish child reaching the religious age of majority. Generally, part of this ceremony involves the child being called to the Torah for the first time as part of a religious service. From this point forward, the child is regarded ritually and ethically as a responsible adult in the Jewish community. The term refers to both the child who is called to the Torah for the first time and the liturgical setting for this event. The female version of this term is *Bat Mitzvah*.

Barechu—A prayer that opens daily and Sabbath services; call to worship.

Baruch haShem—Lit: Blessed is The Name. A phrase used to express gratitude, "thank God."

Bat Kol—Lit: daughter of The Voice. A heavenly voice.

Bimah—Stage or raised platform in a synagogue's worship space.

Brit Milah—Lit: covenant of circumcision. This term refers to the ritual circumcision that Jewish baby boys traditionally undergo eight days after birth. Jewish girls also are also entered into the covenant and thus participate in the covenant (*brit*), but they do not undergo a *Brit Milah*.

Chabad—Hebrew acronym derived from the Hebrew words *Chesed,* *Binah,* and *Da'at,* (compassion, wisdom, and knowledge). Name of a *Hasidic* movement, also called the Lubavitcher movement.

Challah—Braided egg bread traditionally served in pairs as part of the three meals of the Sabbath and on holidays.

Charoset—A sweet mixture of nuts and fruit used as ritual food during the Passover ritual meal (*seder*) to symbolize the hope that sweetened the bitterness of slavery.

Daven—Yiddish. To pray (related to the Latin root "divine").

El Maleh Rachamim—Lit: God full of compassion. Memorial prayer.

Geulah—Redemption.

Gilgulim—Lit: cycles. In certain Jewish mystical traditions, this term refers to a belief in reincarnation, as a soul cycles through various human incarnations over multiple lifetimes. While most Jews do not believe in reincarnation, this belief exists alongside other traditional and contemporary Jewish beliefs about death and the afterlife.

Haftarah—A reading from the books of the Hebrew prophets that accompanies the morning Torah reading on the Sabbath and certain holidays. Often read by a *bar* or *bat mitzvah* child.

Haggadah—Lit: telling. A text that sets forth the order of the Passover *seder.*

Hamotzi—the traditional Hebrew blessing over bread. If a meal includes bread, this blessing is said at the beginning of the meal.

HaMakom—Lit: The Place. Used as a name of God.

Hasidic/Hassidus/Hasidut—Referring to the eighteenth-century Jewish mystical tradition.

Havdallah—Lit: separation. The service conducted after the conclusion of the Sabbath (Saturday after sundown) that separates the Sabbath from the rest of the week.

High Holy Days—The two major Jewish fall holidays, the New Year (*Rosh HaShana*) and the Day of Atonement (*Yom Kippur*).

Holy of Holies—The inner sanctum of the ancient Temple in Jerusalem. Often used metaphorically.

Huppah—Canopy under which Jewish couples stand while getting married, often made of a *tallit* (ritual-shawl) and held by four poles. Can be made of flowers, greenery, or fabric. Symbolizes the home the couple will create.

Im Yirtzeh Hashem—Lit: if God wills it. An expression interjected into statements about the future.

Intifada—Arabic. Lit: shaking off, uprising, rebellion. Historically, the First Intifada refers to the wave of Palestinian protests and street rebellions that took place from 1987–1993. The Second Intifada took place between 2000–2005.

Kabbalah—Lit: what is received. This term refers to the Jewish mystical tradition.

Kaddish—Hebrew prayer used as a conclusion at various points in the prayer service. The *Kaddish* extols God's beneficence. The Mourner's *Kaddish* refers to the final *Kaddish* in the service; it has taken on special meaning for mourners, although it does not mention death. The *Kaddish de Rabbanan* is a version of the *Kaddish* that is said at the conclusion of group study.

Kahal—Congregation.

Kavod—Honor or dignity; glory (usually in reference to an attribute of God).

Kiddush—Lit: sanctification. A prayer said over wine on the Sabbath and holidays

Kippah—Yarmulke (skull cap), traditionally worn by Jewish men and some women.

Kittle—Burial shroud, also worn on *Yom Kippur*, at one's wedding, and when leading a Passover *seder.*

Kosher / *kashrut*—Jewish dietary law and customs.

Lubavitcher—a person who is part of the *Chabad* movement (see above).

Luftmensch—Yiddish. Lit. air-person. One whose mind is often in the clouds, unaware of or unbothered by earthly matters.

Mah Tovu—Lit: how good. Opening prayer of morning services. First line of the prayer derives from Num 24:5.

Maror—Bitter herbs. Used as ritual food during the Passover ritual meal (*seder*) to symbolize the bitterness of slavery.

Maskil—Enlightened one.

Matzah—Unleavened bread. Used as ritual food during the Passover ritual meal (*seder*) in remembrance of the bread the Hebrew slaves hurriedly took with them when they escaped Egypt—bread, which they took from their ovens before it had a chance to rise. *Matzah* is eaten throughout the week-long festival of Passover.

Middah /Middot (pl)—Character trait.

Midrash—Lit: seeking. Commonly refers to classical rabbinic commentaries on the Hebrew Bible, both legal and narrative. Contemporary *midrash* can include any retellings, additions, or interpretations of stories from Torah and tradition.

Minchah—Afternoon prayers.

Minyan / Minyanim (pl)—A prayer quorum of ten adult Jews. In order to recite certain prayers at religious services, traditional Judaism requires the presence of a *Minyan*. In the Orthodox world, a *Minyan* can only be comprised of ten adult Jewish males. In the other movements of Judaism, ten adult Jewish women or men can comprise a *Minyan*.

Mussar—Lit: instruction. Refers to religious ethical teachings generally and, more specifically, to a nineteenth-century Lithuanian movement that focused on character development as the essential spiritual practice.

PaRDeS—Lit: Paradise. A Hebrew acronym formed from the initials of four different approaches to Biblical interpretation.

Passover—English term commonly used to refer to *Pesach*, the Jewish festival of freedom, commemorating the liberation of the ancient Hebrew slaves from Egypt. The festival is observed in the spring.

Pirkei Avot—Collection of rabbinic teachings from around 200 C.E.

Rabbah—Female term for Rabbi, although many use the term "rabbi."

Rebbe—A Rabbi in the Hasidic tradition.

Seder—The ritual meal that commemorates Passover.

Shabbat (Shabbes in Yiddish*)*—The Sabbath, the seventh day. One of the Ten Commandments, *Shabbat* is observed with prayer, celebration, family time, singing, and special meals. Considered the most important Jewish holiday.

Shacharit—Morning prayers.

Shalom—Lit: wholeness. Used as a greeting: peace.

Shehecheyanu—A blessing that thanks God for keeping us alive and allowing us to reach the moment being noted.

Shema—Lit: Listen! A core prayer of Judaism, biblical in origin, recited when arising in the morning and when going to bed at night. Speaks of God's oneness.

Shivah—Lit: seven. Refers to the seven days of mourning following burial.

Shtetl—Yiddish. A small village (from the German *stadt,* meaning town).

Shul—Yiddish. Lit: school. The word came to mean synagogue.

Siddur—Prayerbook (from the Hebrew root *samech—dalet—resh,* meaning order).

Tefillin—A set of two small, black, leather boxes containing scrolls inscribed with selected Hebrew passages from the Torah. Traditionally these are donned during weekday morning prayers. Not worn on Sabbath or festivals. Sometimes called phylacteries in English.

Tikkun Leil Shavuot—A tradition of engaging in Jewish text study, often all night, on the eve of the *Shavuot* holiday in the spring.

Torah—The first five books of the Bible: Genesis, Exodus, Leviticus, Numbers, and Deuteronomy. More generally, the term can refer to Jewish learning.

Tzaddik / Tzaddikim (pl.)—Righteous person.

Tzelem Elohim—The image of God.

Yahrtzeit—Yiddish. Anniversary of the death.

Yeshiva—Place of study.

YHVH—The English rendition of the four Hebrew letters comprising God's unpronounceable name, also known as the Tetragrammaton.

Yizkor—Lit: remember. Prayers for the dead.

Yom Kippur—Day of Atonement.

Zohar—Core books of the Jewish mystical tradition, ascribed to a second century sage, but believed by modern scholars to be the work of the thirteenth-century Spanish sage Moshe de Leon.